Vowel Sounds

a	h**a**d, s**a**t	(HAD) (SAT)
ah	f**ar**, c**a**lm	(FAHR) (KAHM)
air	p**ear**, sc**are**	(PAIR) (SKAIR)
aw	l**aw**, c**au**se	(LAW) (KAWZ)
ay	b**ay**, r**a**te	(BAY) (RAYT)
e	m**e**t, b**e**t	(MET) (BET)
ee	m**e**, fair**y**	(MEE) (FAIR-ee)
er	f**ur**, aft**er**	(FER) (AF-ter)
i	s**i**t, b**i**d	(SIT) (BID)
oh	g**o**, r**ow**b**oa**t	(GOH) (ROH-boht)
oi	**oi**l, b**oy**	(OIL) (BOI)
oo	r**oo**t, s**ou**p	(ROOT) (SOOP)
or	f**or**, b**or**der	(FOR) (BOR-der)
ow	h**ow**, s**ou**nd	(HOW) (SOWND)
u	f**u**n, c**u**p	(FUN) (KUP)
uh	c**ou**ld, p**u**ll	(KUHD) (PUHL)
y	fl**y**, s**igh**t	(FLY) (SYT)
yoo	f**u**se, v**iew**	(FYOOZ) (VYOO)
ə	sod**a**	(SOH-də)
ə	sil**e**nt	(SY-lənt)
ə	penc**i**l	(PEN-səl)
ə	bac**o**n	(BAY-kən)
ə	circ**u**s	(SER-kəss)

Consonant Sounds

ch	**ch**ur**ch**, na**t**ure	(CHERCH) (NAY-cher)
g	**g**et, **g**reat	(GET) (GRAYT)
j	**j**ust, a**g**e	(JUST) (AYJ)
ks	mi**x**, si**x**	(MIKS) (SIKS)
ng	ki**ng**, fi**ng**er	(KING) (FING-ger)
th	**th**ree, **th**in	(THREE) (THIN)
t̲h̲	**th**en, fur**th**er	(T̲H̲EN) (FER-t̲h̲er)
zh	vi**s**ion	(VIZH-ən)

Say the other consonants just as you always do when you find them in a word.

Every time you see a "y" with a vowel following it, sound it like the "y" in "yoo," just as you do in "yet."

6

Volume Six · Stadium through Zoology

The GOLDEN BOOK ILLUSTRATED DICTIONARY

IN SIX VOLUMES

by

Stuart A. Courtis

Professor of Education, Emeritus, University of Michigan

and

Garnette Watters

Formerly Director of the Language Department, Public Schools, Hamtramck, Michigan

Allen Walker Read *Consultant on Pronunciation*

Associate Professor, Columbia University

GOLDEN PRESS

NEW YORK

Library of Congress Catalog Card Number: 61-7080

 Designed and produced by Artists and Writers Press, Inc. Printed in the U.S.A. by Western Printing and Lithographing Company. Published by Golden Press, Inc., Rockefeller Center, New York 20, New York. Published simultaneously in Canada by The Musson Book Company, Ltd., Toronto

sta·di·um (STAY-dee-əm) *n. stadiums.* An outdoor field with many rows of seats built around it.–Football and baseball games are often played in *stadiums.*

staff (STAF) *n. staffs* or *staves.* 1. A pole, stick, or rod.–Little Bo-Peep carried a *staff* to guide the sheep.–The Boy Scouts raised the flag on the flag*staff.*–Tommy made a walking *staff* for Grandfather.
2. (*pl. staffs*) The four spaces and five lines on which notes are put in written music.

3. (*pl. staffs*) A group, especially of workers. –A hospital has a *staff* of doctors.–A school has a *staff* of teachers.
–*v. staffs, staffed, staffing.* Provide workers for.–It is sometimes difficult to *staff* hospitals in Africa because of the lack of doctors and nurses there.

stag (STAG) *n. stag* or *stags.* A male deer that is fully grown. *Stags* have horns.

stage (STAYJ) *n. stages.* 1. A raised platform or floor for public performances.–The children went onto the *stage* to sing "The Farmer in the Dell."
2. The theater; acting.–Mary wants to go on the *stage.* She wants to be an actress more than anything.
3. Degree or period.–A frog goes through a tadpole *stage* of development.–We climbed the mountain by easy *stages.* We would go up a little way, stop to rest, and then go on.
–*v. stages, staged, staging.* Arrange; bring about; put on (a stage).–The boys *staged* a boxing match. They made all the arrangements for having it in public.

stage·coach (STAYJ-kohch) *n. stagecoaches.* A coach or carriage used in olden times to carry passengers and mail.

stag·ger (STAG-er) *v. staggers, staggered, staggering.* 1. Walk unsteadily, or sway back and forth or from side to side.–The sick man *staggered* down the sidewalk.
2. Arrange alternately.–The principal *staggered* our lunch hours. He arranged them one after another so that everyone in the school would not be eating at the same time.

stag·nant (STAG-nənt) *adj.* Not flowing; foul from standing still.–Mosquitoes breed in *stagnant* water.

stain (STAYN) *n. stains.* 1. A soiled spot.–Do not spill blackberry juice on your dress or it will make a *stain.*
2. A coloring or finish.–Father used a maple *stain* for the table.
–*v. stains, stained, staining.* 1. Make a spot.–The juice will *stain* your dress.
2. Color, or put a finish on.–Father *stained* the unpainted table.

stair (STAIR) *n. stairs.* A step.–We go down a flight of *stairs* to get to the basement.

stair·way (STAIR-way) *n. stairways.* A set of steps.–The *stairway* leading to the second floor has a rail at the side.

stake (STAYK) *n. stakes.* 1. A pointed stick or rod pounded into the ground.–The goat was tied to a *stake.*
2. An issue; a thing to be won or lost.–The soldier's life was at *stake.*
3. An interest.–Every citizen has a *stake* in the future of the town.
–*v. stakes, staked, staking.* 1. Mark off with stakes.–Bob *staked* out his garden. He drove sticks into the ground around it to show where his garden ended.
2. Risk.–I would *stake* my life on the prince's loyalty to the king. That is how much I believe in the prince's loyalty.

sta•lac•tite (stə-LAK-tyt) *n. stalactites.* An icicle-shaped formation hanging from the ceiling of a cave. *Stalactites* are formed over very long periods of time by dripping water that contains lime. The water evaporates, but the lime is added to the growing *stalactite.*

sta•lag•mite (stə-LAG-myt) *n. stalagmites.* A formation of lime that looks like an upside-down icicle rising from the floor of a cave. *Stalagmites* are formed over long periods of time by the build-up of lime from water that has dripped to the floor of the cave.

stale (STAYL) *adj. staler, stalest.* 1. Not new or fresh.–This cake is *stale.* It is old and dry.
2. Not keen or vigorous.–Bob played baseball badly because he was *stale* from over-training and from playing in too many games.

stalk (STAWK) *n. stalks.* The main stem of a plant. – Mary broke the *stalk* of the lily.–Bob ate a *stalk* of celery.
–*v. stalks, stalked, stalking.* 1. Try to get near an animal or person without letting that animal or person know it.–The hunter *stalked* the deer in the woods.
2. Walk slowly and proudly. – The cat *stalked* through the door.

stall (STAWL) *n. stalls.* 1. A space in a barn or stable for one horse or one cow.–The horse stands in his *stall* and eats hay from a rack.

2. A booth, or small enclosed counter.–The girls had a *stall* from which to sell candy at the fair.
3. A seat for a member of a church choir.–The minister faced the choir *stalls.*
–*v. stalls, stalled, stalling.* 1. Stop when you don't want it to.–Our motor *stalled* and we couldn't get it started.
2. Delay on purpose.–Mother told Jack to stop *stalling* and to get ready.

stal•lion (STAL-yən) *n. stallions.* A male or he horse.

sta•men (STAY-mən) *n. stamens.* The part in the middle of a flower on which the fine, yellowish powder called pollen is found. Insects take pollen from the *stamens* and carry it to other flowers.

stamp (STAMP) *n. stamps.* 1. A small printed piece of paper sold by the Post Office. It is glued to letters and packages to show that one has paid for sending them.–Before mailing letters or packages, you must put *stamps* on them.

2. A block (usually rubber) with a name, picture, or some other design on it. You can press the *stamp* on an ink pad and then print the design on paper.
3. A mark, signature, or the like pressed upon anything.–The teacher puts a *stamp* on our report cards.
–*v. stamps, stamped, stamping.* 1. Mark with a stamp.–She *stamps* her name on the cards.
2. Put a stamp on.–Remember to *stamp* the letter before mailing it.
3. Beat the ground with the foot; pound or crush with the foot. – The hungry pony *stamped* noisily. – Some little children believe that if you *stamp* on an ant, it will rain.
–*Stamp out* means get rid of.–The mayor did much to *stamp out* crime in the city.

stam•pede (stam-PEED) *v. stampedes, stampeded, stampeding.* 1. Cause to run, scatter, or flee in a sudden rush.–The fire in the barn *stampeded* the cattle.
2. Flee in panic; run headlong in a body.–The crowd *stampeded* out of the smoke-filled theater.

stand (STAND) *n. stands.* 1. A position.–The member of the Safety Patrol took his *stand* at the corner to help the little children cross the street.–What *stand* do you take on this subject? What do you think about it?

2. An outdoor counter where things are sold. –We bought a pound of big red cherries at the fruit *stand*.

bedside stand

fruit stand

3. A small table; a base that something stands on.–Mother put the lamp on the bedside *stand*.
4. A stop to face a military foe.–Custer's last *stand* against the Indians is famous in American history.
–*v. stands, stood, standing*. 1. Rest on one's feet with the body upright.–We lie down to sleep; we sit down to eat our meals; we *stand* to sing "The Star-Spangled Banner."
2. Rise; get to one's feet.–Our teacher has us *stand* up, face the windows, and stretch our arms every hour.
3. Set up on end.–*Stand* the broom there.
4. Rest upright.–The candlestick *stands* on the sideboard.
5. Bear or endure. – Mother cannot *stand* hearing Baby cry.
6. Hold good; remain. – Mother's promise still *stands*.
7. Take or have a position.–Where do you *stand* in your class? How do you compare with the others?

stand•ard (STAN-derd) *n. standards*. 1. A banner or flag.–The boy who carries our flag is our *standard-bearer*. He carries the *standard*.

2. Any post, pole, or the like that stands up straight to support or hold up something.–A flagpole is a *standard*.
3. Something by which things can be judged, measured, or compared; something set up as a rule or model.–Bob's mark on the arithmetic test was not up to his usual high *standard*. He does better most of the time.
–*adj*. 1. Conforming to the usual rule.–The *standard* size for typewriter paper is eight and a half by eleven inches.
2. Of a value generally recognized. – They studied the *standard* authors.
–*Standard time* is the time that has been chosen by law for use by all people in a part of a country or in a whole country.–Detroit has Eastern *Standard time*. The city of Chicago has Central *Standard time*.

stan•za (STAN-zə) *n. stanzas*. A group of lines of a poem, especially of a poem set to music. In a song, the tune is sung once for each *stanza*.–We learned one *stanza* of "The Star-Spangled Banner."

sta•ple (STAY-pəl) *n. staples*. 1. Most important products raised.–Coffee and rubber are the *staples* of parts of South America.
2. A U-shaped piece of metal with the ends pointed.–The farmer fastened the wire fence to the posts with *staples*.

3. A piece of wire that bends over at each end to fasten papers together.–The teacher fastened the pages together with *staples*.
–*v. staples, stapled, stapling*. Fasten with staples.–She *stapled* the booklet. She put the papers together with staples.
–*adj*. Most important; chief.–Among the *staple* articles in a grocery are coffee and tea.

star (STAHR) *n. stars*. 1. A five- or six-pointed figure.–The teacher puts *stars* on our spelling papers if the words are spelled right.
2. A *star* is a large sphere of glowing gas in space. Our sun is a *star*. Other *stars* are so far away that they are seen only as points of light in the night sky.
3. A leading actor or performer. – Mickey Mouse was the *star* of the movie we saw.
4. A person who can do something exceptionally well.–Babe Ruth was a baseball *star*.
–*v. stars, starred, starring*. 1. Be the chief performer.–Mickey Mouse *starred* in the moving picture.
2. Put a star on. – The teacher *starred* the good spelling papers.

starch (STAHRCH) *n. starches*. 1. A white substance found in certain plants that has no taste or odor.–Potatoes, macaroni, rice, and many other foods contain *starch*.
2. A white powder made of this, used to stiffen clothes. – Mother puts *starch* in Father's collars.
–*v. starches, starched, starching*. Stiffen with starch.–Starch is mixed with water and used to *starch* shirts and other clothes before they are ironed.

stare (STAIR) *n. stares*. A steady look with wide-open eyes.
–*v. stares, stared, staring*. Look straight and steadily with eyes wide open.–The hungry girl *stared* at the food on the table.

star•fish (STAHR-fish) *n. starfish* or *starfishes.* A star-shaped animal that lives in the sea.

star•light (STAHR-lyt) *n.* Light coming from the stars.–The *starlight* helped us find our way through the woods.

star•ling (STAHR-ling) *n. starlings.* A brownish-black bird whose feathers look greenish and purplish in the sunlight.

Stars and Stripes (STAHRZ ən STRYPSS). A name for the flag of the United States.

start (STAHRT) *n. starts.* 1. A sudden, startled movement.–A loud crash of thunder made me awake with a *start.*

2. A setting out; beginning. – The whistle blew and Bob was off to a good *start* in the race.

3. A lead.–She had a five minutes' *start,* but I caught up to her.

4. A place of beginning.–In studying world trade, we'll look at our village stores for a *start.*

–*v. starts, started, starting.* 1. Begin; set out. – I *start* to school at eight o'clock. – I *start* working on time. – Bob turned on the radio and the music *started.*

2. Set in motion.–Father *started* the car.

start•er (STAHR-ter) *n. starters.* 1. A person who tells others when to start or begin doing something.–The person who blows a whistle for a race or a game to begin is a *starter.*–A man at the bus station who tells the driver when to start is a *starter.*

2. A mechanical device to set something in motion. – Father worked the *starter* in the car to start the motor.

star•tle (STAHR-tl) *v. startles, startled, startling.* Shock; surprise; frighten for a moment.–The ringing of the doorbell *startled* Mother.

star•va•tion (stahr-VAY-shən) *n.* Being without food.–The farmer's pigs died of *starvation.* He had no food and could not feed them.

starve (STAHRV) *v. starves, starved, starving.* Be without food; die of hunger.–If you do not eat, you will *starve.*

state (STAYT) *n. states.* 1. A group of people who work and live under one government, or the territory in which these people live and work.–The United States is made up of fifty *states.*–The United Nations is made up of member *states,* or countries.

2. A condition. – Mary was in an excited *state* on the night of the class play.

3. Way in which a person of wealth or position lives; grandeur; magnificence. – The Oriental prince lives and travels in *state.*

–*v. states, stated, stating.* Say something by writing or speaking.–The doctor *stated* that Baby had the measles.

–*adj.* Governmental; formal; official. – Mr. Harris is studying the *state* papers of Abraham Lincoln.

stat•ed (STAY-tid) *adj.* Fixed or definite; set. –Most clubs meet at *stated* times and places. Our club meets on Monday evenings at eight in the school gymnasium.

state•house (STAYT-howss) *n. statehouses.* (Sometimes spelled with a capital "S.") The building in which a state legislature meets and conducts its affairs.

state•ment (STAYT-mənt) *n. statements.* 1. A report; a formal account, written or spoken. – The man who saw the accident made a *statement* to the police.

2. A listing showing how much money you owe or how much is due you.–According to my bank *statement,* I have $14.36 in the bank.

stat•ic (STAT-ik) *n.* An electrical disturbance in the air that causes crackling sounds and otherwise interferes with clear reception of radio signals.–It was difficult to hear the broadcast because of the *static.*

–*adj.* Stationary; at rest; standing still.–The water in a river is never *static;* it is always moving.

–*Static electricity* is electricity whose charges do not move in a current. It is produced when certain materials are rubbed together, such as silk and glass. When you walk across a rug on a cold day and receive a shock from the metal door handle, its cause is a charge of *static electricity* created by the rubbing of your shoes on the rug. The charge jumps from you to the door handle.

sta•tion (STAY-shən) *n. stations.* 1. A regular stopping place for trains or buses. – A railroad *station* is a building in which people wait for trains.

2. An appointed place of duty.–The Safety Patrol boys stood at their *stations* to help the little children cross the streets.

–*v. stations, stationed, stationing.* Locate for duty.–My brother is *stationed* at an army camp nearby.

sta•tion•ar•y (STAY-shə-nair-ee) *adj.* 1. Fixed in one place; not movable.—Our wash-tubs are *stationary*. So is the furnace.
2. Not changing in size or number. – The size of our class has been *stationary* all year.

sta•tion•er•y (STAY-shə-nair-ee) *n.* Writing materials, such as paper and envelopes. – Mother keeps her *stationery* in the desk.

sta•tis•tics (stə-TISS-tiks) *n. sing.* and *pl.* 1. (In the *sing.*) The collecting and analyzing of numerical data with the goal of reaching some numerical estimate. One would use *statistics* to estimate anything from how much spinach will be eaten in a certain town in a given year to how many trucks will cross a certain bridge in a given day.
2. (In the *pl.*) Numerical facts or data which have been collected and analyzed.—*Statistics* show that everyone in our town who works is earning twice as much this year as he did five years ago.

stat•ue (STACH-oo) *n. statues.* A carved or molded figure of a person or animal. *Statues* are made of stone, clay, metal, wood, etc. —We saw the *statue* of Abraham Lincoln in Washington.

stat•ure (STACH-er) *n. statures.* Natural height.—Dwarfs are persons of very short *stature.* – Giants are persons of very tall *stature.*

sta•tus (STAY-təss *or* STAT-əss) *n. statuses.* 1. Social or professional position. – He enjoys a high *status* in medical circles. He is highly regarded as a doctor by other doctors. —Mr. Smith's present *status* is that of vice-president of the firm.
2. State or condition; situation.—What is the present *status* of the ball game? Who is winning and what is the score?

stat•ute (STACH-oot) *n. statutes.* A law.—*Statutes* against stealing are part of the law of every land.

stay (STAY) *n. stays.* 1. A time of staying in a place. – We had an enjoyable *stay* at the farm.
2. A support.—*Stays* of rope or wire support the mast.
—*v. stays, stayed, staying.* Remain; live; reside; be (in one place).—You go and I will *stay* here.—Bob has gone to Grandmother's to *stay* for the summer.

stead•y (STED-ee) *adj.; steadily, adv.* 1. Regular; always the same; not jerky.—Grandmother's writing is *steady.*—Father drives the car at a *steady* speed.
2. Firm; not shaky or wavering.—The man's step is *steady.* He doesn't totter or shake when he walks.—The big tree is *steady.*

steak (STAYK) *n. steaks.* A slice of meat (or fish), usually beef, to be fried or broiled.—We got a two-pound *steak* at the butcher's.

steal (STEEL) *v. steals, stole, stealing.* 1. Take something that belongs to another person without his permission.—The Bible tells one not to *steal.*—The dog *stole* the cat's food.
2. Move quietly and secretly.—Bob *stole* into the kitchen to taste the stew.

steam (STEEM) *n.* Water turned into gas or vapor by heat. When water boils, it throws out moisture into the air. This moisture is *steam.* You cannot see *steam.* When *steam* is turning back to water, it forms a white cloud of tiny drops, also called *steam.*—Some homes are heated by *steam.*—Some engines are run by the power of *steam.*
—*v. steams, steamed, steaming.* 1. Treat or cook with steam.—Mother *steams* bread to freshen it. She puts hard bread into a pan with holes in it, sets it over a kettle of boiling water, and covers it up. Foods can be cooked in this way, too.
2. Give off steam.—The water in the teakettle is *steaming.*
3. Go by steam.—The ship *steamed* out of the harbor.

steam•boat (STEEM-boht) *n. steamboats.* A boat which is driven by steam power.

steam en•gine (STEEM en-jən) *steam engines.* An engine driven by steam power. —Many railroad engines are *steam engines.*

steam•er (STEEM-er) *n. steamers.* 1. A ship, boat, or engine that is moved by steam.
2. A kind of pan with holes in it for steaming food.—Mother cooked the pudding in a *steamer.*

steam•ship (STEEM-ship) *n. steamships.* A ship which is driven by steam power.

steed (STEED) *n. steeds.* A horse, especially one of high spirit.—The knight rode a gallant *steed.*

steel (STEEL) *n.* and *adj.* Iron that has been heated and mixed with carbon and other substances to make it harder and stronger. *Steel* is used to make many things that get hard use and must be very strong. – The bodies of most cars are made of *steel.*
–*v. steels, steeled, steeling.* Make strong or tough; make able to resist. – John *steeled* himself against possible disappointment.

steep (STEEP) *v. steeps, steeped, steeping.* Soak.–Tea is better if *steeped* in boiling water.
–*adj. steeper, steepest; steeply, adv.* Slanting sharply.–The boys climbed the *steep* hill.

stee•ple (STEE-pəl) *n. steeples.* The pointed tower on a church roof.

steer (STIR) *n. steers.* The young male of beef cattle. – *Steers* are killed to provide meat.
–*v. steers, steered, steering.* Direct; guide; cause to go in the direction desired. – Bob *steered* his bicycle through the crowded street. – We turn the steering wheel on an automobile to *steer* the car and make it go where we want it to.

stem (STEM) *n. stems.* 1. The main stalk of a plant.–Flowers and leaves are joined to the main *stem* by smaller *stems.*
2. The tube of a smoking pipe through which smoke is drawn into the mouth.
3. A slender support like the stem of a plant. –The glass has a *stem* at the bottom.
–*v. stems, stemmed, stemming.* 1. Remove the stems of.–Jane *stemmed* and pitted the cherries for the pie.
2. Grow out of, as from a stem.–The riots *stemmed* from unemployment.
3. Make headway against.–The ship *stemmed* the tide.
4. Stop; decrease. – The flow of blood was *stemmed* by applying a tourniquet.

sten•cil (STEN-səl) *n. stencils.* 1. A sheet of paper or metal with designs or letters cut through it. When you lay out a *stencil* on paper and brush ink across the *stencil,* the cutout designs or letters will show on the paper.

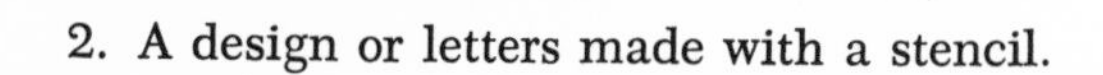

2. A design or letters made with a stencil.

ste•nog•ra•pher (stə-NAHG-rə-fer) *n. stenographers.* A person who can write down spoken words as fast as they are said by a special way of writing called shorthand.

step (STEP) *n. steps.* 1. The placing of one foot forward.–Jack took six *steps* to get to the blackboard.–The distance which one can put one foot forward is also a *step.*
2. A regular movement of the feet in dancing.–Mary taught Jack the new dance *step.*
3. A foot*step* is the sound of feet when walking or running.
4. One footboard of a stairway or ladder.– The first *step* of our hall stairs is covered with a rubber mat.
5. An act; a thing to do; one of a series of such actions.–The first *step* in building a house is to dig the basement.
–*v. steps, stepped, stepping.* Move by placing one foot in a new forward position while the other foot remains where it was, as in walking.–Father *stepped* up one stair.

step•fa•ther (STEP-fah-th̲er) *n. stepfathers.* The husband of one's mother, but not one's real father.–After Bill's father died, his mother married another man. This man is Bill's *stepfather.*

step•lad•der (STEP-lad-er) *n. stepladders.* A ladder with two parts hinged together so it will stand up by itself. A *stepladder* has flat steps instead of rungs to stand on.

step•moth•er (STEP-muth̲-er) *n. stepmothers.* The wife of one's father, but not one's real mother.–After Cinderella's own mother died, her father married another woman. This woman was Cinderella's *stepmother.*

steppe (STEP) *n. steppes.* A vast treeless plain, especially one of those in parts of the Soviet Union.

ster•e•o•phon•ic (stair-ee-ə-FAHN-ik) *adj.* Made by a special process for reproducing sounds with great realism.–Father bought an album of *stereophonic* records.

ster•e•o•scope (STAIR-ee-ə-skohp) *n. stereoscopes.* A viewing instrument by means of which two slightly different pictures of the same subject may be seen as one. Pictures seen through a *stereoscope* have a three-dimensional quality, or a feeling of depth.–My grandmother has a *stereoscope.*

ster•ile (STAIR-əl) *adj.* 1. Free of living germs.—The doctor placed a *sterile* bandage on the wound.
2. Not able to produce crops; not fertile; barren.—It is now possible to irrigate *sterile* desert areas and make them fertile.

ster•i•lize (STAIR-ə-lyz) *v. sterilizes, sterilized, sterilizing.* Make sterile or free from living germs.—The nurse *sterilizes* the doctor's instruments in boiling water.

stern (STERN) *n. sterns.* The back part of a boat.
—*adj. sterner, sternest; sternly, adv.* 1. Strict.—Our teacher plays with us during recess, but during class she is very *stern.* She will not allow any laughing or whispering during our lessons.
2. Harsh; angry.—Jack called his dog away from the smaller dog in a *stern* voice.

steth•o•scope (STETH-ə-skohp) *n. stethoscopes.* An instrument used by doctors for listening to sounds in the body, such as the heartbeat.—The doctor listened to the patient's breathing with his *stethoscope.*

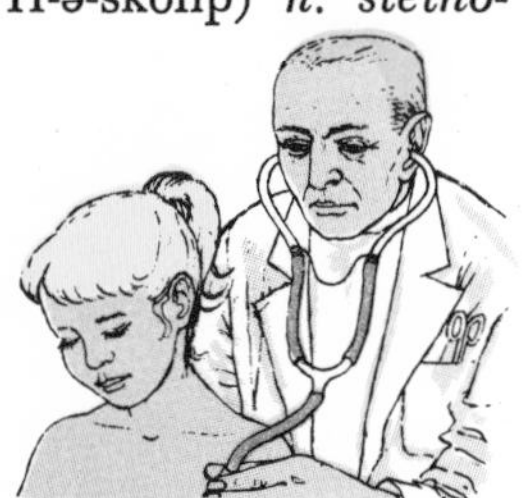

stew (STOO *or* STYOO) *n. stews.* A dish of vegetables and meat boiled together slowly.—Lamb *stew* is Father's favorite dish.
—*v. stews, stewed, stewing.* Cook by boiling slowly.—The cook *stewed* the prunes.

stew•ard (STOO- *or* STYOO-erd) *n. stewards.* 1. An officer on a ship in charge of food and sleeping quarters for passengers and crew.
2. A man on a ship who takes care of rooms, waits on table, and performs other duties, under the direction of a chief *steward.*
3. A man in charge of the dining car on a train.

stew•ard•ess (STOO- *or* STYOO-er-dəss) *n. stewardesses.* 1. A woman steward.
2. A woman on an airplane who looks after the comfort of the passengers and feeds them.

stick (STIK) *n. sticks.* 1. A long, slender piece of wood.—The boys cut *sticks* to make a kite.
2. Something shaped like a stick of wood, as a *stick* of candy, a *stick* of chewing gum, a *stick* of dynamite.—A cane is a walking *stick.*
—*v. sticks, stuck, sticking.* 1. Fasten together with glue or paste.—*Stick* these two pieces of paper together.
2. Hold fast.—The dish *stuck* to the table.
3. Prick; pierce.—Be careful or you will *stick* your finger with the pin.
4. Put or thrust.—The cat *stuck* its nose into the milk.
5. Be unable to continue; fail to work.—The old car *stuck* halfway up the hill.
—*Stick to* sometimes means to keep at.—*Stick to* your work until it is done.

stiff (STIF) *adj. stiffer, stiffest; stiffly, adv.* 1. Not easily bent or moved.—Cardboard is *stiff;* paper is easy to fold.—The boy's sore arm is *stiff* now, but it will soon loosen up as he uses it.
2. Thick; solid; firm.—Gelatin becomes *stiff* when it cools.
3. Hard; harsh.—The troops engaged in a *stiff* battle.—A *stiff* breeze came up.
4. Formal and unbending in manner.—He made a *stiff* bow, without a word of greeting.

stiff•en (STIF-ən) *v. stiffens, stiffened, stiffening.* Make or become stiff or firm.—Mother uses starch to *stiffen* the collars and cuffs on Father's shirts.—The pudding *stiffens* when it cools.—The army's resistance *stiffened* in the face of the attack.

stile (STYL) *n. stiles.* 1. A step or steps used in going over a fence or a wall.—The old woman's pig would not go over the *stile.*
2. A gate that allows only one person to pass through at a time.

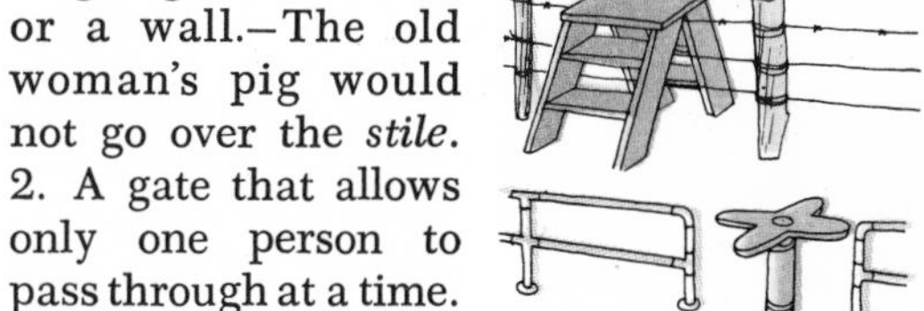

still (STIL) *n. stills.* A device used in purifying water and in making whiskey and other liquors.—You can make fresh water out of salt water with a *still.*
—*v. stills, stilled, stilling.* Quiet; make still.—Mother *stilled* the baby's crying with a lullaby.
—*adj., adv.,* and *conj.* 1. Not moving.—Stand *still.* Do not move.
2. Quiet; silent.—Be *still.* Do not make a sound.
3. Nevertheless; and yet.—Ruth says her tables again and again; *still,* she doesn't seem to know them.
4. Even.—Bob can write well when he writes fast; he can write *still* better when he writes slowly.
5. Yet.—At noon the fire was *still* burning. It had not gone out.

still•ness (STIL-nəss) *n.* Quietness; calm.—The *stillness* of the night is restful.—This lake is known for its *stillness.* The water is never ruffled.

stilt (STILT) *n. stilts.* One of a pair of long poles which has a step or a footrest attached so that the user is elevated above the ground.–Tom learned to walk on *stilts.*

stim·u·lant (STIM-yə-lənt) *n. stimulants.* Something which stimulates, excites, or rouses, usually for a short time. – A cold shower sometimes acts as a *stimulant.*–Various medicines and beverages, including tea and coffee, are *stimulants.*

stim·u·late (STIM-yə-layt) *v. stimulates, stimulated, stimulating.* Rouse to action; stir up; excite.–He was *stimulated* and encouraged by the good news.–The teacher is trying to *stimulate* a classroom discussion.
–*stimulation, n.*

sting (STING) *n. stings.* 1. Bite (of an insect).–Bees and other insects give painful *stings.*
2. The injury made by the bite of an insect.
3. The part of a bee, insect, or animal used for stinging.
4. A sharp, burning pain.–The *sting* of the salt in Jack's eyes made him come out of the water.
5. A sharpness; an intention to hurt.–Tom felt the *sting* of his friend's words of ridicule.
–*v. stings, stung, stinging.* 1. Bite (by an insect).–The mosquito *stung* me.
2. Cause a sharp, burning pain.–Salt *stings* if it gets into a cut on your finger.
3. Hurt by sharpness of word or manner.– Tom was *stung* by his friend's ridicule.

stingray (STING-ray) *n. stingrays.* A flat fish having a long whiplike tail with one or more spines. *Stingrays* live mostly near the bottoms of warm seas. Their tails are used as weapons and are quite dangerous.

stin·gy (STIN-jee) *adj. stingier, stingiest.* Not generous; unwilling to spend or give away money or other things.–The *stingy* man spends money on nobody, not even himself.

stink (STINGK) *n. stinks.* A bad smell; foul odor.–A leak in the gas pipe caused a *stink* in the house.
–*v. stinks, stank* or *stunk, stinking.* Give off a bad odor.–Garbage, if allowed to stand a long time, *stinks.*

stir (STER) *n. stirs.* 1. Excitement.–The accident in the factory caused a *stir.*
2. Movement.–We could hear a *stir* in the kitchen.
3. A mixing.–She gave the batter a *stir.*
–*v. stirs, stirred, stirring.* 1. Move or mix, as with a spoon.–Mother *stirs* the candy when it is cooking to keep it from burning.
2. Move a little.–The wind made the leaves *stir.*
3. Arouse; excite.–The man *stirs* up trouble wherever he goes.

stir·rup (STER- *or* STIR-əp) *n. stirrups.* One of a pair of footrests or supports for the feet of a person riding horseback. *Stirrups* are fastened to the saddle and hang down on each side.

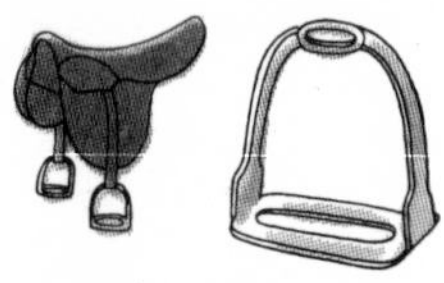

stitch (STICH) *n. stitches.* 1. A single passage of thread through the cloth in sewing.
2. In crocheting or knitting, *stitches* are made by twisting the thread around the needles in certain ways.
3. A sharp, sudden pain.–Grandmother got a *stitch* in her side when she bent over to pick up her glove.
–*v. stitches, stitched, stitching.* Sew; make stitches.–Mother *stitched* the hem in Mary's dress.

stock (STAHK) *n. sing.* and *pl.* Cows, horses, sheep, and other domestic animals. – The farmer keeps his *stock* in the barn.

stock (STAHK) *n. stocks.* 1. Share of investment in a business.–Father buys *stocks,* or lends his money to a business. If the business makes a profit, Father receives a dividend, or share in the profit.
2. Family.–She comes of Irish *stock.*
3. (In the plural) Wooden frame in which wrongdoers in olden times were forced to sit or stand in public for long periods. Many had holes for the hands and feet.
4. A supply, especially of things to sell.– After the Christmas rush, the stores had only a small *stock* left.
–*v. stocks, stocked, stocking.* Have or get a supply of (usually in a store). – Mr. Jones doesn't *stock* hats.

stock•ade (stah-KAYD) *n. stockades.* 1. A defensive enclosure made of high stakes stuck upright in the ground. The early pioneers of America built *stockades* around their dwellings to protect them from Indian attacks.

2. Any such high, fenced enclosure.—The cowboy showed us a cattle *stockade.*

stock•ing (STAHK-ing) *n. stockings.* One of a pair of coverings for the feet and lower legs. —Mary wears wool *stockings* in the winter.

stock•yard (STAHK-yahrd) *n. stockyards.* A yard or enclosure where cattle and sheep are kept before they are sent on to markets or slaughterhouses.

stoke (STOHK) *v. stokes, stoked, stoking.* Tend; put fuel in (a furnace, boiler, etc.).—Father *stokes* the coal furnace. He stirs up the fire and puts coal on when it is needed.

stok•er (STOH-ker) *n. stokers.* A person or a machine that takes care of a furnace by putting coal into it. A *stoker* in a factory or on a ship takes care of the fires which heat the boilers.

stole (STOHL) *n. stoles.* A woman's scarf or shoulder covering, often of fur, wool, or silk. —*v.* One form of the verb *steal.*—The hungry man *stole* food.

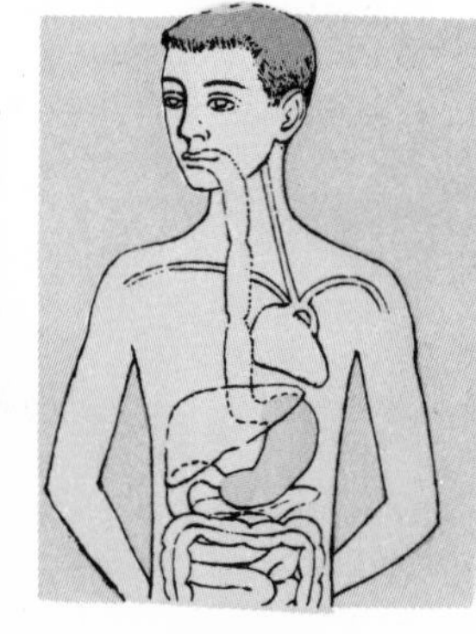

sto•len (STOH-lən) *v.* and *adj.* One form of the verb *steal.* – The jewelry was *stolen.*

stom•ach (STUM-ək) *n. stomachs.* The pouch inside the body into which food goes when swallowed. The *stomach* helps to digest the food.

stone (STOHN) *n. stones* and *adj.* 1. A piece of rock.—The house was built of large *stones.*
2. Rock; a hard mineral material found in the earth.—The house was built of *stone.*
3. A gem.—Rubies, opals, and diamonds are precious *stones* used in jewelry.
4. A large seed in a fruit such as the peach or plum.—Mother took the *stones* out of the peaches before preserving them.
—*v. stones, stoned, stoning.* 1. Throw stones at. —In olden times criminals were sometimes *stoned* to death.
2. Take the seeds out of.—Mary helped Mother *stone* the cherries before preserving them.

stood (STUHD) *v.* One form of the verb *stand.*—The boy *stood* by his chair.

stool (STOOL) *n. stools.* 1. A seat without a back.—Mother sits on a kitchen *stool* to mix the cake.
2. A low footrest with legs.

stoop (STOOP) *n. stoops.* 1. A small entrance porch.—In the summer, Mother sometimes sits on the *stoop.*
2. A slumping posture.—That girl does not stand straight; she has a *stoop.*
—*v. stoops, stooped, stooping.* 1. Let the shoulders and head lean forward.—That girl *stoops.*
2. Bend down.—Can you *stoop* and touch the floor with your fingers without bending your knees?
3. Do something unworthy of oneself.—Do not *stoop* to stealing.

stop (STAHP) *n. stops.* 1. A halt; a standstill. —Bring the car to a *stop* at a red light.
2. A stopping place.—The bus *stop* is at the next corner.
3. A device for controlling the tone or quality of tone of a musical instrument.—You can see the *stops* at the side of an organ keyboard.
—*v. stops, stopped, stopping.* 1. Halt; come to a standstill.—*Stop*, look, and listen before you cross the street.
2. Cease; quit.—The bell *stopped* ringing.
3. Close or stuff up.—The boy *stopped* the leak in the dike by putting his thumb into the hole.
4. Block; prevent from moving.—A big, fat man with packages *stopped* the turnstile.
5. Cause to cease or come to an end.—Mother *stopped* the baby's crying by giving her a cracker.—Father *stopped* the water from running by turning off the faucet.
6. Prevent.—Father caught Baby just in time to *stop* her from falling.
7. Drop in (at); visit.—I *stopped* at the bank to cash a check on my way home.

stop•light (STAHP-lyt) *n. stoplights.* 1. A traffic signal light.—The busy intersection has a *stoplight* to control the flow of traffic.

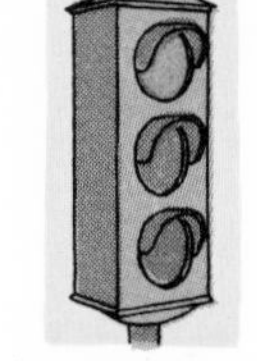

2. A red signal light on the rear end of an automobile.—When a driver steps on his brake, the *stoplight* automatically flashes a warning that the car is slowing or stopping.

stop•per (STAHP-er) *n. stoppers.* A piece of cork, rubber, or glass used to close a bottle or other container.—Mary put the *stopper* in the vinegar bottle.—The perfume bottle has a fancy glass *stopper.*

stop watch (STAHP wahch) *stop watches.* A watch whose hands can be stopped or started at will, usually by pressing a button. *Stop watches* are used especially to time races or other sporting events.

stor•age (STOR-ij) *n.* 1. Being stored; keeping things stored; a place where things may be kept for safekeeping.—We have some furniture in *storage.*—At home our place for *storage* is the attic.

2. The amount paid for storing a thing.—She had to pay twenty-five dollars *storage* on her fur coat.

stor•age bat•ter•y (STOR-ij bat-ə-ree) *storage batteries.* A battery that stores electrical energy. *Storage batteries* can be very easily recharged when they have run down.

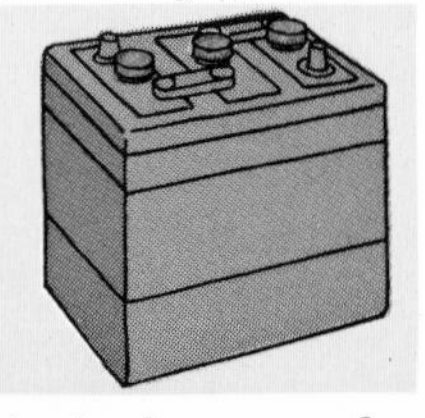

store (STOR) *n. stores.* 1. A shop, or place where things are sold.—Bob went to the fruit *store* to buy a dozen oranges.

2. A supply.—We have quite a *store* of preserved fruit on the cellar shelves.

—*v. stores, stored, storing.* Put or keep in a special place for later use.—We *store* potatoes, onions, and canned goods in the cellar.

stork (STORK) *n. storks.* A wading bird with long legs, a long neck, and a long bill.

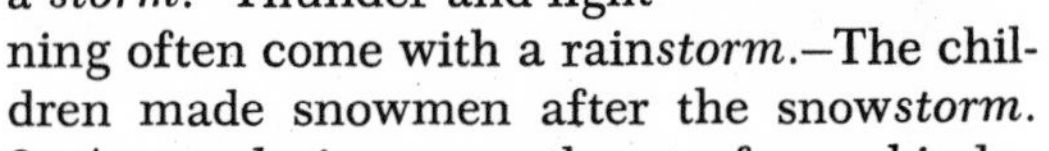

storm (STORM) *n. storms; stormy, adj.* 1. Any strong natural disturbance in the air. Sometimes there is rain, snow, sleet, or hail, and a strong wind blowing during a *storm.*—Thunder and lightning often come with a rain*storm.*—The children made snowmen after the snow*storm.*

2. An explosion or outburst of any kind.—Mary burst into a *storm* of tears.

3. Violent military attack.—The army took the town by *storm.*

—*v. storms, stormed, storming.* 1. Rush into by force and numbers.—The winners of the ball game *stormed* the schoolroom.

2. Rush angrily.—Jack *stormed* into the room and asked who had taken his bicycle.

sto•ry (STOR-ee) *n. stories.* 1. A report of things that have happened, or of imaginary happenings made up by someone.—Sally likes the *story* of Chicken Little.

2. A falsehood; a lie.—If you do something wrong, do not tell a *story* about it; tell the truth.

3. A floor, or a level, of a building.—We live in a house with two *stories.* It has two floors, on two different levels. The kitchen, dining room, and living room are on the first *story.* The bedrooms are on the second *story.*

stout (STOWT) *adj. stouter, stoutest; stoutly, adv.* 1. Heavily built; fat; thick.—Jack Sprat was thin and his wife was *stout.*—The tramp carried a *stout* stick to defend himself against dogs.

2. Sturdy; strong.—The boy set out to seek his fortune with a *stout* heart.

stove (STOHV) *n. stoves.* A box built of iron, brick, or some other material that does not burn, in which a fire can be made, or an electric source of heat turned on, for cooking or heating. There are electric and gas *stoves.*

In some *stoves,* coal or wood is burned. Houses used to be heated by *stoves,* but now *stoves* are used mostly for cooking.

strad•dle (STRAD-l) *v. straddles, straddled, straddling.* To spread the legs far apart; to sit on something with one leg on either side. –Bob *straddled* the horse to ride it.–The boy is *straddling* a stool.

straight (STRAYT) *adj. straighter, straightest* and *adv.* 1. Not crooked; without turns, curves, or bends.–The road goes *straight* for five miles, and then it turns.
2. Right; in order.–Our teacher asked us if we had all our lessons *straight.*–Mother told Mary to put the sofa cushions *straight.*
3. Direct; directly.–Go *straight* to school. Go now and go the shortest way.
4. Honest.–That man is *straight.* You can trust him.
5. Serious.–John kept a *straight* face in the classroom, though he wanted to laugh at the antics of the dog outside.

straight•en (STRAY-tn) *v. straightens, straightened, straightening.* 1. Make straight. –The carpenter *straightened* the crooked nail before he hammered it.
2. Tidy; make neat.–The teacher told us to *straighten* up our desks.

strain (STRAYN) *n. strains.* 1. Injury caused by pulling a muscle or ligament.–Father's injury was only a *strain.*
2. Pressure; weight; tension.–The *strain* on the telephone wires caused by the falling tree made them break.–Mother was under a great *strain* when Father and Baby were sick.
3. (Often in plural) Music; melody.–He recognized the *strains* of "The Star-Spangled Banner."
4. Streak; trace.–There was a *strain* of uneasiness in his voice.
–*v. strains, strained, straining.* 1. Stretch; pull too tight.–The clothesline was *strained* by the wet clothes hanging on it.
2. Sprain; injure by pulling a muscle or ligament.– Father lifted a heavy rock in the garden and *strained* his back.
3. Press through a sieve or strainer to remove little pieces.–Mother *strained* the orange juice to get out the seeds and pulp.
4. Try as hard as possible.–Jack *strained* to lift the table.

strain•er (STRAY-ner) *n. strainers.* A kitchen tool with a fine screen or wire net used for straining things; a pan with small holes at the bottom; a sieve.–Tomatoes, fruits, and soups are often pressed through a *strainer* to take out seeds and pulp.

strait (STRAYT) *n. straits.* 1. A narrow, natural channel of water that joins two larger bodies of water.–The *Strait* of Gibraltar connects the Atlantic Ocean and the Mediterranean Sea.

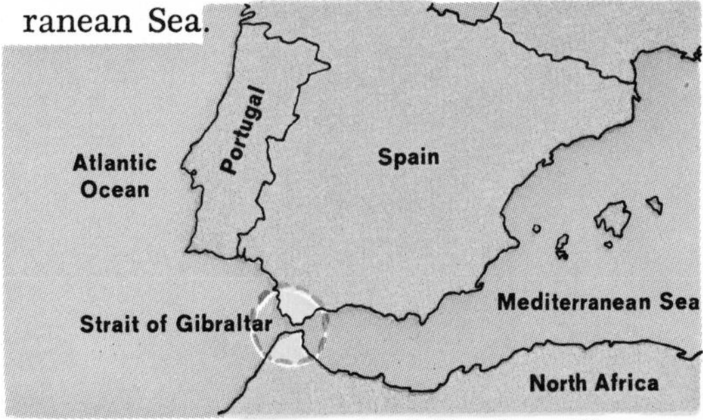

2. (Usually in plural) Difficulty; distress.– The man was in desperate financial *straits* before he found a job.

strand (STRAND) *n. strands.* 1. One of the many fine threads twisted together to make heavier threads, ropes, yarns, and so forth.
2. A string.–Mother wore a *strand* of pearls with her black dress.–Grandmother brushed a *strand* of hair off Mary's forehead.
–*v. strands, stranded, stranding.* 1. Place in a helpless position.–The lost boy was *stranded* in the strange city without money.
2. Force aground.–A ship was *stranded* on the big rocks.

strange (STRAYNJ) *adj. stranger, strangest; strangely, adv.* 1. Not known, seen, or heard of before; new and not familiar.–The man's face was *strange* to Bob.–This part of the city is *strange* to me.
2. Queer; not natural; odd. – Mother felt *strange* after eating the fish. – Mary looks *strange* in a baby bonnet; she's a big girl now.
3. Shy.–The new boy felt *strange* among so many boys he didn't know.

stran•ger (STRAYN-jer) *n. strangers.* 1. A person whom one has never known, seen, or heard of before.–Mother opened the door and found a *stranger* standing on the porch.– This boy is a *stranger* in our school.
2. A person in a place unfamiliar to him.– I am a *stranger* in Boston. Can you tell me how to reach Boston Common?

stran•gle (STRANG-gəl) *v. strangles, strangled, strangling.* 1. Kill or die by choking.– The hero in the story *strangled* the villain. He killed him by holding him tightly by the neck so that he could no longer breathe.–Do not fasten your puppy's collar too tight, or he may *strangle.*
2. Choke; cut off the breath.–Grandfather's cough seems to *strangle* him. It makes him gasp for breath painfully.

strap (STRAP) *n. straps.* A narrow strip of leather or other material that can be bent easily.–Father put a *strap* around the suitcase.–*Straps* of metal are used on boxes to make them stronger.
–*v. straps, strapped, strapping.* 1. Fasten with a strap.–Bob *strapped* the basket onto his bicycle.
2. Whip with a strap.–Long ago students were often *strapped* as punishment.

stra•te•gic (strə-TEE-jik) *adj.; strategically, adv.* 1. Based on careful planning, management, or direction.–The army made a *strategic* withdrawal from the city.–Mary took up a *strategic* position in the school hall, where she could catch Joan and give her a message at lunchtime. She had thought out where Joan would be and how she, Mary, could best reach her.
2. Important or useful, especially in the planning and direction of military projects.–Bridges usually are *strategic* military targets.

strat•o•sphere (STRAT-ə-sfir *or* STRAY-tə-sfir) *n.* The part of the atmosphere that extends from a point about ten miles above earth to a point about sixty miles above earth. Below the *stratosphere* is the troposphere and above it is the ionosphere. Temperature varies very little within the *stratosphere.*

straw (STRAW) *n. straws* and *adj.* 1. A dry stem of wheat, rye, oats, or other grain after the grain has been threshed or taken off.–*Straw* is used as bedding for cattle, to make hats and paper, to pack china, bricks, or other breakable things, and for other purposes.
2. A thin tube of paper.–Bob sips his ice-cream soda through a *straw.*

straw•ber•ry (STRAW-bair-ee) *n. strawberries.* A red berry that grows on creeping vines, close to the ground.

stray (STRAY) *v. strays, strayed, straying.* Wander.–Little Red Riding Hood *strayed* away from the path to pick flowers.
–*adj.* 1. Lost.–Jack found a *stray* puppy.
2. Scattered; loose. – A few *stray* curls showed beneath her hat.

streak (STREEK) *n. streaks.* A line or stripe. –Joe got a *streak* of paint on his face.
–*v. streaks, streaked, streaking.* Mark with long lines or stripes.–The sunset *streaked* the sky with crimson.

stream (STREEM) *n. streams.* 1. A flow of water or other liquid, or gas.–A *stream* of water came from the faucet.
2. A river or brook.–We went to the *stream* to fish.
3. A steady line of people or things. – A *stream* of people poured out of the theater.
–*v. streams, streamed, streaming.* 1. Run or flow.–Light *streamed* from the open door.
2. Wave or blow.–The children marched in the parade with flags and banners *streaming.*
3. Move steadily in large numbers.–Large crowds of people *streamed* out of the theater after the play.

stream•er (STREE-mer) *n. streamers.* A long narrow flag, ribbon, or anything that will wave.–The children carried *streamers* in the parade.

stream•line (STREEM-lyn) *v. streamlines, streamlined, streamlining.* To shape so that surrounding air, water, or gas will pass to the sides without being blocked off, and so not check the speed of movement.–Airplanes must be *streamlined* so that they can fly swiftly.

street (STREET) *n. streets.* An open way in a town or city on which people travel.–Automobiles, bicycles, and people walking filled the narrow *streets.*

street•car (STREET-kahr) *n. streetcars.* A large, public car which runs on tracks in the street.–*Streetcars* are run by electricity.

strength (STRENGKTH *or* STRENGTH) *n. strengths.* The quality of being strong.–The workman had great *strength.* He could lift big rocks.–Grandmother didn't have much *strength* after her sickness.–The *strength* of his argument lay in the fact that his idea would save money.

strength•en (STRENGK- *or* STRENG-thən) *v. strengthens, strengthened, strengthening.* Make or grow strong; give strength to.–The men *strengthened* the bridge by putting more timbers under it.

stren•u•ous (STREN-yoo-əss) *adj.; strenuously, adv.* 1. Very energetic; extremely active.–The senator is a *strenuous* fighter for human rights.

2. Marked by great effort.–The candidates are waging a *strenuous* campaign for election to office.

stress (STRESS) *n. stresses.* 1. Emphasis.–In our school much *stress* was put on spelling. In our class much attention was given to learning to spell.
2. A strain; a force.–The rafters in the building are under constant *stress.*
3. An accent.–He put *stress* on the words "as we, and we alone, may decide."
–*v. stresses, stressed, stressing.* Accent or emphasize.–In some music we *stress* the first note of each measure.–In saying the word "kitten," we *stress* the first syllable. – Our school *stresses* spelling.

stretch (STRECH) *n. stretches.* 1. A reaching out; extension.–He cannot be considered tall by any *stretch* of the imagination.
2. A continuous area; a section.–This is a beautiful *stretch* of road.
–*v. stretches, stretched, stretching.* 1. Extend; reach out.–The children *stretched* their arms high over their heads. – The cat always *stretches* when she wakes up.
2. Spread apart.–Bob had to *stretch* his fingers to play the piano.
3. Reach.–Baby *stretched* out her hand for the glass of milk.
4. Make or get larger under strain.–Mary *stretched* the rubber band to get it around her book.
5. Extend or reach. – Our garden *stretches* from the house to the back fence.

stretch•er (STRECH-er) *n. stretchers.* 1. A person or thing that stretches or makes larger.–Father's shoes were stretched on a shoe *stretcher.*
2. A carrier for injured or sick people, made of two poles with heavy cloth fastened between them. A *stretcher* is carried by two men, one at each end.–The injured boy was carried to the ambulance on a *stretcher* and rushed to a hospital.

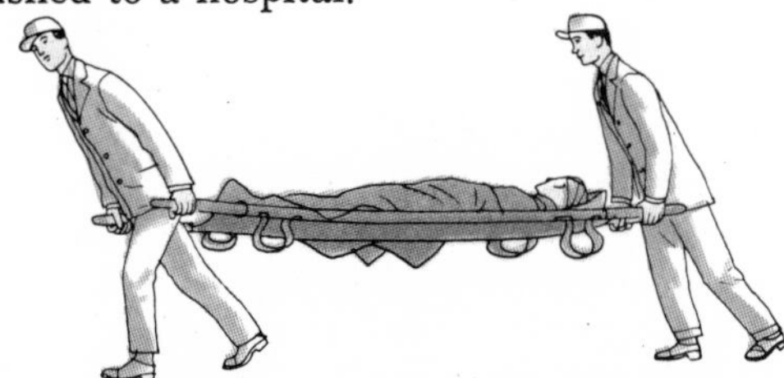

strew (STROO) *v. strews, strewed, strewing.* Scatter.–Do not *strew* your toys all over the house. – When Mary dropped the bag, it *strewed* beans all over the floor.

strict (STRIKT) *adj. stricter, strictest; strictly, adv.* 1. Demanding obedience to rules. – The principal is very *strict.* He makes all the children obey the rules carefully.
2. Exact; just right.–Bob made the measurements for the model airplane with *strict* accuracy.
3. Absolute; total; extremely careful. – The monks observed *strict* silence at their work.

stride (STRYD) *n. strides.* A long step.–Bob measured the field with a hundred *strides.*
–*v. strides, strode, striding.* Walk with long steps.–The teacher *strode* to the back of the room to open the window.

strife (STRYF) *n.* Fighting; struggle; conflict.–The nation was torn by *strife.*

strike (STRYK) *n. strikes.* 1. The sound of a bell or gong.–We heard the *strike* of the clock.
2. A stopping of work by workmen as a group to get more money or better working conditions.–There is a *strike* at the factory now.
3. In baseball, a miss or failure to hit a good pitch when batting.–Bob was called out on *strikes.*
4. In bowling, the knocking down of all the pins with the first ball.–Father bowled last night and had five *strikes* in a row.
–*v. strikes, struck, striking.* 1. Hit; come or bring into sharp contact with.–The boy tried to *strike* me.–The car skidded and *struck* a pole.
2. Light (a match). – Be careful when you *strike* matches.
3. Sound by hitting a bell or gong.–Mary heard the clock *strike* two.
4. Come suddenly to (one's mind).–An idea of how to make a model plane *struck* Bob today.
5. Quit work as a group to get higher pay or better working conditions.–The men at the factory have *struck;* they quit work yesterday and said they would not go back till they were promised more money.
6. Find; come upon.–The miners *struck* gold while digging.–Bob and Mary have *struck* a plan for saving money.
–*Strike out* sometimes means to mark out. –Mary spelled the word wrong and corrected it by *striking out* the wrong letter.
–*Strike out* may mean to start. – The Boy Scouts *struck out* through the woods.
–*Strike out* in baseball means for the batter to fail to hit, or fail to swing at, three good pitches.–Bob *struck out.* The pitcher *struck* him *out.*

string (STRING) *n. strings.* 1. A cord; a light rope; a heavy thread or anything else used for tying or binding.–Bob's kite *string* broke, and his kite blew away.
2. Ornaments on a string.–Mary has a *string* of beads.
3. A fine, strong cord or wire used to make the tones on violins, pianos, and some other musical instruments.

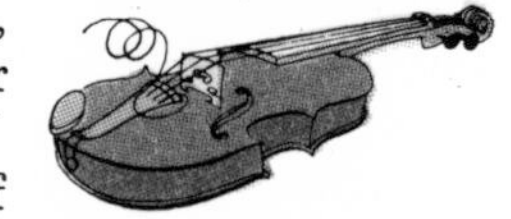

4. A row.–A *string* of stockings was hung near the decorated Christmas tree.
5. Any long, thin piece that looks like a cord. –Mother cooked the candy until the syrup formed *strings* when it dripped from a spoon.
6. A tough threadlike part of a plant.–Beans in the shell, or pod, have *strings* along the sides of the shell.
–*v. strings, strung, stringing.* 1. Remove strings from. – Mother *strings* beans before she cooks them.
2. Put on a string.–Children like to *string* beads to wear when they play "dress up."
3. Put strings on.–The violinist could not play until he had *strung* his violin.
–*String out* means to stretch out like a piece of string.–The parade was *strung out* from the river to the park.
–To *string up* something means to hang up by a string or rope.–The butcher *strung up* a leg of beef.

string bean (STRING been) *string beans.* A pod of beans. Along each side of the pod, or shell, is a stringy part that is pulled off before cooking.

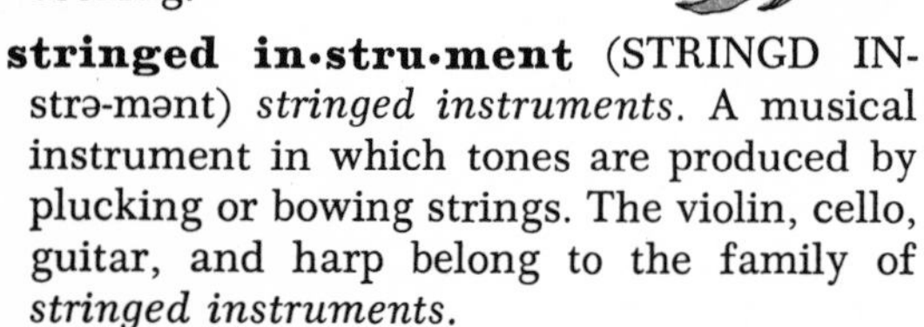

stringed in•stru•ment (STRINGD IN-strə-mənt) *stringed instruments.* A musical instrument in which tones are produced by plucking or bowing strings. The violin, cello, guitar, and harp belong to the family of *stringed instruments.*

strip (STRIP) *n. strips.* A long, narrow piece. –Mary cut off a *strip* of paper to write her spelling words on.
–*v. strips, stripped, stripping.* 1. Undress.– Mother *stripped* Baby to give her a bath.– The doctor asked the boys to *strip* before he examined them.
2. Peel off, or cut off, in strips.–The hunter *stripped* the skin from the rabbit he had shot that afternoon.
3. Make bare or empty.–The hungry children *stripped* the cupboard of all the food that had been in it.

stripe (STRYP) *n. stripes.* A broad line; a long, narrow band or strip.–The American flag has red and white *stripes.*
–*v. stripes, striped, striping.* Cover or mark with stripes. – The boys *striped* the pole with paint so it could be used for a Maypole on May Day.

strive (STRYV) *v. strives, strove, striving.* 1. Make a great effort; try or work very hard.– The man is *striving* to complete his task.
2. Battle; struggle; fight.–The firemen *strove* in vain against the flames.

stroke (STROHK) *n. strokes.* 1. A blow. – Bob chopped the piece of wood in two with one *stroke* of the ax.
2. A kind of sudden illness which often makes a person helpless.–The old man had a *stroke* last night.
3. A complete movement made over and over in a certain activity, such as skating, swimming, or rowing.–Tom rowed with long, even *strokes.*
4. A single movement, as the *stroke* of a pen, brush, pencil, etc.; the visible result of such a movement that makes a mark.–The artist's brush *strokes* in that painting are graceful and delicate.
5. A sound caused by striking.–Santa Claus came at the *stroke* of twelve by the clock.
6. A gentle caress.–Tom gave Pussy's head an affectionate *stroke.*
–*v. strokes, stroked, stroking.* Rub gently and caressingly.–Mother *stroked* Baby's head.

stroll (STROHL) *n. strolls.* A slow walk for pleasure.–The girls have gone for a *stroll.*
–*v. strolls, strolled, strolling.* Walk slowly for pleasure.–They *strolled* about for an hour.

strong (STRAWNG) *adj. stronger, strongest; strongly, adv.* 1. Not weak; having strength or force.–Prize fighters are *strong.*
2. Forceful.–A *strong* wind is blowing the ships about.–The need of money is a *strong* reason for going to work.
3. Large and able; sufficient. – The United States has a *strong* navy. It has many men and ships, and much equipment.
4. Sharp; keen; powerful.–This cheese has a *strong* taste.–The *strong* smell filled the man with disgust.
5. Concentrated.–Father likes *strong* coffee, but Mother likes it with more water in it.
6. Tough; not easily broken.–The kite string is *strong.*–The old chair is *strong,* however it may look. It will hold your weight.

strop (STRAHP) *n. strops.* A leather strap on which straight razors are sharpened.
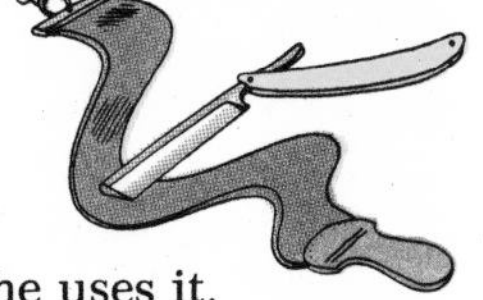
–*v. strops, stropped, stropping.* Sharpen on a strop. – The barber *strops* his razor before he uses it.

struck (STRUK) *v.* One form of the verb *strike.*–The clock *struck* four.

struc•ture (STRUK-cher) *n. structures.* 1. Anything built, as a factory or bridge. – We saw many large *structures* as we came nearer the city.
2. The way in which anything is formed or shaped.–The *structure* of Mary's face is like that of Mother's.

strug•gle (STRUG-əl) *n. struggles.* A strong effort or fight.–The men put up a great *struggle* to keep the fire from spreading. It was hard work.
–*v. struggles, struggled, struggling.* Work very hard; fight against difficulties.–The poor man had to *struggle* to feed his children.–The lion *struggled* to get out of his cage.

strung (STRUNG) *v.* One form of the verb *string.*–We *strung* popcorn for the Christmas tree.

strut (STRUT) *n. struts.* 1. A brace or support.–One of the plane's wheel *struts* was damaged in the emergency landing.
2. A haughty walk; a proud gait.–The rooster must think he is king of the barnyard, judging by his *strut.*
–*v. struts, strutted, strutting.*–Walk with exaggerated pride.–The peacock *strutted* in the garden, his tail spread wide.

stub (STUB) *n. stubs.* 1. Short, dull piece left after the main part is gone.–Mary has used the pencil down to a *stub.*–Father threw the *stub* of his cigar away.
2. A pen with a blunt point.–Mary likes a sharp pen, but Bob likes a *stub.*
3. A short part of a bill or ticket that is torn off and given to the buyer as a receipt. – Tickets such as theater tickets and train tickets have *stubs.* Checks have *stubs* that are left in the checkbook as a record.
–*v. stubs, stubbed, stubbing.* Bump (one's toe). –Don't *stub* your toe against the low step.

stub•born (STUB-ern) *adj.; stubbornly, adv.* Refusing to give in to others or to change one's mind; obstinate.–Father told Jack he was solving the problem in the wrong way, but Jack was *stubborn.* Jack insisted that he could do it his own way.

stuck (STUK) *v.* One form of the verb *stick.* –Bob *stuck* the stamp on the envelope.

stu•dent (STOO- *or* STYOO-dənt) *n. students.* A person who studies; a pupil.–There are five hundred *students* in our school. – People who study law are *students* of law. – Our minister is a *student* of the Bible.

stu•di•o (STOO- *or* STYOO-dee-oh) *n. studios.* 1. A room where a painter, musician, or other artist works.

2. A place where radio and television programs are broadcast.
3. A place where movies are made.

stud•y (STUD-ee) *n. studies.* 1. A room used for reading, learning, or writing.–The writer went into his *study* to work on his new book.
2. A subject that one tries to learn.–Geography, English, and history are some of Bob's *studies.*
3. A written work produced as the result of research.–The botanist did a *study* on the uses of palm trees.
–*v. studies, studied, studying.* 1. To try to learn or understand by reading, thinking, or practicing.–Ann is *studying* French.
2. Try to figure out; think about.–Bob *studied* the puzzle. He tried to think out a way to solve it.
3. Look at carefully. – Sally picked up the snail and *studied* it closely.

stuff (STUF) *n. stuffs.* 1. The material that things are made of.–Cotton is the best *stuff* for children's clothes. – The teacher thinks Bob has the *stuff* in him to be an engineer.
2. Material or objects of any kind.–If there were less *stuff* in this room, it would look prettier.
–*v. stuffs, stuffed, stuffing.* Fill.–She *stuffed* the doll with cotton.

stuff•ing (STUF-ing) *n. stuffings.* 1. A material used for filling a thing.–Cotton and sawdust are *stuffings* used for dolls.
2. A dressing usually made of bread crumbs mixed with seasonings and put into chicken, turkey, or other meat or food.

stum•ble (STUM-bəl) *v. stumbles, stumbled, stumbling.* 1. Trip by catching the foot.—Mary *stumbled* on the garden hose.
2. Walk unsteadily; walk shakily.—Baby is learning to walk and often *stumbles.*
3. Make a mistake.—Mary *stumbled* in spelling the long word.

stump (STUMP) *n. stumps.* 1. The short part left in the ground after a tree or plant has been cut down. —The squirrel sat on a tree *stump* and ate a nut.—Ed looked at the age rings on the *stump.*

2. The part of anything that is left when the main part is gone.

stump•y (STUMP-ee) *adj. stumpier, stumpiest.* Short and thick like a stump.—A *stumpy* little man came waddling down the street.—Jack's dog likes to thump his *stumpy* tail on the floor.

stun (STUN) *v. stuns, stunned, stunning.* 1. Make senseless or unconscious.—A blow on the head *stunned* the boy. For a time he knew nothing.
2. Shock; surprise.—We were *stunned* by the news of the accident.

stung (STUNG) *v.* One form of the verb *sting.*—A bee *stung* Grandmother.

stunt (STUNT) *n. stunts.* An unusual trick; something that is hard to do.—Acrobats and clowns amuse people by doing *stunts.*
—*v. stunts, stunted, stunting.* Check or stop (growth).—Too little exercise and too little fresh air may *stunt* one's growth.

stu•pid (STOO- *or* STYOO-pid) *adj. stupider, stupidest; stupidly, adv.* Dull; not bright or smart.—Because the child is too shy to talk much, he sometimes seems *stupid.* — The things the thoughtless man said were *stupid.*

stur•dy (STER-dee) *adj. sturdier, sturdiest; sturdily, adv.* 1. Strong; well-made; able to endure things.—This is not a very *sturdy* chair to sit on; it may not hold you.—Mary is not so *sturdy* as Sally; Mary gets sick more easily.
2. Firm.—Jack has a *sturdy* belief that his dog will come back; he really believes it, although the dog has been gone nearly a year.

stur•geon (STER-jən) *n. sturgeon* or *sturgeons.* A kind of fish that is good to eat.

sty (STY) *n. sties.* 1. A pen built for pigs. —Mother said the house was as dirty as a *sty.*

2. A red, swollen sore on the edge of the eyelid.

style (STYL) *n. styles.* 1. Fashion.—High-button shoes are not in *style.*
2. A way of doing something. — There are many different *styles* of handwriting among the students at school.

styl•ish (STYL-ish) *adj.; stylishly, adv.* Fashionable. — *Stylish* clothes are the kind that well-dressed people are wearing.—The clothes worn a hundred years ago are not *stylish* now.

sub•due (səb-DOO *or* -DYOO) *v. subdues, subdued, subduing.* Overpower; conquer. —The sheriff and his deputies *subdued* the band of rustlers.

sub•ject (SUB-jikt) *n. subjects.* 1. The person or thing about which one is talking, writing, thinking, or studying.—The *subject* that Mary and Bob were talking about was the party for Tuesday.—The *subject* of Linda's story was "Life as a Movie Star."—My favorite *subject* is arithmetic.
2. A citizen of a kingdom.—Mr. Jones is a British *subject,* a *subject* of the British Queen.

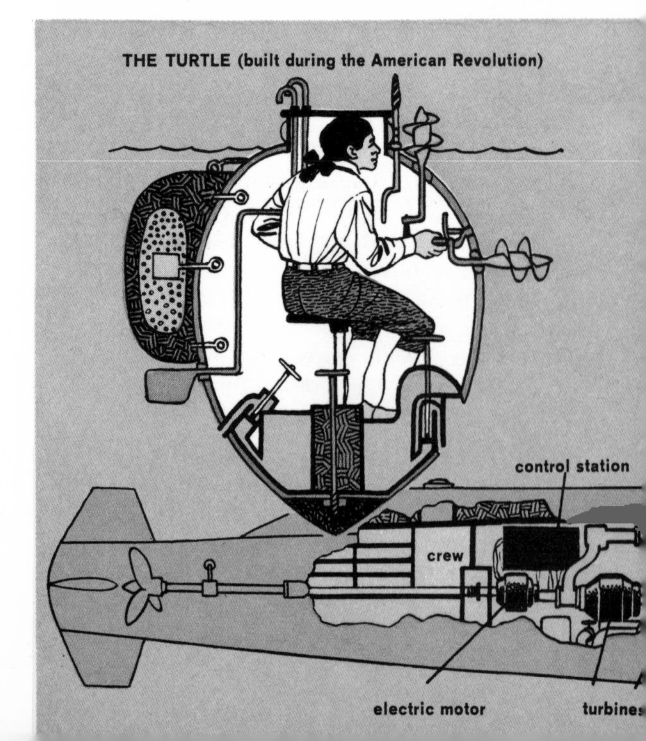

–(səb-JEKT) *v. subjects, subjected, subjecting.* Force to endure or submit.–The explorers were *subjected* to great hardships. – The king's armies *subjected* all the small surrounding countries to his rule.
–(SUB-jikt) *adj.* 1. Apt to have.–Father is *subject* to colds. He catches cold easily.
2. Depending upon or resting on.–I accept your invitation, *subject* to Mother's consent. I shall come if Mother will let me.

sub•ma•rine (SUB-mə-reen) *n. submarines.* A boat that can run under water.
–(sub-mə-REEN) *adj.* Being or used under water in the sea or ocean; having to do with the depths of the sea or ocean.–Scientists study *submarine* life. They study plants and animals that live in the sea.

sub•merge (səb-MERJ) *v. submerges, submerged, submerging.* 1. Cover with water. – The flood *submerged* roads and cars.
2. Sink; dive beneath the surface of the water.–The submarine captain gave the command to *submerge.*

sub•mit (səb-MIT) *v. submits, submitted, submitting.* 1. Give in or surrender.–The boy *submitted* to having his tooth pulled.
2. Hand in or offer.–Mary *submitted* a report to her teacher.

sub•or•di•nate (sə-BOR-də-nit) *adj.* 1. Of a lower rank, position, or order; of less importance.–Tom rose from a *subordinate* job in the firm to the position of office manager.
2. Under the command or authority of a superior.–A private in the army is *subordinate* to his officers.

sub•scribe (səb-SKRYB) *v. subscribes, subscribed, subscribing.* 1. Agree to take and pay for.–Mother has *subscribed* to the daily paper and a monthly magazine.
2. Make a written promise to give a certain amount.–We *subscribed* five dollars to the Red Cross.
3. Agree (to); approve.–I *subscribe* to the proposal that the town build a swimming pool.

sub•scrib•er (səb-SKRYB-er) *n. subscribers.* A person who promises to take and pay for something, as a magazine or newspaper.–Jack now has fifty *subscribers* on his newspaper route.

sub•scrip•tion (səb-SKRIP-shən) *n. subscriptions.* 1. Agreement to take something and pay for it.–Mother has renewed her *subscription* to the paper for another year.
2. An amount promised.–Our *subscription* to the Red Cross was five dollars.

sub•side (səb-SYD) *v. subsides, subsided, subsiding.* Become less.–The wind *subsided* in the evening.

sub•stance (SUB-stənss) *n. substances.* 1. What a thing is made of; a material. – The Indians smeared their faces with a reddish *substance.*
2. The main part. – The *substance* of the committee's report deals with education.
3. The actual meaning; the essential idea or ideas.–The *substance* of his philosophy is "Do unto others as you would have others do unto you."
4. Property; wealth.–Mr. Jones is a man of *substance.*

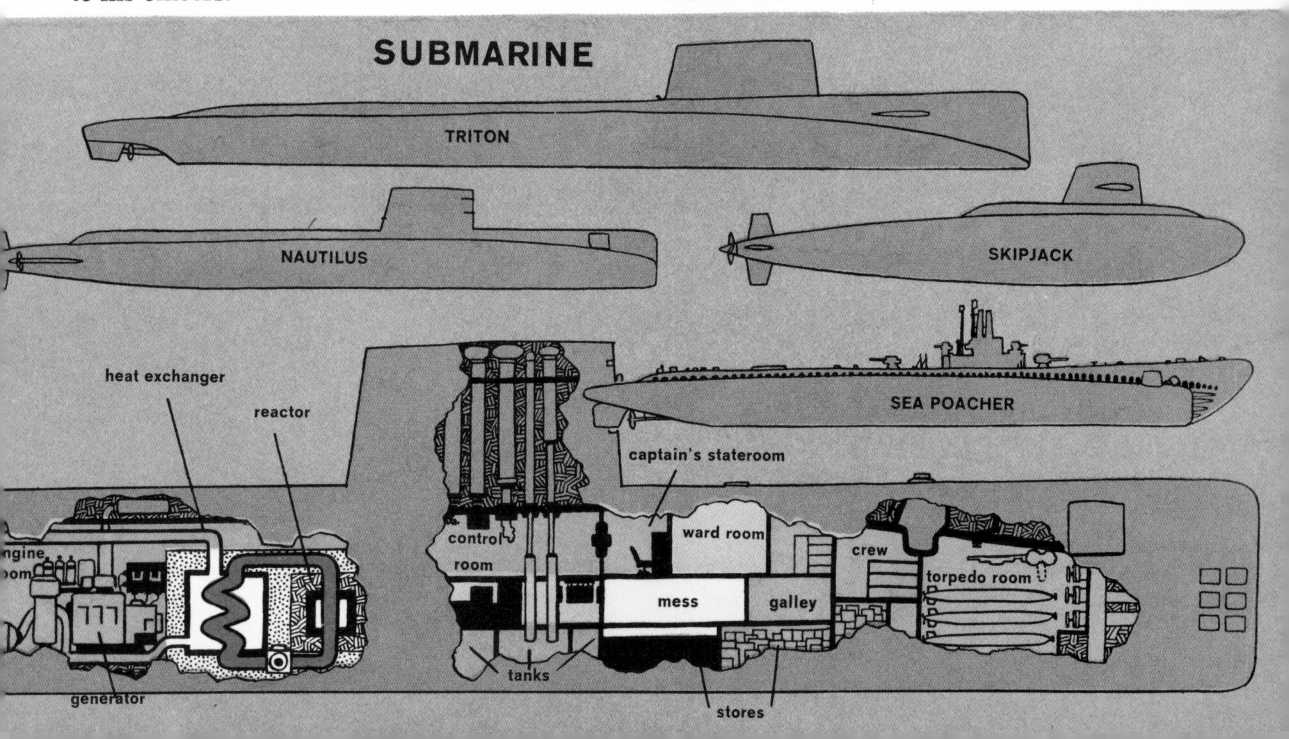

sub•stan•tial (səb-STAN-shəl) *adj.; substantially, adv.* 1. Strong and solid; firm.–It was a small but *substantial* house.
2. Large; considerable. – Harry received a *substantial* increase in salary.
3. Real; not imaginary.–The figure Ann saw proved to be *substantial* after all, and not a ghost as she had thought.
4. Of wealth or means.–Mr. Jones is a *substantial* businessman.

sub•sti•tute (SUB-stə-toot *or* -tyoot) *n. substitutes.* A person or thing serving in place of another.–The doctor could not come, so he sent a *substitute.* He sent another doctor.–Father didn't have a saw, so he used a knife as a *substitute.*–Bill is a *substitute* on the school football team. He sometimes plays in place of one of the regular players.
–*v. substitutes, substituted, substituting.* Provide in place of.–They didn't have chocolate ice cream, so they *substituted* vanilla.
–*substitution, n. substitutions.*

sub•tract (səb-TRAKT) *v. subtracts, subtracted, subtracting.* Take away.–One *subtracted* from four leaves three.

sub•trac•tion (səb-TRAK-shən) *n.* Taking one thing from another.–"One from four leaves three" is an example of *subtraction.*

sub•urb (SUB-erb) *n. suburbs.* A section or small community on the edge of a city. – We could not get a house in the city, so we live in a *suburb.*

sub•way (SUB-way) *n. subways.* An electric railroad that runs under the ground. – We went into the city by *subway.*

suc•ceed (sək-SEED) *v. succeeds, succeeded, succeeding.* 1. Come after.–Miss Jones was our first teacher; then Miss Smith *succeeded* her.
2. Win a desired goal; finish a thing satisfactorily.–"If at first you don't *succeed,* try, try again."

suc•cess (sək-SESS) *n. successes; successful, adj.; successfully, adv.* 1. Getting what one wants; doing what one wants to do satisfactorily.–William had *success* in making his kite.
2. Fame; fortune.–The man won *success* by working very hard.
3. A person or thing that succeeds or turns out well.–The singer was a great *success.* She was famous because she sang well.–The fire drill was a *success.* All the children left the building quickly and calmly.

suc•ces•sion (sək-SESH-ən) *n. successions; successive, adj.; successively, adv.* 1. The happening or coming of one thing right after another.–In the circus parade, the elephants walked in *succession.* They followed one another without anything between them.
2. Right to follow or inherit. – After the king's death, the *succession* to the throne was in doubt. It was not certain who had the right to be the next king.

such (SUCH) *adj.* 1. So bad; so good; so big; so much.–Baby is *such* a comedian!–The boy is *such* an eater!
2. Of a certain kind.–Bob had *such* vegetables as corn, peas, and cabbage in his garden. –Mary reads *such* stories as "The Three Bears" and "Cinderella" to Sally.
–*pron.* 1. This or that which has already been spoken of.–Mother said no, and *such* was her decision.
2. Such a thing or person.–What we thought Bob had meant as a criticism was not intended as *such.*

suck•er (SUK-er) *n. suckers.* 1. A lollipop or hard piece of candy, usually fastened to a stick. – All the children at Sue's birthday party were given *suckers* as favors.
2. The little shoots or stems that come up from the roots of trees and bushes.–We cut down the *suckers* from the bush so the main bush would be stronger.
3. A kind of fish.

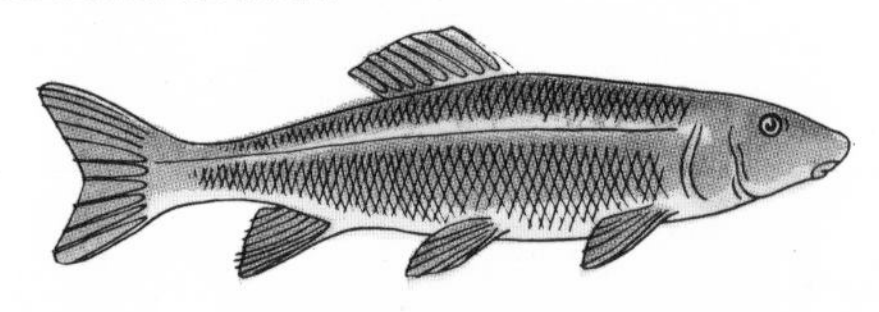

suc•tion (SUK-shən) *n.* and *adj.* Sucking the air out of something to create a vacuum which draws other things in.–When Mary drinks an ice-cream soda through a straw, the liquid reaches Mary's mouth through *suction.*–A vacuum cleaner picks up dirt by *suction.*

sud•den (SUD-n) *adj.; suddenly, adv.* 1. Unexpected.–A *sudden* clap of thunder made us jump.
2. Quick; rapid.–Father made a *sudden* trip to the country.
–*All of a sudden* means suddenly or unexpectedly.–*All of a sudden* the door opened.

suds (SUDZ) *n. pl.* Water with enough soap in it to make bubbles.–Mother washed the clothes in *suds.*

sue (SOO *or* SYOO) *v. sues, sued, suing.* Take action against someone through the courts.–The man would not pay for the damage he had done, so Father had to *sue* him. Father started action against him in court to get him to do the right thing.

su•et (SOO- *or* SYOO-it) *n.* Hard fat taken from the meat of cattle and sheep. *Suet* is used for cooking and for making candles.

suf•fer (SUF-er) *v. suffers, suffered, suffering.* 1. Feel great pain.–Grandmother *suffered* when she broke her arm.
2. Endure; undergo.–The poor man has *suffered* many hardships during the cold winter.
3. Be harmed or hurt.–The farmers' crops have *suffered* because we have had no rain.

suf•fi•cient (sə-FISH-ənt) *adj.; sufficiently, adv.* Enough; as much as is needed. – We have *sufficient* coal for the winter. We have plenty of coal for the winter.

suf•fo•cate (SUF-ə-kayt) *v. suffocates, suffocated, suffocating.* 1. Kill or die by stopping the breath.–The killer *suffocated* his victim.
2. Choke or smother. – The firemen wore masks so that the heavy smoke would not *suffocate* them.

sug•ar (SHUHG-er) *n. sugars.* A sweet substance made from sugar beets or sugar cane. –We put *sugar* in coffee, on fruit, and on breakfast food to make them sweet.
–*v. sugars, sugared, sugaring.* 1. Make sweet by adding sugar.–Father *sugared* the cereal for Baby. He sprinkled sugar on it.
2. Turn to sugar.–The jelly has *sugared* from being boiled too long.

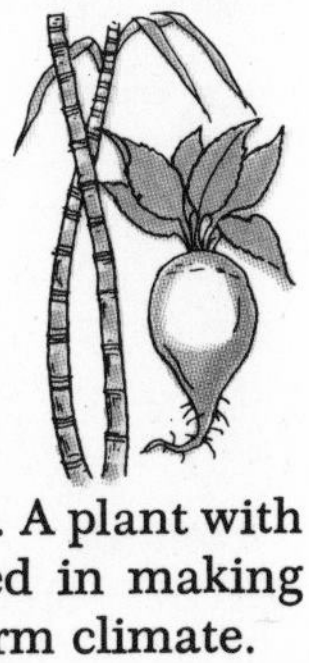

sug•ar beet (SHUHG-er beet) *sugar beets.* A large, white kind of beet used in making sugar.

sug•ar cane (SHUHG-er kayn). A plant with tall, hollow stalks that are used in making sugar. It usually grows in a warm climate.

sug•ar ma•ple (SHUHG-er may-pəl) *sugar maples.* A maple tree that gives a sweet sap. When this sap is boiled for a long time, it becomes a sugar called maple sugar.

sug•gest (səg-JEST) *v. suggests, suggested, suggesting.* 1. Bring up or mention as a possible and desirable thing to do. – The teacher *suggested* that we read the story before going home.–Bob *suggested* that we work first and then play.
2. Bring something to someone's mind or attention.–If I say "cloud" to you, what does it *suggest?* It *suggests* rain.

sug•ges•tion (səg-JESS-chən) *n. suggestions.* 1. A thought or idea that someone has and suggests or offers to someone else.–Mary gave us a *suggestion* as to how we might save paper.
2. A bringing to mind; a hint.–There is a *suggestion* of unhappiness in her manner and her speech.

su•i•cide (SOO- *or* SYOO-ə-syd) *n. suicides.* 1. Killing of oneself.–The man's death was not an accident; it was *suicide.* He killed himself purposely.
2. A person who kills himself. – The man was a *suicide.*

suit (SOOT *or* SYOOT) *n. suits.* 1. A set of clothing worn together, as a jacket, vest, and trousers.–Father's new *suit* is brown.
2. In a pack of playing cards, all those cards that have spots of the same shape.–Hearts, clubs, spades, and diamonds are the four *suits.*
–*v. suits, suited, suiting.* 1. Satisfy or please. –A picnic on the last day of school *suited* the children very well. They liked it.
2. Go well with; match.–A yellow dress *suits* a person with brown hair and brown eyes.

suit•a•ble (SOO- *or* SYOO-tə-bəl) *adj.; suitably, adv.* Proper; fit.–Men's straw hats are not *suitable* for winter weather.–Overalls are *suitable* for farm work.

suit•case (SOOT- *or* SYOOT-kayss) *n. suitcases.* A flat traveling bag. – Mother packed our clothes in a *suitcase* when we went to Grandmother's.

suite (SWEET) *n. suites.* 1. A group or a set. –A special *suite* of hotel rooms is being reserved for the President.–Mother bought a *suite* of furniture for the bedroom.
2. A staff of followers or attendants.–The prince and his *suite* will arrive at the hotel tomorrow.

suit•or (SOO- *or* SYOO-ter) *n. suitors.* A man who wants to marry a certain woman.–The woman's *suitor* called on her every night last week.

sul•fur or **sul•phur** (SUL-fer) *n.* A yellowish substance that burns easily and gives off a strong odor that makes it hard for one to breathe.–The heads of some matches have *sulfur* in them.

sulk (SULK) *v. sulks, sulked, sulking.* Show bad humor by keeping quietly and gloomily to oneself.–The girl *sulks* when she does not get her own way.

sulk•y (SUL-kee) *n. sulkies.* A small, two-wheeled carriage often used for racing.
–*adj. sulkier, sulkiest; sulkily, adv.* Cross; bad-tempered.–Mother said that no one likes a *sulky* person.

sul•len (SUL-ən) *adj.; sullenly, adv.* 1. Quietly angry.–Baby is *sullen* when she can't have her own way.
2. Dull; gloomy. – The *sullen* skies made everyone feel unhappy at the picnic.

sul•tan (SUL-tn) *n. sultans.* A ruler in certain countries of the East.

sul•try (SUL-tree) *adj. sultrier, sultriest.* Hot and damp.–A *sultry* day is one that is hot and moist, with very little breeze.

sum (SUM) *n. sums.* 1. The number made by adding numbers.–The *sum* of four and two is six.
2. (In the plural) Arithmetic problems.–Bob sometimes has trouble doing his *sums.*
3. An amount of money.–Mary has a small *sum* of money to spend each week.
–*v. sums, summed, summing. Sum up* means to tell in a few words.–The teacher asked us to *sum up* what we had learned during the day.

su•mac or **su•mach** (SHOO- *or* SOO-mak) *n. sumacs* or *sumachs.* A bush that has large, reddish blossoms and, later, red berries on it. The berries are not good to eat. The leaves of *sumac* turn a bright red in the fall.

sum•ma•rize (SUM-ə-ryz) *v. summarizes, summarized, summarizing.* Briefly give the main points of a speech, discussion, piece of writing, or series of events.–A speaker often *summarizes* at the end of his talk to remind his listeners of the points he has made.
–*summary, n. summaries.*

sum•mer (SUM-er) *n. summers.* One of the four seasons.–The seasons of the year are spring, *summer,* autumn, and winter.–In our part of the world, *summer* is the hottest season.

sum•mit (SUM-it) *n. summits.* The top; the highest point.–It is a hard climb to the *summit* of the hill.
–A *summit meeting* refers to a meeting of the heads of state of leading nations, usually the United States, Britain, France, and the Soviet Union. The purpose of such a meeting is to discuss world problems in the hope of finding solutions acceptable to all.

sum•mon (SUM-ən) *v. summons, summoned, summoning.* Call or send for.–The teacher *summoned* the boy to her desk.

sun (SUN) *n. suns.* 1. The brightest body we see in the sky; the star which gives the earth light and heat.–The earth goes around the *sun* once in a year.–We see the stars shining at night. We see the *sun* shining during the day.
2. Heat and light of the sun.–The *sun* makes the plants grow.–The living room faces the east, so it gets the morning *sun.*
–*v. suns, sunned, sunning.* Expose to the light of the sun. – Father sat on the sand and *sunned* himself.

sun•beam (SUN-beem) *n. sunbeams.* A ray of sunlight.–A *sunbeam* danced on the wall.

sun•bon•net (SUN-bahn-it) *n. sunbonnets.* A bonnet with a broad brim. –A *sunbonnet* is usually worn to keep the hot sun off the face and the neck.

sun•burn (SUN-bern) *n. sunburns.* A burn made by the sun's rays.–Mary put a cream on her *sunburn.*
–*v. sunburns, sunburned, sunburning.* Have the skin reddened or blistered by the sun's rays.–People with light skins are apt to *sunburn* easily.

Sun•day (SUN-dee) *n. Sundays.* The first day of the week. *Sunday* is the Christian Sabbath, or day of rest.

sun•di•al (SUN-dy-əl) *n. sundials.* An instrument for telling time by the sun's shadow. The sun makes a shadow that points towards numbers on the dial. The numbers on which the shadows fall tell what time it is.

sun•down (SUN-down) *n.* The time when the sun goes down out of sight; sunset. –Mother told us to be home by *sundown.*

sun•fish (SUN-fish) *n. sunfish* or *sunfishes.* A small, somewhat brightly colored fish that is good to eat.

sun•flow•er (SUN-flow-er) *n. sunflowers.* A tall plant that has large, yellow flowers with large, brown centers which are full of seeds.

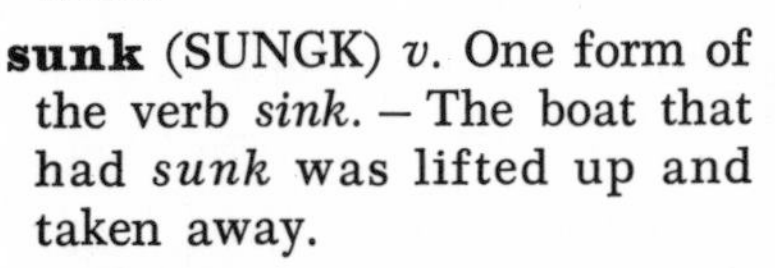

sung (SUNG) *v.* One form of the verb *sing.* – We sing the song "America" in school. We have *sung* it every day this week.

sunk (SUNGK) *v.* One form of the verb *sink.* – The boat that had *sunk* was lifted up and taken away.

sun•light (SUN-lyt) *n.* Light of the sun.–We sat in the *sunlight* to get warm.

sun•ny (SUN-ee) *adj. sunnier, sunniest.* 1. Filled with sunshine.–This is a *sunny* day.
2. Bright; pleasant.–Sally has a *sunny* smile.

sun•rise (SUN-ryz) *n. sunrises.* 1. The time of day when the sun comes up.–Grandfather gets up at *sunrise.*
2. Dawn; light in the sky when the sun comes up.–We watched the *sunrise* from the mountaintop.

sun•set (SUN-set) *n. sunsets.* 1. The going down of the sun.–Take down the flag just before *sunset.*
2. The changing light and color in the sky when the sun goes down.–We watched the *sunset* over the lake.

sun•shine (SUN-shyn) *n.* Light from the sun.–The *sunshine* came into the window.

su•per•in•tend•ent (soo- *or* syoo-prin-TEN-dənt) *n. superintendents.* A person who oversees or directs workers.–A *superintendent* of schools directs and guides teachers, and sees that school business is taken care of. –The *superintendent* of an apartment house sees that the house is kept clean, heated, and in good condition.

su•pe•ri•or (sə- *or* soo-PIR-ee-er) *n. superiors.*
1. A person higher in position than another. –The principal is our teacher's *superior.*
2. A person better than another or others in some respect.–John is Bob's *superior* at tennis. John plays tennis better than Bob does.
–*adj.* 1. Higher in position. – A major is *superior* to a captain. – A superintendent of schools is *superior* to a teacher.
2. Better.–Our team has *superior* players on it.–Bill thinks he is *superior.* He acts as though he were better than the other boys.

su•per•mar•ket (SOO- *or* SYOO-per-mahr-kit) *n. supermarkets.* A large shopping center or food store, usually operated on a self-service basis.–Mother goes to the *supermarket* once a week to shop for our food.

su•per•son•ic (soo- *or* syoo-per-SAHN-ik) *adj.* Capable of traveling at a speed faster than that of sound, or faster than about 738 miles an hour.–The Air Force has many *supersonic* aircraft.

su•per•sti•tion (soo- *or* syoo-per-STISH-ən) *n. superstitions.* 1. A false belief or fear.–It is an old *superstition* that it is bad luck for a black cat to cross a path ahead of you.–Educated people today know that *superstitions* are not true.
2. The habit of believing in mysterious powers or forces which do not really exist.–*Superstition* makes people think it is unlucky to walk under a ladder.–Science tries to fight *superstition.*

su•per•sti•tious (soo- *or* syoo-per-STISH-əss) *adj.; superstitiously, adv.* Believing in and fearful of unknown powers.–*Superstitious* people think it is bad luck for thirteen people to sit at a table.

sup•per (SUP-er) *n. suppers.* The last meal of the day. – Some people have dinner at noon. In the evening they have *supper,* a lighter meal.

sup•ply (sə-PLY) *n. supplies.* An amount or quantity on hand.–The stores have a *supply* of shoes for the winter season.–Father has our *supply* of coal in the coal bin.
–*v. supplies, supplied, supplying.* 1. Give; produce; provide.–The farmers *supply* food for the people of the city.–City people *supply* clothing, machines, and other things to the farmer.
2. Add or furnish.–Mary got all the words in the puzzle but one. Bob *supplied* that one.
3. Fill.–The store tries to stock enough coats to *supply* the demand.

sup·port (sə-PORT) *n. supports.* 1. Anything that holds something up.–A clothesline pole or prop is a *support* because it holds up the clothesline.
2. Help in getting food, clothing, and the things necessary for living; getting a living.–Children depend on their parents for *support.*
–*v. supports, supported, supporting.* 1. Hold up; keep (a thing) from falling.–A clothesline pole *supports* a clothesline.–Posts *support* the roof of the porch.
2. Furnish a home, food, and clothing for, or everything necessary for living. – The father *supports* his children.
3. Help; encourage.–The sick man was *supported* by the good wishes of his neighbors. –Mother said she would *support* Jack's plan to go camping.
4. Be in favor of; uphold.–Father *supports* Mr. Jones for mayor.

sup·pose (sə-POHZ) *v. supposes, supposed, supposing.* 1. Believe; guess.–I *suppose* Jack will come to the party.
2. Imagine. – Just *suppose* you were on a desert island. What would you do?
3. Expect or presume.–The children are *supposed* to be in bed. It is their usual time for sleeping, but I do not know if they have actually gone to bed yet.

su·preme (sə- *or* soo-PREEM) *adj.; supremely, adv.* 1. Greatest.–This news is of *supreme* importance to us.
2. Highest in position or power. – In the United States the *Supreme* Court is the highest court.

sure (SHUHR) *adj. surer, surest.* 1. Certain; positive.–Mary is *sure* that she heard Mother call.
2. Dependable. – This is a *sure* recipe for chocolate cake. It will not fail.
3. Confident. – Jack is *sure* of making the team. He is certain he will.
4. Firm; safe. – The mountain climbers crossed the ridge with *sure* steps.

sure·ly (SHUHR-lee) *adv.* Certainly.–*Surely* that was Father we saw; I am sure it was.

surf (SERF) *n. surfs.* Waves of the sea hitting or washing against the shore.–We stood on the rocks and watched the *surf.*

sur·face (SER-fəss) *n. surfaces.* 1. A side; the outside.–The *surface* of a brick is rough.
2. A top, or flat upper part.–The *surface* of the table needs to be painted.–A stick was floating on the *surface* of the water.
3. Outside; outward appearance. – On the *surface,* Mary thought the problem looked easy. But when she began to work on it she realized that it was quite difficult.

surge (SERJ) *n. surges.* A sudden great wave or rush.–A *surge* of water carried the tiny boat to shore.
–*v. surges, surged, surging.* Roll up and fall. –During the storm, the waves *surged* over the rocks on the coast.

sur·geon (SER-jən) *n. surgeons.* A doctor who operates on people.–A *surgeon* operated on Mary. He took out her tonsils.

sur·plus (SER-pluss) *n. surpluses* and *adj.* Extra amount.–We had a *surplus* of money this week. We had some left over.

sur·prise (ser-PRYZ) *n. surprises.* 1. Something not expected.–Father had a *surprise* in his pocket for Sally.
2. A feeling caused by something that was not expected.–A look of *surprise* came over Bob's face when he saw his new bicycle.
–*v. surprises, surprised, surprising.* 1. Come upon suddenly and unexpectedly.–The policeman *surprised* the robbers in their hideout.
2. Amaze; take unaware.–Mother was *surprised* to see us.
–*adj.* Not expected.–We are planning a *surprise* party for our teacher. She doesn't know about it or expect it.

sur·ren·der (sə-REN-der) *n. surrenders.* A giving up.–The *surrender* of the enemy came when their supplies ran out.
–*v. surrenders, surrendered, surrendering.* Give up.–The enemy held the town for a long time, but at last they had to *surrender* it.–The robbers *surrendered* to the police.

sur·rey (SER-ee) *n. surreys.* A four-wheeled carriage with two seats. *Surreys* are drawn by horses.

sur·round (sə-ROWND) *v. surrounds, surrounded, surrounding.* 1. Enclose. –A fence *surrounds* the garden. It goes all the way around the garden to keep the chickens from getting in.
2. Close in on all sides.–When the sheriff's men *surrounded* him, Robin Hood blew his horn for his Merry Men to come to his aid.

sur•round•ings (sə-ROWN-dingz) *n. pl.* Things or conditions all about one. – The children have always lived in pleasant *surroundings*. They have had a pretty home in the country, with pleasant neighbors.

sur•vey (SER-vay) *n. surveys.* A study; examination; comparison.–The teachers made a *survey* of the parents' opinion of the progress of their children. They tried to find out what the parents thought.
–(ser-VAY) *v. surveys, surveyed, surveying.* 1. Look over; examine.–The teacher *surveyed* the room to see that everything was neat and orderly.
2. Measure carefully to get the size, shape, and position of an area and to determine where the boundaries are. – The men are *surveying* the lot next to our house.

sur•vey•or (ser-VAY-er) *n. surveyors.* A person who uses surveying instruments to measure land for size, shape, and position.

sur•vive (ser-VYV) *v. survives, survived, surviving.* 1. Remain alive after; live through.–All the families *survived* the flood.
2. Live longer than. – Mrs. Jones *survived* Mr. Jones. When Mr. Jones died, Mrs. Jones was still alive.
3. Last through.–The old flag has *survived* three wars. We still have it.
–*survival, n. survivals.*

sur•vi•vor (ser-VY-ver) *n. survivors.* A person who is still alive.–The ship sank, and two sailors were the only *survivors*. All the others were drowned.

sus•pect (SUSS-pekt) *n. suspects.* A person thought guilty of something.–The policeman arrested one *suspect* for the murder.
–(sə-SPEKT) *v. suspects, suspected, suspecting.* 1. Guess; imagine.–I *suspect* that you have had enough to eat.
2. Think or believe to be guilty without being able to prove it.–The boy *suspected* his pet crow of taking the clip, but he couldn't be sure because he hadn't seen him do it.
3. Doubt.–Father *suspected* the stranger's honesty.

sus•pend (sə-SPEND) *v. suspends, suspended, suspending.* 1. Hang. – The swing was *suspended* from a broad branch of the tree.
2. Stop; put off.–Work on the road was *suspended* because of the rain.
3. Temporarily not allow to attend or to perform one's work.–Bill was *suspended* from school for smoking between classes.

sus•pend•ers (sə-SPEN-derz) *n. pl.* Straps worn over the shoulders and buttoned or clamped onto the trousers to keep them up.– Father wears *suspenders*, but Bob wears a belt.

sus•pen•sion bridge (sə-SPEN-shən brij) *suspension bridges.* A bridge hung from cables.

sus•pi•cious (sə-SPISH-əss) *adj.; suspiciously, adv.* 1. Thinking someone has done wrong, or that something is wrong, without real proof.–The policeman is *suspicious* of the man standing in front of the bank.
2. Causing one to doubt or suspect. – The man's sneaky habits are *suspicious*. They make people think he is not to be trusted.
–*suspicion, n. suspicions.*

swal•low (SWAHL-oh) *n. swallows.* 1. A small bird that flies swiftly and smoothly. –Some *swallows* build their nests in barns. 
2. As much as one can drink in one gulp.–The thirsty boy asked for a *swallow* of water.
–*v. swallows, swallowed, swallowing.* 1. Take into the stomach through the throat. – Do you want some water to help you to *swallow* the pill?
2. Believe too easily. – The boy *swallows* everything anyone tells him.

swam (SWAM) *v.* One form of the verb *swim*. –Ducks swim in the pond. One duck *swam* all the way across the pond.

swamp (SWAHMP) *n. swamps; swampy, adj.* Soft, wet, marshy land.–We gathered cattails in the *swamp*.
–*v. swamps, swamped, swamping.* 1. Fill with water and sink.–A big wave *swamped* the little boat.
2. Overwhelm. – Mother said she was *swamped* with work. She had too much to do.

swan (SWAHN) *n. swans.* A large water bird with short legs and a long neck.–The graceful *swans* swim in the pond at the park.

swap (SWAHP) *v. swaps, swapped, swapping.* Trade; exchange. – The girls *swap* books with the other girls after they have read them.–Bob *swapped* a ball for a bat.
–*swap, n. swaps.*

swarm (SWORM) *n. swarms.* A large group; a crowd.–A *swarm* of bees is a group that leaves the beehive and flies away together to form a new colony somewhere else. –*Swarms* of people rushed to the fire.
–*v. swarms, swarmed, swarming.* 1. Gather into a big group.–Bees are *swarming* in the flower garden.
2. Be crowded or full.–The barn is *swarming* with flies.

swarth•y (SWOR-thee) *adj. swarthier, swarthiest.* Dark in color.–People who are outdoors much of the time in the hot sun are apt to have a *swarthy* skin.

swat (SWAHT) *n. swats.* Hard blow or hit.–The boy gave the mosquito a *swat.*
–*v. swats, swatted, swatting.* Hit; knock.–The ballplayer *swatted* the ball out of the park.

sway (SWAY) *v. sways, swayed, swaying.* 1. Move or swing slowly back and forth or from side to side.–The trees *swayed* in the wind.
2. Influence; cause to change one's mind.–Nothing could *sway* the boy from his resolve to become a sailor.

swear (SWAIR) *v. swears, swore, swearing.* 1. Make a statement asking God or some sacred being to witness the truth of what you say.–The witness in court *swore* to tell the truth.
2. Vow or promise.–When Bob joined the Boy Scouts, he had to *swear* to obey certain rules.
3. Curse; use sacred names without reverence.

sweat (SWET) *n.* 1. Perspiration; moisture which comes through the skin.–*Sweat* ran from the man's forehead.
2. Moisture; droplets of water. – *Sweat* formed on the cold glasses of water.
–*v. sweats, sweated, sweating.* 1. Perspire; give off moisture through the skin.–We *sweat* when we run or exercise and become warm.
2. Collect moisture.–Cold water pipes *sweat* when it is very warm. Drops of water form on the pipes.

sweat•er (SWET-er) *n. sweaters.* A knitted wool garment worn on the upper body. – Mother is knitting a *sweater* for Bob.–The teacher asked the children to take off their *sweaters* in school so that they would not get too warm.

sweep (SWEEP) *n. sweeps.* A cleaning with a broom.–Mother said that a daily *sweep* was all that the floor needed.
–*v. sweeps, swept, sweeping.* 1. Brush with a broom.–Mary likes to *sweep* the porch.
2. Push or carry along or away.–The rushing water *swept* away everything in its path.
3. Pass over lightly.–The teacher *sweeps* her hand over her desk each morning to see if there is dust on it.
4. Pass over or through rapidly.–Fire *swept* the forest. It passed quickly through.

sweet (SWEET) *adj. sweeter, sweetest; sweetly, adv.* 1. Of the pleasant taste of sugar.–Sugar is *sweet.* Vinegar is sour.
2. Pleasing.–Roses have a *sweet* smell.
3. Fresh.–Baby likes *sweet* milk, milk that isn't sour or spoiled.
4. Not salted.–*Sweet* butter has no salt.
5. Soft and pleasing. – Mary has a *sweet* voice.–The sounds of the violin were *sweet.*
6. Lovable; good and pleasant. – Baby is *sweet.*

sweet•en (SWEE-tn) *v. sweetens, sweetened, sweetening.* Make sweet by adding sugar or syrup.–*Sweeten* the cherries while they are still cooking.

sweet•heart (SWEET-hahrt) *n. sweethearts.* 1. A loved one. – Baby is Mother's *sweetheart.*
2. A beau.–Aunt Ruth had a *sweetheart.*

sweet po•ta•to (SWEET pə-tay-toh) *sweet potatoes.* A kind of large yellow root that is somewhat sweet. *Sweet potatoes* are good to eat when baked, candied, or boiled.

sweet Wil•liam (sweet WIL-yəm) *sweet Williams.* A kind of flower of many colors that grows in flat clusters. *Sweet William* belongs to the family of pinks.

swell (SWEL) *n. swells.* A long wave or waves out at sea.–The ship tossed in the *swell.*
–*v. swells, swelled, swelling.* Become larger in size, amount, force, or sound.–The mosquito bite made Mary's hand *swell.* – A balloon *swells* when air is blown into it.–The river *swells* when the snow melts.–Music *swells* when it becomes louder and louder.

swell•ing (SWEL-ing) *n. swellings.* A swollen place; a place that is puffed up. – The *swelling* on Father's finger has gone away.

swel•ter (SWEL-ter) *v. swelters, sweltered, sweltering.* Suffer from the heat.–People in the city often *swelter* in the summer.

swept (SWEPT) *v.* One form of the verb *sweep.*–Mary *swept* the front porch.

swift (SWIFT) *adj. swifter, swiftest; swiftly, adv.* 1. Very fast.–The race horse is *swift.*
2. Prompt; quick.–Mother had a *swift* reply to her letter.

swift•ness (SWIFT-nəss) *n.* Speed. – The messenger delivered the letter with great *swiftness.*

swim (SWIM) *n. swims.* A period of swimming.–The boys went for a *swim* in the lake.
–*v. swims, swam, swimming.* 1. Move through the water by moving the arms and legs, or

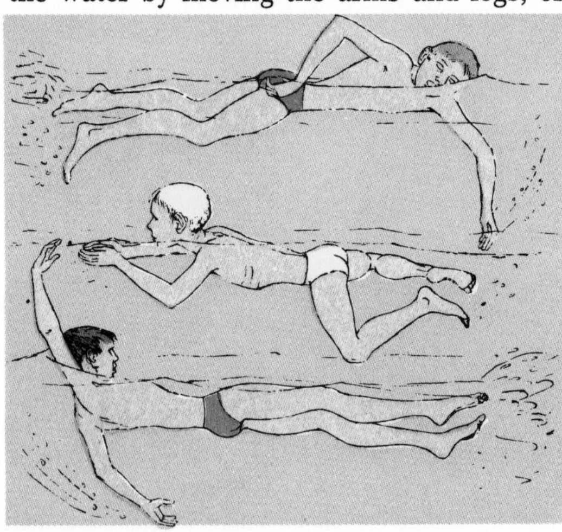

fins and tail.–A fish *swims* by moving its fins and tail.–A duck *swims* with its feet.
2. Cross by swimming.–The boys could not *swim* the wide river.
3. Glide smoothly.–The balloon went *swimming* through the air.
4. Float about.–Rings of butter *swim* on the soup. They float. They stay on the top.
5. Be covered. – Mary's favorite dessert is berries that are *swimming* in cream.
6. Be dizzy.–My head is *swimming* from excitement.

swim•mer (SWIM-er) *n. swimmers.* An animal or person who swims.

swin•dle (SWIN-dl) *v. swindles, swindled, swindling.* Cheat or get something dishonestly.–The crooked salesman tried to *swindle* Father by selling him a car that was no good.
–*swindle, n. swindles.*

swin•dler (SWIN-dler) *n. swindlers.* A person who gets things by dishonesty or cheating.–Father had the *swindler* arrested for trying to sell him a car that was no good.

swine (SWYN) *n. sing.* and *pl.* A hog or pig.

swine•herd (SWYN-herd) *n. swineherds.* A person who cares for swine as a shepherd cares for sheep.

swing (SWING) *n. swings.* A seat hung so that it can move back and forth. – Father hung the *swing* from a branch of the largest tree in our backyard.

–*v. swing, swung, swinging.* 1. Move back and forth in a swing.–Children like to *swing.*
2. Move or cause to move in a circle or part of a circle.–A golfer *swings* the golf club to hit the ball.–Can you stand on one foot and *swing* the other?

swish (SWISH) *n. swishes.* A whispering sound; a rustle. – We heard the *swish* of Mother's taffeta skirt as she entered the room.
–*v. swishes, swished, swishing.* Move with a whistling or rushing noise.–The lion tamer's whip *swished* through the air.

switch (SWICH) *n. switches.* 1. A whip, or a small branch of a tree used for whipping.
2. On a railroad, a mechanical device that shifts part of a track so that a train can move from one track to another.

3. A device for turning off and on.–Electric lights are turned on by a *switch.*
–*v. switches, switched, switching.* 1. Whip.–The cruel man *switched* the dog.
2. Swing back and forth or up and down like a whip.–A cow *switches* her tail to drive the flies off.
3. Change over; transfer. – The engine *switched* from one track to another. – Bob *switched* coats with Jack. Bob wore Jack's coat and Jack wore Bob's.
4. Turn (on or off) with a switch.–*Switch* the light on so you can see to read.

swol•len (SWOH-lən) *v.* One form of the verb *swell.*—John's finger had *swollen* as a result of the infection.

swoop (SWOOP) *v. swoops, swooped, swooping.* Move swiftly and smoothly down.—The barn swallow *swooped* down to catch an insect.

sword (SORD) *n. swords.* A weapon that has a long blade sharpened on one or both edges.

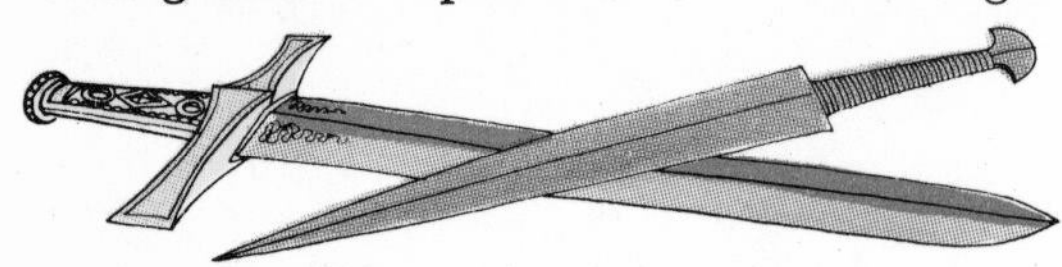

swore (SWOR) *v.* One form of the verb *swear.* —Billy *swore* that he would uphold the rules of the club.

sworn (SWORN) *v.* One form of the verb *swear.*—Billy has *sworn* to uphold the rules of the club.

swung (SWUNG) *v.* One form of the verb *swing.*—The monkey *swung* by his tail from a branch.

syc•a•more (SIK-ə-mor) *n. sycamores.* A kind of tree with scaly bark.

syl•la•ble (SIL-ə-bəl) *n. syllables.* 1. A part of a word that is pronounced separately. We say the word "criticism" in four parts: (KRIT-ə-siz-əm). Each part is a *syllable.* We say the word "man" in only one part: (MAN). "Man" has only one *syllable.*
2. In writing, a part of a word that can be separated at the end of a line. Each *syllable* contains at least one vowel. In this dictionary these *syllables* are marked by dots in each entry word, as: crit·i·cism. Words that appear without dots, like "man," cannot be separated at the end of a line.

sym•bol (SIM-bəl) *n. symbols.* 1. A thing that stands for something else.—A white flag is a *symbol* of surrender.—The American flag is the *symbol* of the United States.
2. A mark which has a definite meaning.—In arithmetic we use + as a *symbol* for addition and − as a *symbol* for subtraction.

sym•bol•ize (SIM-bəl-yz) *v. symbolizes, symbolized, symbolizing.* 1. Be a symbol of; stand for.—An olive branch *symbolizes* peace to most people.
2. Represent by a symbol.

sym•pa•thet•ic (sim-pə-THET-ik) *adj.; sympathetically, adv.* Sharing the feelings of others, and feeling kindly toward them.—Mother is *sympathetic* toward the sick woman. She seems to know how the woman feels, and feels sorry for her.

sym•pa•thize (SIM-pə-thyz) *v. sympathizes, sympathized, sympathizing.* Feel sympathy for; share the feelings of.—When Bob is sick, he wants you to *sympathize* with him. He wants you to show that you understand how he feels.

sym•pa•thy (SIM-pə-thee) *n. sympathies.* 1. A kind feeling that one person has for another. A person shows *sympathy* for another person when he feels that person's sorrows and troubles.
2. Agreement.—Father is in *sympathy* with our plans for vacation.
3. A state of understanding and sharing ideas and feelings about things.—If music makes both Bob and Mary feel happy at the same time, they are in *sympathy* with each other.

sym•pho•ny (SIM-fə-nee) *n. symphonies.* A long piece of music, usually in four parts, written for an orchestra.

symp•tom (SIMP-təm) *n. symptoms.* A sign; an indication.—The doctor did not find any *symptoms* of measles when he examined the baby; he found no red spots.

syn•o•nym (SIN-ə-nim) *n. synonyms.* One of two or more words that mean the same or nearly the same thing.—"Small" and "little" are *synonyms.*—"Big" and "large" are also *synonyms.*

syr•up or **sir•up** (SIR- *or* SER-əp) *n. syrups* or *sirups.* A thick, sticky, sweet liquid containing much sugar and sometimes fruits and other flavoring.—Mary wanted chocolate *syrup* on her ice cream and Bob asked for pineapple *syrup.*—Bob and Mary always eat lots of maple *syrup* with their pancakes.

sys•tem (SISS-təm) *n. systems.* 1. An orderly plan or method.—Mother has a *system* for doing her housework.
2. A whole body.—The doctor said that Bob's *system* was unusually strong.
3. A network.—Uncle Joe is an announcer for a radio and television broadcasting *system.*
4. An arrangement; an order.—The United States and Britain have democratic *systems* of government.

T t

T, t (TEE) *n. T's, t's.* The twentieth letter of the alphabet.

ta•ble (TAY-bəl) *n. tables.* 1. A piece of furniture with a flat top resting on legs.–We set lamps on *tables* in the living room.

2. A list of things, or information given in a very short form.–We looked in the *table* of contents in the front of the book to find out what stories were in the book.–In arithmetic we learn the multiplication *table:*

$$2 \times 1 = 2$$
$$2 \times 2 = 4$$
$$2 \times 3 = 6$$

ta•ble•cloth (TAY-bəl-klawth) *n. tablecloths.* A cloth spread on a dining table before the dishes and foods are put on.–Mary put the *tablecloth* and napkins on the table.

ta•ble•spoon (TAY-bəl-spoon) *n. tablespoons.* A large spoon.–Mother serves the vegetables with a *tablespoon.*

tab•let (TAB-lət) *n. tablets.* 1. A pad.–A writing *tablet* has many sheets of paper fastened together at the top.
2. A sheet or thin piece of metal, stone, or wood with something written on it.–The school children put up a *tablet* in the main hall in honor of the first principal of the school.
3. A small, flat pill.–The *tablets* which the doctor gave Father were easy to swallow.

tab•u•late (TAB-yə-layt) *v. tabulates, tabulated, tabulating.* Make a table or arrangement of numbers, words, or facts.–The results of the election were *tabulated* to show at a glance the names of all the candidates and the number of votes each received.
–*tabulation, n. tabulations.*

tack (TAK) *n. tacks.* A short nail with a large flat or rounded head.–The children used thumb*tacks* to fasten their drawings to the wall.
–*v. tacks, tacked, tacking.* 1. To fasten with tacks.–The drawings were *tacked* onto the wall.
2. Sew loosely and temporarily. – Mother *tacked* the hem of Mary's dress. She put in loose stitches until she could sew it permanently.

tack•le (TAK-əl) *n. tackles.* 1. Things used for doing a job.–Fishing *tackle* is the equipment used by a fisherman for fishing.
2. Ropes specially arranged for lifting heavy loads.
3. One of the players on a football team.–John is right *tackle* on the school team.
–*v. tackles, tackled, tackling.* 1. Grab; get hold of.–One football player *tackled* the other.
2. Try to do; undertake.–Father will *tackle* the work that has to be done as soon as he gets home.

tact (TAKT) *n.; tactful, adj.; tactfully, adv.* A person who has *tact* knows how to do and say things without annoying people or hurting their feelings.

tad•pole (TAD-pohl) *n. tadpoles.* The young of a frog or toad. *Tadpoles* have tails which disappear before they become full-grown frogs or toads.

taf•fe•ta (TAF-ə-tə) *n. taffetas.* A stiff silk cloth.–Grandmother has a dress of brown *taffeta* that makes a rustling or whispering sound when she walks.

taf•fy (TAF-ee) *n.* A candy. *Taffy* is made of sugar or molasses, water, and vinegar.

tag (TAG) *n. tags.* 1. A small piece of cardboard fastened to anything to give a name, directions for use, price, etc.–The clerk told us we could find the price of the skates by looking at the *tag.*–The children tied Christmas *tags* to their gifts to tell who was to get each gift and whom it was from.
2. A game in which one player, who is "it," chases the others until he touches one.
–*v. tags, tagged, tagging.* 1. Fasten a tag to.–After the gifts were *tagged,* they were put under the Christmas tree.
2. Follow close behind.–Jack's dog always *tags* after him.
3. To touch in the game of tag.–Mary *tagged* Ruth, and then Ruth was "it."

tail (TAYL) *n. tails.* 1. A part which grows on the back or rear end of many animals.–Cows switch their *tails* to keep the flies away.
2. The last or back part of anything, as the *tail* of an automobile, the *tail* of an airplane, the *tail* of a person's coat or shirt.

tai•lor (TAY-ler) *n. tailors.* A man who makes or alters clothes.–Mother took her suit to the *tailor* to have it shortened.

take (TAYK) *v. takes, took, taking.* 1. Hold; clasp; grasp.–The children *take* each other's hands when playing "The Farmer in the Dell."
2. Accept.–Grandfather said that he would not *take* the money that Bob offered to pay for the pony.
3. Choose; select; pick for yourself.–*Take* the book you want.–*Take* any seat you wish.
4. Carry; bring.–We *take* our lunch to school.
5. Receive; get; win.–Mary will surely *take* the prize for the best story.–The girls won the first game, but the boys *took* the second.
6. Capture.–The police *took* the robbers at their hideout.
7. Use up; need.–Bread *takes* an hour to bake. It needs to be baked an hour.
8. Rent or buy.–The boys will *take* the boat for the day.
9. Accompany; escort.–I will *take* you to school. I will go with you.–Father *takes* Mother out to dinner on Thursdays.
10. Go on.–Father *took* the train to town.
–*Take off* means to remove.–Mother *took* the dishes *off* the table.

talc (TALK) *n.* A soft, soaplike mineral. *Talc* is used in making talcum powder, soap, and lubricating products.

tal•cum (TAL-kəm) *n. talcums.* A kind of smooth white powder used on the face or body to soothe the skin.

tale (TAYL) *n. tales.* 1. A story.–Grandfather told an exciting *tale* about the bear he fought.
2. A bad report about someone, told to get him into trouble.–Mary likes to carry *tales* to Mother about Jack.

tal•ent (TAL-ənt) *n. talents.* A natural ability to do a thing easily.–Mary has a *talent* for music.

tal•ent•ed (TAL-ən-təd) *adj.* Having a special natural ability.–Mary is *talented* in music. She learns music easily and quickly.

talk (TAWK) *n. talks.* 1. A discussion.–Let's have a *talk* about your problems.
2. A speech; a lecture.–The policeman gave a *talk* on safety.
3. A rumor.–There is *talk* of school closing early this year.
–*v. talks, talked, talking.* Speak; put ideas or thoughts into spoken words.–We *talk* to our friends about things we're interested in.

talk•a•tive (TAWK-ə-tiv) *adj.* Likely to talk much; fond of talking.–Some children are *talkative.* They talk a great deal.

tall (TAWL) *adj. taller, tallest.* 1. Long or high from head to foot.–One boy is short; the other is *tall.*–A person who stands seven feet high is very *tall.*
2. High.–The Empire State Building is *tall.*

tal•low (TAL-oh) *n.* The fat of cows, sheep, and some other animals. *Tallow* is used in making soap and candles.

tal•ly (TAL-ee) *n. tallies.* 1. A piece of paper or a card on which a score in a game, or a count of anything, is kept.
2. A score or count.–During the game, Mary kept the *tally.*
3. A mark used in keeping count or score.–Each mark that Mary made was a *tally.*
–*v. tallies, tallied, tallying.* 1. Match or agree.–Bob's answer *tallies* with Mary's; Bob and Mary both think the answer is 369.
2. Make a count; keep score.–Bob and Mary *tallied* the votes for class president.

tal•on (TAL-ən) *n. talons.* A claw, especially of a bird that kills other birds or animals for food.–Hawks have long, sharp *talons.*

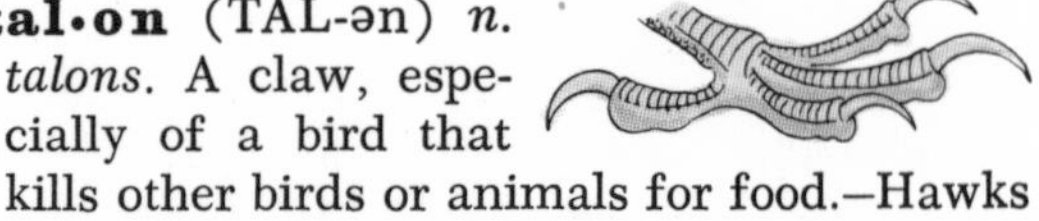

tam•a•rack (TAM-ə-rak) *n. tamaracks.* A tree of the larch family.

tam•bou•rine (tam-bə-REEN) *n. tambourines.* A very small drum with only one head and with flat pieces of metal fastened loosely to the rim. It is played by tapping it with the fingers while shaking it to make the metal pieces jingle.

tame (TAYM) *v. tames, tamed, taming.* Make gentle and obedient; accustom to people.–Some animals, such as horses, that were once wild have been *tamed* so people can use them.
–*adj. tamer, tamest; tamely, adv.* 1. Not wild; accustomed to people.–The squirrels in the park are *tame.* They aren't afraid of people. 2. Not exciting; dull.–Mary said the book was so *tame* that she did not finish it.

tam-o'-shan•ter (tam-ə-SHAN-ter) *n. tam-o'-shanters.* A flat, round cap with the top larger than the head band. Some *tam-o'-shanters* are crocheted from yarn and others are made from wool or felt.

tam•per (TAM-per) *v. tampers, tampered, tampering.* Meddle with something; try to fix or repair something without knowing how.–Father never *tampers* with the clock. He has it repaired by someone who is an expert on clocks.

tan (TAN) *n. tans.* A light-brown color.
–*v. tans, tanned, tanning.* 1. Turn to a brownish color from exposure to the sun.–The children played outdoors so much that their faces *tanned.*
2. Make (hides) into leather.–The hides and skins of certain animals are *tanned.*

tan•a•ger (TAN-ə-jer) *n. tanagers.* A kind of sparrow-like bird. The male *tanager* has beautiful, bright-colored feathers.

tan•ge•rine (tan-jə-REEN) *n. tangerines.* A kind of small, sweet orange which peels easily.

tan•gle (TANG-gəl) *n. tangles.* A twisted knot.–Ellen got a *tangle* in her sewing thread and had to break it.
–*v. tangles, tangled, tangling.* Knot and twist together.–Bob has *tangled* the string of his kite so badly that he will have a hard time straightening it.

tank (TANGK) *n. tanks.* 1. A large container for liquid.–We have a hot-water *tank* in the basement.
2. A heavily armored war machine mounted with guns. A *tank* can travel over very rough ground.

tank•er (TANGK-er) *n. tankers.* A cargo vessel fitted with tanks for carrying such things as oil and gasoline.

tan•nic ac•id (TAN-ik ASS-id). A chemical that is used in medicines, inks, tanning, and dyeing. *Tannic acid* is obtained from certain plants, often from oak bark.

tan•ta•lize (TAN-tə-lyz) *v. tantalizes, tantalized, tantalizing.* Tease, as by making promises that are not kept, or by showing something desirable and then keeping it out of reach.–Mother *tantalized* Father with the pie she had baked. She pretended to offer him a piece, but then she told him he could not have any until after dinner.

tan•trum (TAN-trəm) *n. tantrums.* A fit or sudden outburst of bad temper.–The baby had a *tantrum* when she wasn't allowed to have any more cookies. She screamed and cried.

tap (TAP) *n. taps.* 1. A light knock.–We heard a *tap* on the door.
2. A faucet; a valve for controlling the flow of a liquid.–We turned on the *tap* to get a drink of water.
3. A cap that screws on.–The workmen put a *tap* over the end of the pipe to keep the water from coming out.
–*v. taps, tapped, tapping.* 1. Strike or hit lightly.–*Tap* on the box to open it.
2. Make a hole to let the liquid out.–The men *tapped* the sugar maple trees so that the sap would flow out.

tape (TAYP) *n. tapes.* 1. A long, narrow strip of cloth, paper, steel, etc.
2. A narrow strip of paper or cloth with glue on one side.–The teacher mends books with *tape.*–The nurse put *tape* over the cut.
–*v. tapes, taped, taping.* Put a tape on; bind with tape.–The doctor *taped* the boy's foot so that he could walk.

tape•line (TAYP-lyn) *n. tapelines.* A strip of steel or cloth marked off into inches for measuring. It is also called a tape measure.

ta•per (TAY-per) *n. tapers.* A long, thin candle.
–*v. tapers, tapered, tapering.* Become smaller toward one end.–The end of a sharpened pencil *tapers* toward the point.

tape re•cord•er (tayp ri-KOR-der) *tape recorders.* An instrument used to record music, voices, or other sounds on a special kind of tape. A *tape recorder* can play back what it has recorded.

tap•es•try (TAP-iss-tree) *n. tapestries.* A piece of cloth with figures or pictures woven into it. *Tapestries* are hung on the walls just as painted or printed pictures are.

tap•i•o•ca (tap-ee-OH-kə) *n.* A kind of starchy food made from the roots of a tropical plant. *Tapioca* is used to make tasty puddings.

ta•pir (TAY-per) *n. tapirs.* A large hoglike animal found in Central America, South America, and Malaya. The *tapir* has a flexible snout, lives in forests, and eats only plants.

taps (TAPSS) *n.* A traditional tune played on a drum, a bugle, or a trumpet telling soldiers or sailors to put out the lights and go to bed. *Taps* is also sounded when a soldier or a sailor is buried.

tar (TAHR) *n. tars.* 1. A thick, sticky, black substance made from coal.–*Tar* is used in pavements, and to waterproof roofs.
2. A sailor.–The old *tar* likes to tell the children sea stories.
–*v. tars, tarred, tarring.* Put tar on.–The men *tarred* the road.

ta•ran•tu•la (tə-RAN-chə-lə) *n. tarantulas.* A large, hairy spider.

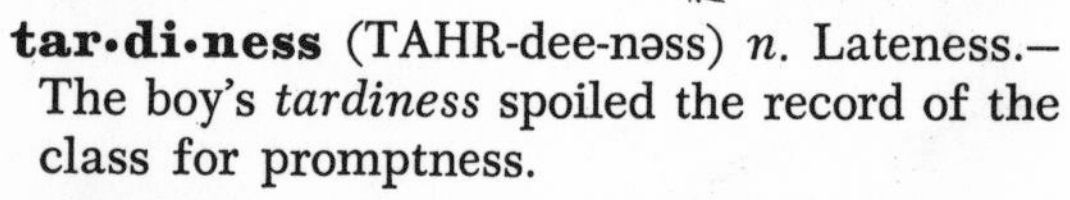

tar•di•ness (TAHR-dee-nəss) *n.* Lateness.–The boy's *tardiness* spoiled the record of the class for promptness.

tar•dy (TAHR-dee) *adj. tardier, tardiest; tardily, adv.* Late.–Mary has not been *tardy* once this school year. She has always been on time.

tar•get (TAHR-gət) *n. targets.* Anything used to shoot or aim at.–The boys put a tin can on the post for a *target;* they tried to hit the can with the stones they were throwing.

tar•iff (TAR-if) *n. tariffs.* 1. A system of taxes or duties fixed by the government on imported goods.
2. A tax or duty.–What is the *tariff* on bicycles?

tar•nish (TAHR-nish) *v. tarnishes, tarnished, tarnishing.* 1. Lose brightness; turn dark on the surface.–Silver *tarnishes* when left out in the air.
2. Cause to turn dark.–Gas will *tarnish* silver. It will make it lose its brightness.

tar•pau•lin (tahr-PAW-lin) *n. tarpaulins.* A large sheet of waterproof canvas.–When it rains, the grounds keeper at the ball park puts *tarpaulins* over the baseball diamond.

tar•ry (TAR-ee) *v. tarries, tarried, tarrying.* Be slow; waste time; wait.–Do not *tarry* on the way. Come right home.

tart (TAHRT) *n. tarts.* A small baked crust of pastry filled with fruit, jelly, or jam.–Grandmother makes *tarts* from pie crust that is left over from making pies.
–*adj. tarter, tartest.* Sour; biting or sharp to the taste.–Grapes that are not ripe are *tart.*

tar•tar (TAHR-ter) *n.* A substance that gathers and hardens on the teeth. *Tartar* consists of tiny particles of food, saliva, and lime. It is usually removed by the dentist when he cleans your teeth.

task (TASK) *n. tasks.* A piece of work.–If a *task* is once begun, never leave it till it's done.
–Bob's weekly *task* is cutting the grass.

tas•sel (TASS-əl) *n. tassels.* 1. An ornament made of a number of cords fastened together at one end and loose at the other. A *tassel* hangs down.–Mary's hat has a *tassel* on the side.
2. The silky threads on an ear of corn.

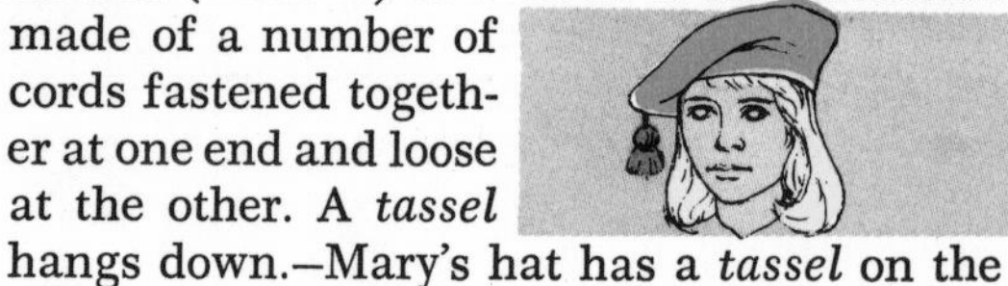

taste (TAYST) *n. tastes.* 1. The sensation or feeling one gets when food or drink is in the mouth.–The *taste* of sugar is sweet; the *taste* of vinegar is sour.
2. Judgment and understanding of beauty, or of what is good or proper.–Mary has good *taste* in clothes. She always picks clothes that are attractive and appropriate.

—v. tastes, tasted, tasting. 1. Test the flavor of food or drink by putting a little into the mouth.—Mary *tasted* the soup and said it was too salty.
2. Have a particular flavor.—This medicine *tastes* bitter.—Sea water *tastes* salty.

tat•tered (TAT-erd) *adj.* Ragged and torn.—The scarecrow's clothes were *tattered.*

tat•too (ta-TOO) *v. tattoos, tattooed, tattooing.* Mark the skin with colors which will not come off.—The sailor had a picture of a clown *tattooed* on his arm.
—tattoo, n. tattoos.

taught (TAWT) *v.* One form of the verb *teach.*—Mother *taught* Mary how to sew.

taut (TAWT) *adj. tauter, tautest; tautly, adv.; tautness, n.* Tightly stretched.—The clothesline was so *taut* that it broke in two.

tav•ern (TAV-ern) *n. taverns.* 1. A place where beer, wine, and other alcoholic drinks are served.
2. An inn; a hotel.—An old *tavern* stood on the side of the hill.

tax (TAKS) *n. taxes.* Money that must be paid by a person or company to help with the cost of government. Firemen and policemen are paid from *taxes* collected by a city. The Army, Navy, and Air Force are paid for by *taxes* collected by the Federal government in Washington.
—v. taxes, taxed, taxing. Require a tax from.—A person is *taxed* according to the amount of money he earns.

tax•i (TAK-see) or **tax•i•cab** (TAK-see-kab) *n. taxis* or *taxicabs.* An automobile, driven by a regular driver, that can be hired to carry passengers. Most *taxis* have a meter to show how long the trip is and how much one must pay.

tax•i•der•mist (TAK-sə-der-mist) *n. taxidermists.* A person who prepares, stuffs, and mounts the skins of animals. The animals stuffed and mounted by a good *taxidermist* look almost alive.

tea (TEE) *n. teas.* 1. A shrub grown mainly in China, Japan, and India; the dried leaves of this plant.
2. A drink made by pouring boiling water over the dried leaves of this plant.—Mother drinks *tea.*
3. A late afternoon party where tea and other refreshments are served.—Mother is going to a *tea* at our neighbor's home.

teach (TEECH) *v. teaches, taught, teaching.* 1. Instruct; show how; help one to learn.—Miss Jones will *teach* you how to sew.—Father *teaches* the boys to play baseball.—Our teacher *teaches* us reading, arithmetic, and spelling.
2. Give lessons in.—Mr. Smith *teaches* art.

teach•er (TEECH-er) *n. teachers.* A person who instructs others, or helps others to learn something.—Mary takes singing lessons from a music *teacher.*

teach•ing (TEECH-ing) *n. teachings.* 1. Instruction; the work of teachers.—Our teacher finds *teaching* very pleasant work.
2. A thing taught or preached.—The *teachings* in the Bible are good rules to live by.
—v. One form of the verb *teach.*—Father is *teaching* Bob to skate.

team (TEEM) *n. teams.* 1. A number of people who work, play, or act together.—One *team* plays against another *team.*
2. Two or more horses or other animals harnessed to one carriage or machine.
—v. teams, teamed, teaming. Join or work together for something.—Two dancers *teamed* up in one act of the show.

team•ster (TEEM-ster) *n. teamsters.* A person who drives a team of horses or a truck.—The *teamsters* loaded up their trucks and drove off.

team•work (TEEM-werk) *n.* Work or effort performed by a team, or by a group of persons as a whole.—The coach believes that good *teamwork* is the key to victory. He believes that everyone must work together in order to win.

tea•pot (TEE-paht) *n. teapots.* A container something like a kettle, made of metal or china, for making and pouring out tea.—Grandmother has a pretty china *teapot.*

tear (TAIR) *n. tears.* A rough, jagged cut.—Father hit his arm against the saw and made a long *tear* in his sleeve.
—v. tears, tore, tearing. 1. Pull apart; rip.—Father *tore* his sleeve on the saw.
2. Pull hard; pull hard on.—The angry artist *tore* down the pictures.—The wind *tore* the leaves from the tree.
3. Run wildly; rush.—Bob *tore* across the field to get his kite.

tear (TIR) *n. tears.* A drop of salt water that comes out of one's eyes.—Big *tears* fell on the baby's cheeks when she cried.

tear gas (TIR gass). A gas that irritates the eyes so that tears begin to flow. *Tear gas* causes temporary blindness. It is used in war, and sometimes it is used by the police as an aid in capturing criminals and breaking up riots.

tease (TEEZ) *v. teases, teased, teasing.* 1. Lightly make fun of.–Mary *teases* Father about getting fat.
2. Beg.–Baby *teases* Mother for lollipops.

tea•spoon (TEE-spoon) *n. teaspoons.* A small spoon.–We use a *teaspoon* to eat ice cream, pudding, and other soft foods.

tech•ni•cal (TEK-nə-kl) *adj.; technically, adv.* Having to do with the special methods and skills of a particular science, art, or field. –Jim has always been interested in engineering, but he has not yet had any *technical* training in the field.

te•di•ous (TEE-dee-əss) *adj.; tediously, adv.* Dull, tiresome, and boring.–The long speech was *tedious.*

teeth (TEETH) *n. pl.* More than one *tooth.* The sharp, white, bony points that grow in two rows in the mouths of people and many animals; the points of a rake or a comb.– We chew our food with our *teeth.*–A rake has *teeth* to comb the grass.

tel•e•cast (TEL-ə-kast) *v. telecasts, telecast* or *telecasted, telecasting.* Broadcast by television.–The program is being *telecast* across the entire nation.

tel•e•gram (TEL-ə-gram) *n. telegrams.* Written message sent over wires by electricity.– Father's *telegram* read, "Home Saturday night in time for supper. Love. Father."

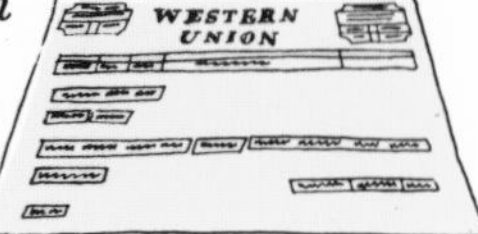

tel•e•graph (TEL-ə-graf) *n. telegraphs· telegraphic, adj.; telegraphically, adv.* A device or way by which written messages are sent over wires by electricity.–Father sent Mother a message by *telegraph* when he was away. –*v. telegraphs, telegraphed, telegraphing.* Send a written message over wires by electricity.–Father *telegraphed* Mother.

tel•e•phone (TEL-ə-fohn) *n. telephones.* A device which carries sound, such as that of voices or music, over wires by electricity.– Sally talked to Father on the *telephone.*

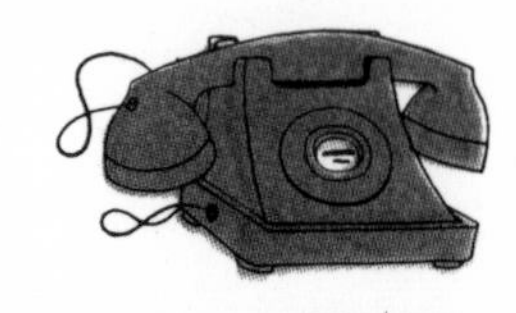

–*v. telephones, telephoned, telephoning.* Talk to someone or call someone on the telephone. –Mother *telephoned* Father to ask him when he would be home.

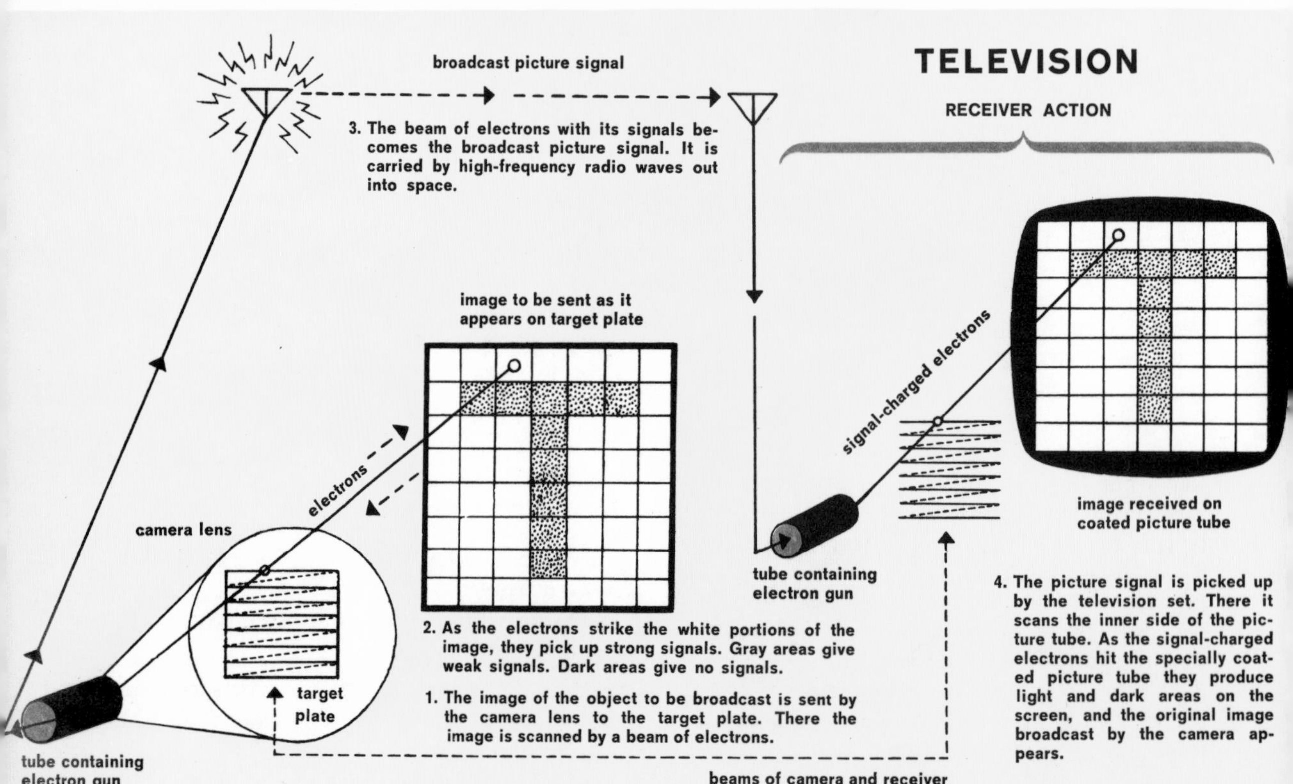

tel•e•scope (TEL-ə-skohp) *n. telescopes.* An instrument which, when looked through, makes faraway objects look larger, clearer, and closer to you. *Telescopes* are used to study the stars. – We looked through a *telescope* at the moon and saw the mountains on it.

Tel•e•type (TEL-ə-typ) *n. Teletypes.* A telegraphic instrument that works like a typewriter. As the operator types on the instrument's keyboard, the *Teletype* sends out the message letter by letter. The message is received and automatically printed by another *Teletype.*

tel•e•vise (TEL-ə-vyz) *v. televises, televised, televising.* Transmit or receive by television. –The championship fight was *televised* from coast to coast.

tel•e•vi•sion (TEL-ə-vizh-ən) *n.* A method of sending pictures of people or objects in motion by radio waves. The moving pictures appear on a screen which is part of the receiving set.–Father sat at his new *television* set, watching and listening to the baseball game being played in Chicago.

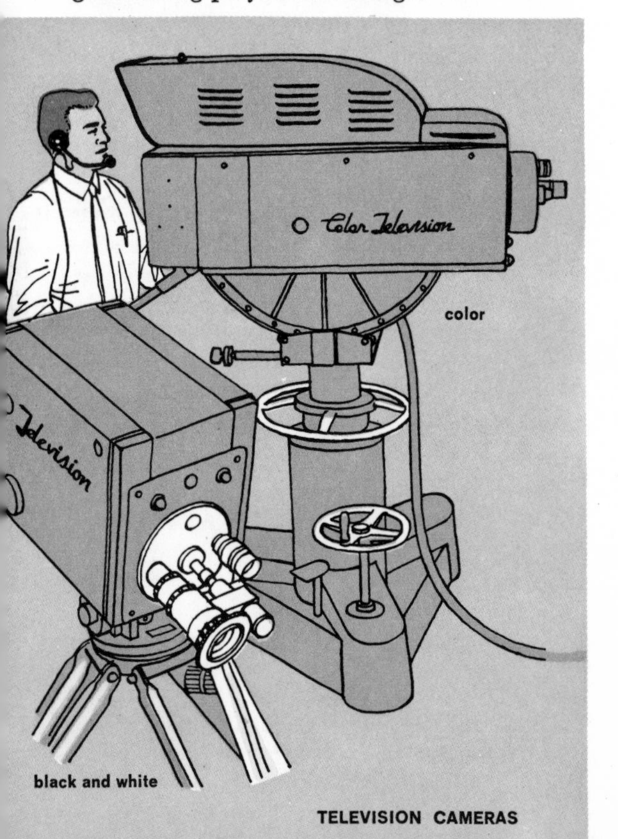

TELEVISION CAMERAS

tell (TEL) *v. tells, told, telling.* 1. Say or speak about something.–I will *tell* you about my trip.–I will *tell* you a story.
2. Show.–The speedometer on the car *tells* how fast you are going.
3. Order; command.–Father *told* the man to leave.
4. Let know; inform.–*Tell* me how far it is to school.

tell•er (TEL-er) *n. tellers.* 1. Someone who tells.–Grandfather is known as a fine *teller* of stories.
2. A bank employee who receives deposits and counts and gives out money.–Frank is working as a *teller* in the bank downtown this summer.

tem•per (TEM-per) *n. tempers.* 1. One's behavior or way of acting.–Mother has an even *temper.* She is calm and is not easily disturbed or made angry.
2. An angry mood.–Jack flies into *tempers* quickly, and he always feels very sorry afterward.

tem•per•ate (TEM-per-ət) *adj.* Mild; not extreme or excessive.–We live in a *temperate* climate, where the weather is not usually very hot or very cold.–Father is a man of *temperate* eating habits; he likes to eat, but doesn't eat too much.

tem•per•a•ture (TEM-per-ə-cher) *n. temperatures.* Heat as measured in degrees; hotness or coolness. *Temperature* is measured by a thermometer.–Mother set the oven control for a *temperature* of 400 degrees (400°).–Water boils when its *temperature* is about 212° Fahrenheit.–When the *temperature* is 0° Fahrenheit, it is very cold.

tem•pest (TEM-pəst) *n. tempests.* A very bad, windy storm.–A *tempest* kept the ships from sailing.

tem•ple (TEM-pəl) *n. temples.* A sacred building used for religious worship.

tem•po (TEM-poh) *n. tempos.* 1. In music, the rate of speed at which a composition is to be played or sung.–The *tempo* increased during the last movement of the symphony.
2. In general, any rate of work or activity; rhythm.–The boy who was behind in his studies tried to work at a faster *tempo* in order to catch up with the others.

tem•po•rar•y (TEM-pə-rair-ee) *adj.; temporarily, adv.* Not permanent; lasting for a little while only.–Jack will take a *temporary* job during his summer vacation.

tempt (TEMPT) *v. tempts, tempted, tempting.* 1. Lead someone to want to do wrong or evil.–The dollar which the man left out on his desk *tempted* the hungry boy to steal.
2. Make one want something; attract.–The cold pool *tempted* the thirsty hiker. It made him long for water.

temp•ta•tion (temp-TAY-shən) *n. temptations.* A thing that leads one to want to do something though he tries not to do it.–An open box of chocolates on the table is a *temptation* to eat.

ten (TEN) *n. tens* and *adj.* The number [10] coming after 9 and before 11.–Five and five make *ten.*

ten•ant (TEN-ənt) *n. tenants.* Someone who pays rent for the use of land or any kind of building.–Grandfather has *tenants* on his farm.–We are *tenants.* We pay rent for our apartment.

tend (TEND) *v. tends, tended, tending.* 1. Look after.–Mary *tends* the baby when Mother is away.–Bob *tends* the front lawn in the summer.
2. Be usually.–Bill *tends* to be lazy; he is usually lazy.

ten•der (TEN-der) *adj. tenderer, tenderest; tenderly, adv.; tenderness, n.* 1. Soft; easily cut or broken.–Some meat is tough, but this piece is *tender.*
2. Not strong; delicate; easily harmed.–Baby has *tender* skin.
3. Kind; easily moved; sympathetic.–Grandmother has a *tender* heart. She shares other people's sorrows and troubles.
4. Sore.–Baby has a *tender* spot on her head where she bumped it.

ten•der•foot (TEN-der-fuht) *n. tenderfoots* or *tenderfeet.* 1. A person without experience; a beginner; a novice.–Newcomers among the pioneers of the United States were called *tenderfeet* by the oldtimers.
2. A beginning rank among Boy Scouts.

ten•don (TEN-dən) *n. tendons.* A strong cord that fastens a muscle to a bone. – The football player pulled one of the *tendons* in his leg and had to leave the game.

ten•dril (TEN-dril) *n. tendrils.* The thin leafless stem by which climbing plants attach themselves to objects for support.–The grape *tendrils* are coiled around the trellis.

Ten•nes•see (ten-ə-SEE) *n.* A state in south central United States noted for its beautiful mountains, valleys, and plains. Its important industries are mixed farming, cattle raising, lumbering, shipping, and manufacturing textiles and hardwood products.

ten•nis (TEN-iss) *n.* A game played by hitting a ball back and forth over a net with a kind of paddle called a racket.

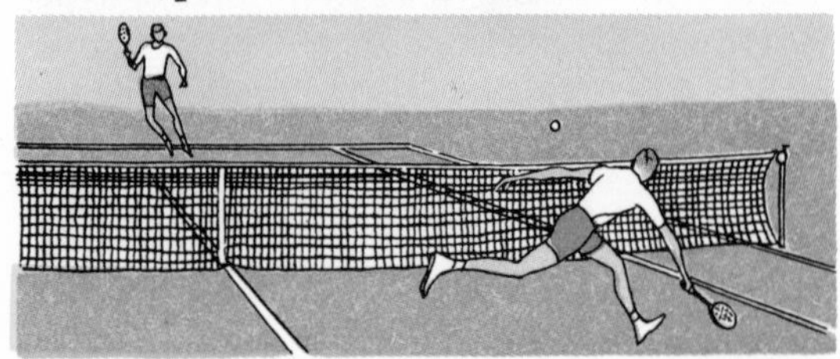

ten•or (TEN-er) *n. tenors* and *adj.* The highest singing voice that a grown man can have; a man with such a voice.–Father sings *tenor.* He is a *tenor.*

tense (TENSS) *n. tenses.* Any of various verb forms used to show the time of an action or happening.–The past *tense* of "come" is "came." John came to see me yesterday. "Came" shows that John's visit happened in the past.
–*adj. tenser, tensest; tensely, adv.; tenseness, n.* Strained; stretched tightly; taut. – The wires were so *tense* that they snapped.–Excitement may cause one to have *tense* nerves.

ten•sion (TEN-shən) *n. tensions.* 1. The act or condition of being strained, tightly drawn, or stretched.–The *tension* on the clothesline was eased when Mother took off the heavy blanket.
2. Mental or nervous strain; worry; anxiety. –The good news relieved the woman's *tension,* and she at last was able to sleep.

tent (TENT) *n. tents.* A movable shelter, usually made of a heavy cotton cloth called canvas. It is held up by poles and fastened to the ground by pegs.–Boy Scouts, soldiers, and campers often sleep in *tents.*

ten•ta•cle (TEN-tə-kəl) *n. tentacles.* 1. A long, flexible projection, usually on the head or near the mouth of an animal; a feeler. *Tentacles* are used for holding, feeling, or moving.–An octopus has eight *tentacles.*
2. Any sensitive hairlike projection on a plant.

tenth (TENTH) *n. tenths.* One of 10 equal parts.–If you divide anything into ten equal parts, each part is one *tenth.* It may be written 1/10.
–*adj.* Coming as number 10 in a series.

te•pee (TEE-pee) *n. tepees.* A pointed tent made of poles and buffalo hides and lived in by the American Indians of the Great Plains.

tep•id (TEP-id) *adj.* Not too warm and not too cool; lukewarm.–Father wouldn't drink the *tepid* water. He wanted cold water.

term (TERM) *n. terms.* 1. A set length of time.–In our school the first *term* is from the eighth of September until the last of January.
2. A word or expression.–We must know the meaning of certain *terms* in order to understand arithmetic. Plus, minus, add, and subtract are *terms* used in arithmetic.
3. A condition; a thing agreed to.–Bill did not live up to the *terms* of the bargain.

ter•mi•nal (TER-mə-nəl) *n. terminals* and *adj.* 1. The end; the part which forms an end. –A bus *terminal* is a station at the end of a bus line.
2. An electrical connecting device at the end of a cable or wire.–The television antenna is connected to a *terminal* in back of the set.

ter•mi•nate (TER-mə-nayt) *v. terminates, terminated, terminating.* Put an end to; end or come to an end. – The chairman *terminated* the discussion.

ter•mite (TER-myt) *n. termites.* A light-colored, soft-bodied, destructive insect. *Termites* live in colonies and feed on wood and paper.

ter•race (TAIR-əss) *n. terraces.* A flat piece of ground that is raised like a broad step.

ter•ra•pin (TAIR-ə-pin) *n. terrapins.* Any of various turtles found in the fresh or tide waters of North America. *Terrapins* are used for food.

ter•rar•i•um (tə-RAIR-ee-əm) *n. terrariums.* A gardenlike enclosure, usually glass-walled, in which small land animals are kept. A *terrarium* is for land animals what an aquarium is for fish.

ter•ri•ble (TAIR-ə-bəl) *adj.; terribly, adv.* Causing great fear or awe.–The car crash was a *terrible* accident.

ter•ri•er (TAIR-ee-er) *n. terriers.* A small, short-haired dog. *Terriers* were once used for hunting small animals that live in the ground.

ter•rif•ic (tə-RIF-ik) *adj.; terrifically, adv.* Terrible; awful; dreadful. – A *terrific* fire broke out in the factory.

ter•ri•fy (TAIR-ə-fy) *v. terrifies, terrified, terrifying.* Frighten very much.–The loud barking of the dog *terrified* the baby so much that she shrieked.

ter•ri•to•ry (TAIR-ə-tor-ee) *n. territories.* 1. A large stretch of land; a part of a country. –Some *territory* in North America is covered with forests.
2. A part of the United States which did not belong to any state, but was governed by men chosen by the President.–Alaska and Hawaii used to be United States *territories.* Now they are states.

ter•ror (TAIR-er) *n. terrors.* 1. Great fear.–*Terror* came over the crowd when the lion got loose.
2. A thing that causes great fear.–The escaped lion was a *terror.*

test (TEST) *n. tests.* A trial or examination which shows how much a person knows about a thing.–Our teacher gave us a spelling *test.*
–*v. tests, tested, testing.* Examine by trial.–The teacher *tested* our spelling ability by giving us a test.

tes•ta•ment (TESS-tə-mənt) *n. testaments.* 1. A legal document telling what a person wishes done with his property after he dies; a will.–The lawyer is planning to read the dead man's *testament* to a gathering of his relatives.
2. (Spelled with a capital "T.") One of the two portions of the Bible, either the New *Testament* or the Old *Testament.*

tes•ti•fy (TESS-tə-fy) *v. testifies, testified, testifying.* Make a solemn statement; tell what one knows to be true.–Bob *testified* that he saw the man pay the money.

tes•ti•mo•ny (TESS-tə-moh-nee) *n. testimonies.* 1. A sworn statement made by a witness in court.–The *testimony* of the first witness stated that the accused man had been in Boston on the day of the crime.
2. Proof; evidence.–What *testimony* do you have to support your statement?

test tube (TEST toob *or* tyoob) *test tubes.* A thin tube of glass closed at one end, usually used for containing liquids. – The scientist used a *test tube* to hold the chemical he was about to use in the experiment.

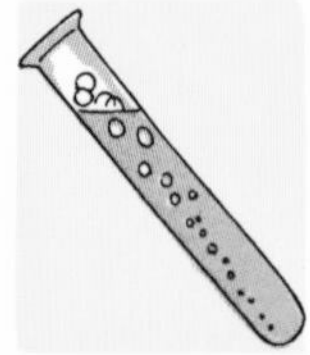

tet•a•nus (TET-n-əss) *n.* A dangerous and often fatal disease, usually caused by infection of wounds. *Tetanus* is marked by pain, stiffness of various muscles, and violent spasms.–Tom has been inoculated to protect him from *tetanus.*

teth•er (TETH-er) *v. tethers, tethered, tethering.* Attach an animal with a rope, chain, or rein so that it can move or graze only within limits.–The cowboy *tethered* his horse to a tree.

Tex•as (TEK-səss) *n.* The second largest state in the United States and the greatest farming state, located in the south central part of the United States. It produces cotton, grain, rice, petroleum, and much meat. *Texas* claims the largest cattle ranch in the world.

text•book (TEKST-buhk) *n. textbooks.* A schoolbook; a book that one studies from in school.–Our school is using a new *textbook* for geography.

tex•tile (TEKS-til *or* -tyl) *n. textiles.* A woven cloth.–Some *textiles* are woven from wool.
–*adj.* Having to do with weaving.–The big *textile* plant weaves many kinds of textiles.

tex•ture (TEKS-cher) *n. textures.* 1. Structure; arrangement of the parts of a substance. *Texture* may be soft or hard, rough or smooth, coarse or fine.
2. The way a fabric is woven; the arrangement of threads in a woven fabric.–Silk has a fine, tight *texture.*

than (THAN *or* thən) *conj.* The word *than* is used in comparing things.–Baby is smaller *than* Mary.–I would rather sleep *than* eat.

thank (THANGK) *v. thanks, thanked, thanking.* Tell that one is grateful; show gratitude. –Bob *thanked* his grandmother for the gift by saying "*Thank* you."

Thanks•giv•ing (thangks-GIV-ing) *n.* A holiday in the United States on the last Thursday in November. It is a day set aside to give thanks to God for the many things we have to be thankful for.

that (THAT *or* thət) *adj.* 1. A person or thing pointed out or noted before.–*That* boy I spoke about yesterday has returned home.
2. One of two or more persons or things. – Although the shelf was filled with many books, I took only *that* book off the shelf.
3. Opposite of this, usually referring to some thing or person not seen.–*That* tree was a maple; this one is an oak.
–*adv.* To a certain extent or degree; so.–No child should eat *that* much.–I don't want to walk *that* far. It's too far, and I'm too tired.
–*conj. That* is used to connect two parts of a sentence and show how they are related.– Bobby said *that* he would come. – Mother knew *that* Father would be late. She knew because Father had told her.–The baby ate so much *that* she got sick.
–*pron. those.* Who, whom, or which.–He is the boy *that* sells papers.–The boy *that* you saw was Jack.

thatch (THACH) *n. thatches.* Grass or straw used as roofing.
–*v. thatches, thatched, thatching.* Cover (a roof) with straw in overlapping layers. – The farmer *thatched* the roof of the hut.

that's (THATSS). That is.–*That's* the best book I ever read.

thaw (THAW) *n. thaws.* A time when snow and frost melt.–We had an early *thaw* in February.
–*v. thaws, thawed, thawing.* Melt; become soft.–If the ice *thaws,* we cannot go skating.

the (THEE *or* thi *or* thə) *adj.* or *art.* *The* is used in speaking of some particular person or thing.—*The* dog with Bob is black.—I read *the* book you gave me.

the•a•ter or **the•a•tre** (THEE-ə-ter) *n. theaters* or *theatres.* 1. A building where something is presented for people to see or hear.—Tom saw a play in the new *theater.*
2. Drama.—Mother enjoys the *theater.* She goes to plays as often as she can.

3. A place of action; a place where great things happen.—Europe and the Pacific areas were *theaters* of war in World War II.

thee (THEE) *pron. Thee* is an old way of saying you, meaning one person only. It is used in the Bible, in prayer, and in some poetry.—"Blessings on *thee,* little man, barefoot boy with cheeks of tan."

theft (THEFT) *n. thefts.* Stealing; robbery. —The newsboy reported the *theft* of his money to the police.

their (THAIR *or* thər) *adj.* Belonging to them.—Bob and Jack could see *their* house from the top of the hill.

theirs (THAIRZ) *pron.* Something belonging to them.—This bicycle is yours and that one is *theirs.*

them (THEM *or* thəm) *pron.* The things or animals or people already mentioned or spoken of.—The boys took the dog with *them.* "*Them*" refers to the boys.—Grandmother had three spotted kittens, but she gave *them* away.

them•selves (thəm-SELVZ) *pron.* The children *themselves* prepared the dinner. Nobody helped them.—The boys *themselves* admitted they had done wrong. Even the boys admitted it. – Mother told the children to dress *themselves.* Each child was to dress himself.

then (THEN) *adv.* 1. At that time.—If you want me to come to your house at three o'clock, I will be there *then.*
2. Soon or immediately afterward.—We arrived home, and *then* it started to rain.
3. Next.—First came the band and *then* the horses.
4. Therefore; because of that.—If you play this morning, *then* you must study this afternoon.

the•o•ry (THEE-ə-ree *or* THIR-ee) *n. theories.* 1. The principles, ideas, or methods of an art or science.—Mary has been studying music *theory.* As soon as she has a piano, she will be able to apply and practice what she has learned.
2. A carefully thought-out explanation based on facts or observations.—After the police had studied all the clues, they offered their *theory* of how the crime had been committed.
3. A possible explanation; an opinion or idea.—Everyone seemed to have a different *theory* on how to raise money for the party.

there (THAIR) *adv.* 1. In that place.—Put the basket *there.*
2. At that place.—Stop *there* for lunch.
3. To that place.—The circus is in town. We were just going *there* when it started to rain.
4. Used to point out or call attention to.—*There* is Father now!—*There* is the trouble.
5. *There* are ten more days until Christmas. —Is *there* room for one more in your car?

there•af•ter (thair-AF-ter) *adv.* After that; afterward.—The child burned his hand playing with matches, and *thereafter* he was always careful of matches.

there•fore (THAIR-for) *adv.* For that reason; because of that.—Mary had a bad cold, and *therefore* could not go to school.

there's (THAIRZ). There is.—*There's* a circus in town this month.

ther•mom•e•ter (ther-MAHM-ə-ter) *n. thermometers.* An instrument for measuring one's temperature, or for telling how cold or hot it is. – Mother took the baby's temperature with a *thermometer* when he was sick. – We have a *thermometer* in the kitchen to tell us how warm or how cold the room is.

Ther•mos bot•tle (THER-məss baht-l) *Thermos bottles.* Trademark name of a bottle so made that it will keep cold things cold and and hot things hot for hours. – Father carries a *Thermos bottle* of hot soup with his lunch. – The boys took a *Thermos bottle* of cold milk on their hike.

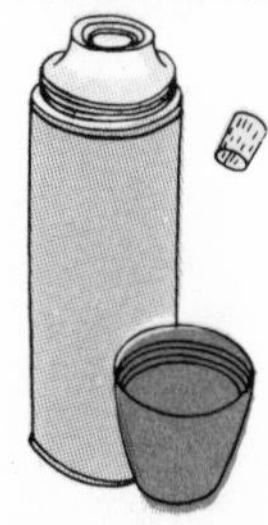

ther•mo•stat (THER-mə-stat) *n. thermostats.* An instrument that makes a heating or air-conditioning unit work just enough to keep a building from getting too warm or too cold.–If you set your *thermostat* for 70°, the temperature in your house will stay near 70°.

these (THEEZ) *adj.* and *pron.* Plural of *this,* used when we point out or speak of more than one person or thing that is nearer to us than some others are.–*These* yellow daisies are from my garden.–*These* are the children who live next door.

they (THAY) *pron. pl.* Used in speaking about persons or things or animals already named. –The boys work hard so that *they* will get good marks.

they'll (THAY-əl). They will.–The girls said they would come early; so *they'll* be here soon.

they're (THAY-er *or* THAIR). They are.–The boys are usually early, but today *they're* late.

they've (THAYV). They have.–We expect the children, but *they've* been delayed.

thick (THIK) *adj. thicker, thickest; thickly, adv.* 1. Not thin; not slender; plump.–One book is thin, the other is *thick.* The *thick* one is wider from cover to cover.
2. Close together; crowded together. – The plants in the garden are too *thick* to have room to grow.–The weeds are *thick* in the garden.
3. Partly solid; not completely liquid.–Water is thin. Gravy is *thick.*
4. Foggy; heavy; clouded.–The air was *thick* with smoke. You could hardly see through it.
5. Husky, deep, or hoarse.–When Father had a cold, his voice was *thick.*

thick•en (THIK-ən) *v. thickens, thickened, thickening.* 1. Make thick or more solid. – Mother *thickens* the pudding with cornstarch.
2. Become thicker. – The ice on the windshield *thickened* as we drove.

thick•et (THIK-it) *n. thickets.* A thick growth of underbrush and bushes.–We had to cut our way through the *thicket* with our jackknives.

thick•ness (THIK-nəss) *n. thicknesses.* 1. Distance from top side to bottom side.–What is the *thickness* of this board? I have measured its length and width, but how thick is it?
2. A layer.–The nurse put six *thicknesses* of bandage on the boy's sore arm.

thief (THEEF) *n. thieves.* A robber; a person who steals.–The policeman caught the *thief* as he left the store with the stolen rings and watches.

thieves (THEEVZ) *n. pl.* More than one *thief;* robbers. – The *thieves* were soon caught.

thigh (THY) *n. thighs.* The part of one's leg between the knee and the hip.

thim•ble (THIM-bəl) *n. thimbles.* A cap usually worn on the middle finger when sewing, to push the needle through the cloth, and to protect the finger. *Thimbles* are made of metal or other hard materials.

thin (THIN) *v. thins, thinned, thinning.* Make smaller, less fat, less thick, or less dense; reduce in size or abundance.–Father *thinned* the carrots in the garden. He pulled out some to give the others more room to grow. – Mother *thinned* the gravy with hot water.
–*adj. thinner, thinnest; thinly, adv.* 1. Slender; not thick.–One book is thick, the other is *thin.* The *thin* book has less distance from cover to cover.–Mother likes bread cut in *thin* slices.
2. Lean; having little flesh or fat.–Mother is *thin,* but Father is stout.
3. Scattered; far apart.–The grass is still *thin* in April. The blades are not close together.
4. (Of a liquid) Easily poured.–We use *thin* cream for coffee, and heavy cream for whipping.
5. Not strong or deep.–The little old lady has a *thin* voice.

thine (THYN) *pron.* An old way of saying *yours.*–The sword was *thine,* not mine.

thing (THING) *n. things.* Any object, idea, deed, or matter. – Furniture, clothes, and other objects are *things.*–There are marbles, pencils, paper, crayons, and many other *things* on the teacher's desk.–He talked of every*thing* except the *thing* on his mind.–Interrupting a person is not a polite *thing* to do.

think (THINGK) *v. thinks, thought, thinking.* 1. Use one's mind.–To work a problem, to learn to spell, or to study anything, one must *think.*
2. Believe.–I *think* it pays to be honest.
3. Get an idea.–Can you *think* of anything to do now that it is raining?

third (THERD) *n. thirds.* One of 3 equal parts of anything. – If an apple is cut into three equal parts, each part is one *third* of the apple. It may be written 1/3.
–*adj.* Coming as number 3 in a series.–Mary was first, Bob was second, and Bill was *third.*

thirst (THERST) *n. thirsts.* 1. A dry feeling in the throat and mouth caused by the need of liquid.–The explorers lost in the desert nearly died of *thirst.*
2. A great desire.–A scholar has a *thirst* for learning about things.

thirst•y (THERSS-tee) *adj. thirstier, thirstiest; thirstily, adv.* Feeling thirst; needing water.–Baby is *thirsty.* She wants a drink.

thir•teen (ther-TEEN) *n. thirteens* and *adj.* The number [13] coming after 12 and before 14.–Ten and three make *thirteen.*

thir•teenth (ther-TEENTH) *n. thirteenths.* One of 13 equal parts.–If a thing is divided into 13 parts all the same size, each part is called one *thirteenth.* It may be written 1/13.
–*adj.* Coming as number 13 in a series.–Jack was the *thirteenth* person in line.

thir•ty (THER-tee) *n. thirties* and *adj.* The number [30] coming after 29 and before 31.
–Three times ten equals *thirty.*

this (THISS) *adj.* and *pron. these.* The one at hand or the one just mentioned. The word *this* is used to speak of or to point out a person or thing that is present, very near, or has just been spoken of.–*This* boy is Bob's cousin; that boy over there is *this* boy's friend. – *This* is my book.

this•tle (THISS-əl) *n. thistles.* A prickly plant that has purple flowers.

thong (THAWNG) *n. thongs.* A strip of leather used for fastening, and as the tail end of a whip.–*Thongs* are often used for lacing shoes.

tho•rax (THOR-aks) *n. thoraxes* or *thoraces.* 1. In higher animals (including human beings), the section of the body between the neck and abdomen; the chest; the cavity within the chest, or enclosed by the ribs.

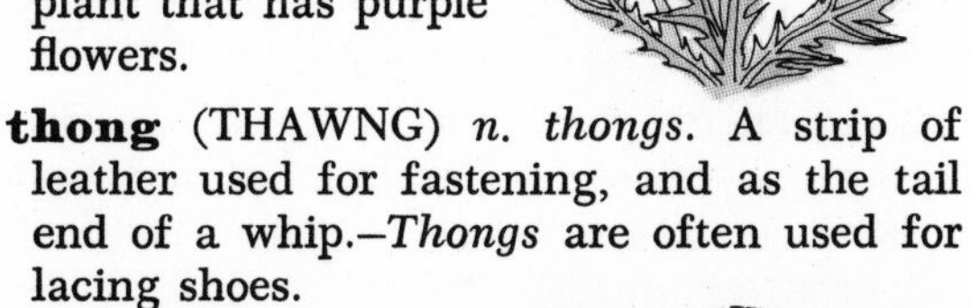

2. In insects, the section of the body between the head and abdomen.

thorn (THORN) *n. thorns.* A prickle; a sharp point on a rosebush or some other plant.

thor•ough (THER-oh) *adj.; thoroughly, adv.; thoroughness, n.* 1. Doing all that should be done.–The girl is very *thorough* with her work. She does it all very carefully.
2. Done completely.–That girl did a *thorough* job.

thor•ough•bred (THER-ə-bred) *adj.* Bred from the finest animals of its kind.–Tom's dog is a *thoroughbred* collie.

thor•ough•fare (THER-ə-fair) *n. thoroughfares.* 1. A public highway or main road. – Turnpikes, freeways, and throughways are *thoroughfares.*

2. A street, road, or passage with an entrance and an exit; a way through.

those (THOHZ) *adj.* and *pron.* Plural of *that,* used in speaking of or pointing out more than one person or thing farther away than some others.–*Those* apples are the best. These are not so good. *Those* apples over there are better than the apples right here.

though (THOH) *adv.* However. – You may have spoken to me; I didn't hear you, *though.*
–*conj.* 1. Even if.–We will come to the party *though* we will be late.
2. In spite of the fact that.–Bob was on time, *though* he got up late.
–*As though* means as if. – Mother spoke *as though* she expected us to go.

thought (THAWT) *n. thoughts.* 1. An idea; anything one thinks about. – He kept his *thoughts* secret.–The man has some good *thoughts* about building airplanes.
2. Thinking; working of the mind.–Father said he would give the problem some *thought.*
–*v.* One form of the verb *think.*–We *thought* of you on your birthday.

thought•ful (THAWT-fuhl) *adj.; thoughtfully, adv.; thoughtfulness, n.* 1. Busy thinking; in the habit of thinking. – George is *thoughtful* about beginning college next month. He has been thinking about it.
2. Careful of the welfare or feelings of others.–Mother said it was *thoughtful* of Mary to send the birthday card to Grandmother.

thought•less (THAWT-ləss) *adj.; thoughtlessly, adv.; thoughtlessness, n.* 1. Careless.–A *thoughtless* person is always making mistakes.
2. Not careful of the welfare or feelings of others.–The *thoughtless* boy played the radio when his father was trying to sleep.

thou•sand (THOW-zənd) *n. thousands.* The number represented by 1 followed by three zeros. Ten one hundreds make a *thousand.*
100 is one hundred.
1,000 is one thousand.

thrash (THRASH) *v. thrashes, thrashed, thrashing.* 1. Separate grain from its stalk by beating; thresh.–The farmer *thrashes* his grain.
2. Beat; whip.–In olden times some prisoners were *thrashed* for crimes.

thread (THRED) *n. threads.* A fine string made by twisting strands of such material as silk and cotton.–This is a spool of *thread.*
–We use *thread* for sewing.
–*v. threads, threaded, threading.* Put thread through (a needle).–Mother *threads* her needle before she starts to sew.

threat (THRET) *n. threats.* A promise to do harm.–Peter was not frightened by the *threat* of force.–The *threat* of rain made us go into the house.

threat•en (THRET-n) *v. threatens, threatened, threatening.* 1. Promise to do harm to.–The pirates *threatened* to attack the ship.
2. Give notice of; warn of.–The wind *threatens* a storm. It warns that a storm may come.

three (THREE) *n. threes* and *adj.* The number [3] coming after 2 and before 4.–Two and one make *three.*

thresh (THRESH) *v. threshes, threshed, threshing.* Separate grain from its stalk by beating; thrash.–The farmer *threshes* his grain. He separates the grain from the straw with a machine.–In olden times, grain was *threshed* by beating it with a jointed stick called a flail.

thresh•old (THRESH-hohld) *n. thresholds.* 1. The piece of wood or stone at the bottom of a doorway.–Baby sat on the *threshold* and watched for Father.
2. Beginning.–The scientist knew that he was at the *threshold* of a discovery.

threw (THROO) *v.* One form of the verb *throw.*–Bob *threw* the ball to Jack after Bill had thrown it to him.

thrice (THRYSS) *adv.* Three times.–The old woman told the prince to knock *thrice* on the door.

thrift (THRIFT) *n.* Avoiding waste; habit of saving.–*Thrift* is a good habit to form.

thrill (THRIL) *n. thrills.* A shivery or excited feeling.–The sight of the flag gave Jack a *thrill.*
–*v. thrills, thrilled, thrilling.* Cause to feel excited.–The music *thrilled* the boy. It gave him a tingling, excited feeling.

thrive (THRYV) *v. thrives, thrived* or *throve, thriving.* 1. Grow strong and be healthy.–The plants will not *thrive* unless you water them.
2. Be successful; grow or improve; get along well.–Father's new business is *thriving.*

throat (THROHT) *n. throats.* 1. Front part of the neck. – Mother puts cream on her *throat* to keep it from wrinkling.–Ed has a bandage on his *throat.*

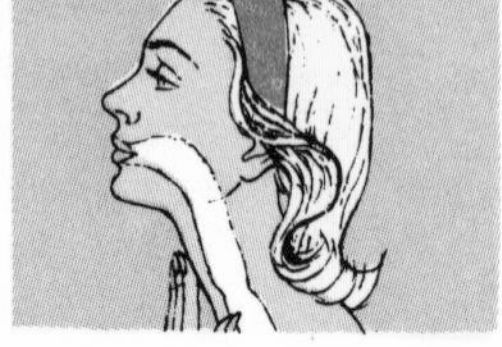

2. The passage inside the neck.–When one swallows food, it passes through the *throat.*

throb (THRAHB) *v. throbs, throbbed, throbbing.* Beat fast or hard; pound.–The boy's heart *throbbed* after he ran the race.

throne (THROHN) *n. thrones.* 1. A chair, usually on a dais, used by a king, queen, or other ruler.
2. The office or rank of a king.–The boy prince came to the *throne* during the war. He became king.

throng (THRAWNG) *n. throngs.* A crowd.–A *throng* gathered for the game.
–*v. throngs, thronged, thronging.* Crowd. – People *thronged* the ball park.

throt•tle (THRAHT-l) *n. throttles.* A valve, lever, pedal, or other means of controlling the flow of fuel to an engine.–The racer opened the *throttle,* thereby increasing the speed of the motorboat.

through (THROO) *adj.* 1. Express; nonstop.–We took the *through* train to the city.
2. Finished.–Mother will be *through* soon.
–*adv.* 1. The whole distance. – We went *through* to California. We went across the entire United States, from New York to California.
2. From beginning to end; from start to finish.–Have you read that book *through,* or have you only read parts of it?

–prep. 1. In one side and out the other.–The train went *through* the tunnel.–Grandmother put the thread *through* the eye of the needle.–Jim looked *through* the microscope.
2. Among; in the midst of; between.–The birds fluttered *through* the trees.–We walked *through* the tall sunflowers.
3. Along; from one end to the other; in.–We walked *through* the halls to go from one class to another.
4. During; throughout.–The baby cried all *through* the night.–We worked *through* the day. We worked all day.
5. Because of.–Tom became sick *through* overeating.
6. By means of.–I didn't tell you directly; I told you *through* him. I told him to tell you.

throw (THROH) *n. throws.* The act of hurling.–Bob's fine *throw* to first base won the game.
–v. throws, threw, throwing. Hurl; fling; cast; pitch.–The pitcher *throws* the ball to the catcher.–*Throw* your waste paper into the basket.–The car stopped suddenly and we were *thrown* from our seats.

thrush (THRUSH) *n. thrushes.* One of a group of songbirds known for their sweet singing. A robin is one kind of *thrush.*

thrust (THRUST) *n. thrusts.* 1. Hard push.–David threw open the door with a quick *thrust.*
2. Stab.–One *thrust* of the knife killed the wildcat.
–v. thrusts, thrust, thrusting. 1. Push hard; shove.–The boy *thrust* his way through the crowd.–The workman *thrust* his shovel deep into the sand.
2. Stab; pierce.–The hunter *thrust* his knife into the wildcat.

thud (THUD) *n. thuds.* Dull, bumping sound. –We heard the *thud* as the book fell to the floor.
–v. thuds, thudded, thudding. Make a dull, bumping sound. – The book *thudded* onto the floor.

thumb (THUM) *n. thumbs.* 1. The short, thick finger set apart from the other fingers.
2. A place for the thumb.–Mittens have *thumbs* but not separate fingers.
–v. thumbs, thumbed, thumbing. Turn (pages of) with the thumb.–Mary *thumbed* through the book looking for pictures.

thun•der (THUN-der) *n. thunders.* 1. The loud rumbling or cracking sound that often follows a flash of lightning.–The dog hides under the bed when he hears *thunder.*
2. A noise like thunder.–We heard the *thunder* of the enemy's guns.
–v. thunders, thundered, thundering. 1. Make the noise of thunder.–It *thundered* during the storm.
2. Speak very loudly. – "Where have you been?" Father *thundered.*

thun•der•storm (THUN-der-storm) *n. thunderstorms.* A storm with thunder and lightning.–We ran to get home before the *thunderstorm.*

Thurs•day (THERZ-dee) *n. Thursdays.* The day after Wednesday. *Thursday* is the fifth day of the week.

thus (THUSS) *adv.* 1. In this way.–If you do the work *thus,* you will get through sooner.
2. Therefore.–He started early; *thus* he was on time.
3. So; this.–You may go *thus* far, and no farther.

thy (THY) *pron.* Your (used of one person only). *Thy* is used in the Bible, in praying, and in old poems. – Thou shalt love *thy* neighbor as *thy*self.

thy•roid (THY-roid) *n. thyroids* and *adj.* A gland in the neck. The *thyroid* is divided into two round parts, one on each side of the windpipe. The *thyroid* secretes a substance which has a great affect on the body's growth, and on one's physical and mental activity.

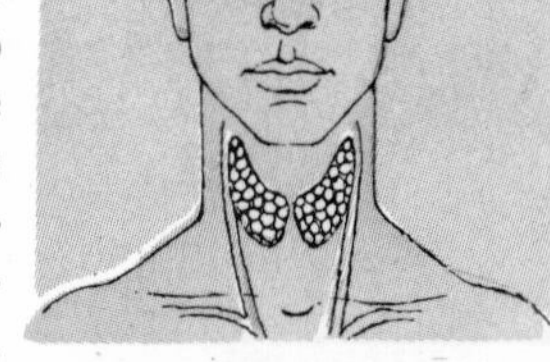

thy•self (thy-SELF) *pron.* An old form of the word *yourself.*

tick (TIK) *n. ticks.* 1. A small insect or spider that sucks the blood of animals and people.
2. A light beat; a sharp, quick click.–We heard the *tick* of the watch.

–v. ticks, ticked, ticking. 1. Make light, quick sounds over and over, like *tick*-tock, *tick*-tock, *tick*-tock.–The clock *ticks.*
2. Make marks to record something; check; count.–The teacher asked us to *tick* off the important points of the things we had copied off the blackboard.–The stop watch *ticked* off the seconds left in the last minute of the game.

tick•et (TIK-it) *n. tickets.* 1. A printed card or paper which shows that one has paid to ride on a train, go into a moving picture, see a football game, etc.
2. A tag.–The clerk put a price *ticket* on each of the different pieces of jewelry.

tick•le (TIK-əl) *n. tickles.* An uneasy, tingling feeling.–Father had a *tickle* in his throat which made him cough.
–*v. tickles, tickled, tickling.* 1. Touch lightly, causing a tingling feeling. – Bob *tickled* Baby's neck with a feather.
2. Amuse; delight.–The clown's performance *tickles* the children. – The kitten's antics *tickled* the whole family.

tick•lish (TIK-lish) *adj.; ticklishness, n.* 1. Sensitive to being tickled. – Sally's feet are *ticklish.*
2. Difficult to do and handle right; requiring tact or great care.–It will be a *ticklish* job to get the teacher's consent to have a party during school hours.–Pasting the small pictures in the scrapbook is *ticklish* work.

tid•al wave (TYD-l wayv) *tidal waves.* A tremendous ocean wave. *Tidal waves* are usually caused by earthquakes or very strong winds. *Tidal waves* can cause great damage when they sweep over the land.

tide (TYD) *n. tides.* 1. The rising and the falling of the ocean. When the *tide* is low, the water is not so deep at the shore line. When

the *tide* is high, the water is deeper and higher up on the shore line. The *tide* is caused by the pulling power, or attraction, of the moon and the sun.
2. A current, or movement of water.–The rowboat was carried out to sea by the *tide.*
–*Tide over* means to help out, carry over, or piece out. – Grandmother loaned us two quarts of milk to *tide* us *over* until the milkman came.

ti•dy (TYD-ee) *v. tidies, tidied, tidying.* Make neat; put in order.–Mary helps Mother *tidy* up the house on Saturday morning.
–*adj. tidier, tidiest.* Neat and in order.–Bob has a *tidy* desk.

tie (TY) *n. ties.* 1. A necktie; a strip of cloth extending around the neck under the collar and knotted in front.–Father likes to wear a red *tie.*
2. An equal score. – The ball game ended in a *tie;* the score was one to one.
3. A large piece of wood to which the rails of a railway are fastened.
–*v. ties, tied, tying.* 1. Fasten; bind; make a knot or bow of.–Baby is too little to *tie* her own shoelaces.–The children *tied* up their Christmas gifts with red ribbon.–The organ-grinder *tied* the monkey to the hand organ.
2. Make the score of one team equal to that of the other.–Jack's home run *tied* the score in the seventh inning.

tier (TIR) *n. tiers.* One of several rows placed one above the other; a layer.–We sat in the top *tier* of seats at the play. – The wedding cake had three *tiers.*

ti•ger (TY-ger) *n. tigers.* A large wild animal of the cat family with yellow fur striped with black. *Tigers* eat the flesh of other animals. At the zoo, the *tigers* are kept in strong cages.

tight (TYT) *adj. tighter, tightest; tightly, adv.; tightness, n.* 1. Close-fitting; too close-fitting; snug. – Baby's feet have grown so much that her shoes are too *tight.*–Screw the nozzle on *tight* if you don't want the hose to leak.
2. Stretched taut.–The clothesline is *tight.*
3. Firm; hard; difficult to undo.–Baby pulled her shoestring into a *tight* knot.
4. A thing that is air*tight* will not let air in. Anything water*tight* will not let water in.
–*adv.* Firmly; closely.–The apples were packed *tight* in the box.

tight•en (TYT-n) *v. tightens, tightened, tightening.* Make firmer, tighter, or more close-fitting. – The workmen *tightened* the rope. They pulled it hard and tied it securely so that it did not sag.–Mother *tightened* the top on the jar.

tight•rope (TYT-rohp) *n. tightropes.* A tightly stretched rope on which one or more acrobats perform. – The circus acrobat rode a bicycle across the *tightrope.*

tights (TYTSS) *n. pl.* A close-fitting garment for the legs and hips, usually worn by acrobats, dancers, and other performers. *Tights* fit smoothly over the skin.

ti•gress (TY-grəss) *n. tigresses.* A female tiger.–The *tigress* defended her three cubs fiercely.

tile (TYL) *n. tiles.* 1. Baked clay or stone in thin pieces, used for roofs, floors, walls in bathrooms, and many other things.
2. A large, earthen pipe for drains and drainage ditches.

till (TIL) *n. tills.* A drawer in which money and other valuables are kept.–The grocer put the money in the *till.*

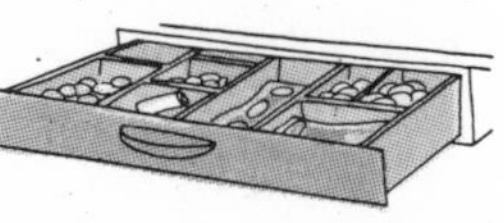

–*v. tills, tilled, tilling.* Plow; turn (earth) to prepare for planting.–The farmer *tilled* the ground before he planted his crops.
–*conj.* Until; up to the time when.–Wait *till* Father gets home.
–*prep.* Until; up to the time of.–Must we wait *till* evening?

tilt (TILT) *v. tilts, tilted, tilting.* 1. Slant; tip; lean to one side.–The telephone pole is not straight up and down. It *tilts.*
2. Tip; set at an angle.–Do not *tilt* your chair back or you may fall.

tim•ber (TIM-ber) *n. timbers.* 1. Wood used for building.–Most houses are made of *timber.*
2. A strong, thick piece of wood.–Large *timbers* were used in building the bridge.
3. Woods or forest where trees grow.–The *timber* burned down.

time (TYM) *n. times.* 1. A measured period that something lasts; duration. – Minutes, hours, days, weeks, months, and years are all measures of *time.* They answer the question "How long?"
2. A part of a measured period.–Morning is a *time* of day.–Spring is a *time* of the year.
3. A definite point or moment (of or in time). –Noon is the *time* for lunch.
4. In music, time means the regular beat.–A waltz is in three-quarter *time.* It has three beats in each measure.
5. An occasion; a repeated happening.–We heard the whistle three *times.*
–*v. times, timed, timing.* Measure the duration or length of.–The teacher *timed* our test. She watched the clock and told us when to start and when to stop.
–*Times* means multiplied by.–Six *times* two is twelve.

time•piece (TYM-peess) *n. timepieces.* A clock or watch.–We tell time by a *timepiece.*

time•ta•ble (TYM-tay-bəl) *n. timetables.* A list showing when trains, planes, buses, etc., arrive and depart.

tim•id (TIM-id) *adj.; timidly, adv.; timidity, n.* Shy; bashful; afraid of people and things. –Baby is *timid* around strangers.

tin (TIN) *n. tins.* A light, soft metal used in making such things as pans, kettles, cans.

tin•der (TIN-der) *n.* Anything, such as paper or soft, dry wood, that catches fire easily.

tine (TYN) *n. tines.* One of the slender, pointed fingerlike pieces on a fork.

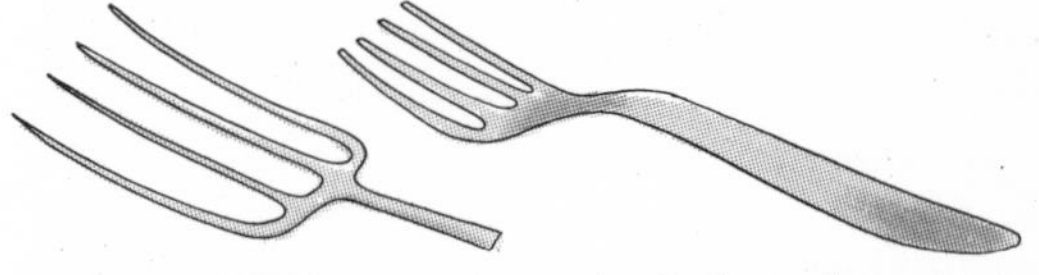

tinge (TINJ) *n. tinges.* A slight color or quality (of).–Mary's hat has a *tinge* of red in it. The hat is mainly blue, but there is some red in it, also.
–*v. tinges, tinged, tingeing* or *tinging.* Add a touch or trace of color to; color slightly; tint. –Mary drew a picture of a sailboat and *tinged* the water with blue.

tin•gle (TING-gəl) *n. tingles.* A stinging or prickly feeling caused by such emotions as excitement or fear.–Bill felt *tingles* running up and down his spine when he entered the haunted house.
–*v. tingles, tingled, tingling.* Have a prickly feeling.–The sound of the fire truck makes Tom *tingle* with excitement.

tin•kle (TINGK-əl) *n. tinkles.* A soft ringing sound.—We heard the *tinkle* of the cowbell.
—*v. tinkles, tinkled, tinkling.* Make or cause something to make ringing sounds.—The boy *tinkled* his knife and fork by hitting them together. The fork *tinkled* when struck.

tin•sel (TIN-səl) *n.* 1. Long strings of glistening threads made of bright metal. — The children trimmed the Christmas tree with *tinsel.*

2. A sparkling cloth with shiny metal threads woven into it.

tint (TINT) *n. tints.* A light or pale color.—Pink, light blue, and pale green are *tints.*—When the sun sets, the clouds have many reddish *tints.*
—*v. tints, tinted, tinting.* Color lightly; put light colors on.—Mary likes to *tint* her pictures with chalks.

ti•ny (TY-nee) *adj. tinier, tiniest.* Very small, as a *tiny* shell or a *tiny* flower.—Baby's hand looks *tiny* next to Mother's.

tip (TIP) *n. tips.* 1. An end.—The seal balanced the ball on the *tip* of his nose.
2. A small piece put on the end of something, as the cap on the end of a cane or umbrella.
3. Money given for service or for some favor done.—Father gave a *tip* to the boy who brought him the message.
—*v. tips, tipped, tipping.* 1. Put a tip on.—Uncle *tipped* his cane with a rubber cap.
2. Tilt; slant.—Baby *tipped* her glass of milk so far that it fell over.
3. Raise or lift (a hat).—Gentlemen *tip* their hats when they meet a lady.
4. Give money for service or for some favor done.—Father *tipped* the boy who brought the message.

tip•toe (TIP-toh) *n. tiptoes.* The end of the toe; the ends of the toes.—Mary walked on her *tiptoes* because the baby was asleep.
—*v. tiptoes, tiptoed, tiptoeing.* Walk on the toes, softly and with caution.—Mary *tiptoed* across the room.

tire (TYR) *n. tires.* 1. An outer rim of rubber that fits onto the rim of a wheel. — Father bought new tires for the car.
2. Any rim on which a wheel rolls. — The wheels of some wagons have iron bands for *tires.*
—*v. tires, tired, tiring.* Become tired or weary.—Do not work too fast or you will soon *tire.*

tis•sue (TISH-oo) *n. tissues* and *adj.* 1. A section of living matter with a particular structure and use, such as bone *tissue,* muscle *tissue,* and brain *tissue.* Your body is made of *tissues.*
2. Tissue paper.

tis•sue pa•per (TISH-oo pay-per) *tissue papers.* Very thin, soft paper.—The children wrapped their gifts in *tissue paper.*

ti•tle (TY-tl) *n. titles.* 1. The name of a book, story, song, picture, etc.—The title of the book is "Man and Power."
2. A special name used before a person's name to show his position or occupation, as "Dr." Smith, "Mrs." Jones, "King" George, "Lord" Byron, "Sir" Galahad.
3. Legal ownership, or papers showing such ownership.—Father paid for the car and has the *title* to it.
—*v. titles, titled, titling.* Name; give a title to.—The author *titled* his new book "Man and Power."

to (TOO *or* tuh *or* tə) *prep.* 1. Give it *to* me. It is mine.
2. I want *to* go. Children like *to* play.
3. Bob walked *to* the woods.
4. Our class won the game four *to* three.
5. Baby can count *to* five.
6. Send the letter *to* Grandmother.
7. The girls danced *to* lively music.
8. Mother rocked the baby *to* sleep.
9. He plays *to* win.
10. Bob tied the horse *to* the post.

toad (TOHD) *n. toads.* A froglike animal. It can live in the water, but usually lives on land. *Toads* eat worms, insects, and slugs.

toad•stool (TOHD-stool) *n. toadstools.* A mushroom, especially one that is poisonous.

toast (TOHST) *n. toasts.* A piece of bread dried and browned by heat.—We eat *toast* for breakfast.
—*v. toasts, toasted, toasting.* 1. Make brown by heating.—The children *toasted* the marshmallows over the campfire.

2. Make warm. – Grandmother sat by the stove and *toasted* her feet.
3. Drink in honor of something or someone. –Everyone *toasted* Bill. Everyone drank in his honor.

toast•er (TOHSS-ter) *n. toasters.* A device for toasting bread, for browning it by heat.

to•bac•co (tə-BAK-oh) *n. tobaccos* or *tobaccoes.* A plant with large leaves which are dried for smoking or chewing. Cigarettes and cigars are made from the leaves of the *tobacco* plant.

to•bog•gan (tə-BAHG-ən) *n. toboggans.* A flat sled that has no runners.–The children like to slide downhill on a *toboggan.*

–*v. toboggans, tobogganed, tobogganing.* – Slide on a toboggan.–We will *toboggan* down the long hill after school.

to•day (tə-DAY) *n. todays.* This day.–*Today* is Monday.–*Today* Mother does the laundry.
–*adv.* 1. On this day.–It is hot *today.*
2. Nowadays; at the present time.–Many women work in factories *today.* Years ago only men worked in factories.

toe (TOH) *n. toes.* 1. One of the parts at the end of the foot. We have five *toes* on each foot.
2. The end of the shoe, stocking, or boot that covers the toes.–Mary had a hole in the *toe* of her stocking.

to•ga (TOH-gə) *n. togas.* A loose outer garment worn by citizens of ancient Rome.

to•geth•er (tə-GETH-er) *adv.* 1. With one another; in a group.–The children play well *together.*–We sat *together* on the bus.
2. In one group or pile.–We put our money *together.*
3. Into one unit or one large piece made of smaller pieces.–The men put the parts *together* to make the automobile.

toil (TOIL) *n. toils.* Any hard work.–Grandfather doesn't mind the *toil* of plowing the land. He is a farmer and is used to hard work.
–*v. toils, toiled, toiling.* Work very hard.–The farmer is *toiling* in the fields.

toi•let (TOI-lit) *n. toilets.* 1. A bathroom or water closet.
2. A bathroom fixture for disposing of bodily waste matter.
–*Make one's toilet* means to bathe, dress, comb one's hair, etc.

to•ken (TOH-kən) *n. tokens.* 1. A sign.–A white flag is a *token* of surrender.
2. A keepsake; a souvenir. – When Ruth moved away, she gave Ann a ring as a *token.*
3. A piece of metal, shaped like a coin, bought and used instead of a ticket.–You can buy streetcar *tokens* in some cities.

told (TOHLD) *v.* One form of the verb *tell.*–Mother *told* us a story yesterday.

tol•er•ance (TAHL-er-ənss) *n.; tolerant, adj.* The act or practice of being fair towards those whose beliefs, religion, and customs are different from one's own.

tol•er•ate (TAHL-ə-rayt) *v. tolerates, tolerated, tolerating.* 1. Permit or allow. – The police will not *tolerate* violation of the law.
2. Endure; put up with.–It is difficult to *tolerate* people with bad manners.

toll (TOHL) *n. tolls.* 1. Ringing.–Each *toll* of the bell told us that an hour had passed.
2. Money paid for the right to use something. –Father had to pay a *toll* to cross the bridge.
–*v. tolls, tolled, tolling.* Ring or sound, slowly and evenly.–The church bells *tolled* at the end of the wedding ceremony.–The clock is *tolling* the hour.

tom•a•hawk (TAHM-ə-hawk) *n. tomahawks.* A hatchet or a lightweight ax that was used by some Indians in North America. –The Indian hurled his *tomahawk* at his enemy.

to•ma•to (tə-MAY-toh) *n. tomatoes.* A red or yellow fruit that grows on a low plant or vine. *Tomatoes* have many seeds in them. The juice of *tomatoes* is good to drink.

tomb (TOOM) *n. tombs.* A grave; a place where the bodies of the dead are kept. – *Tombs* are often built of marble or other hard stone.

to•mor•row (tə-MAHR-oh *or* tə-MOR-oh) *n. tomorrows.* The day following today.–Today is Monday. *Tomorrow* will be Tuesday.
–*adv.* On or for the day following today.–Grandmother will arrive *tomorrow.*

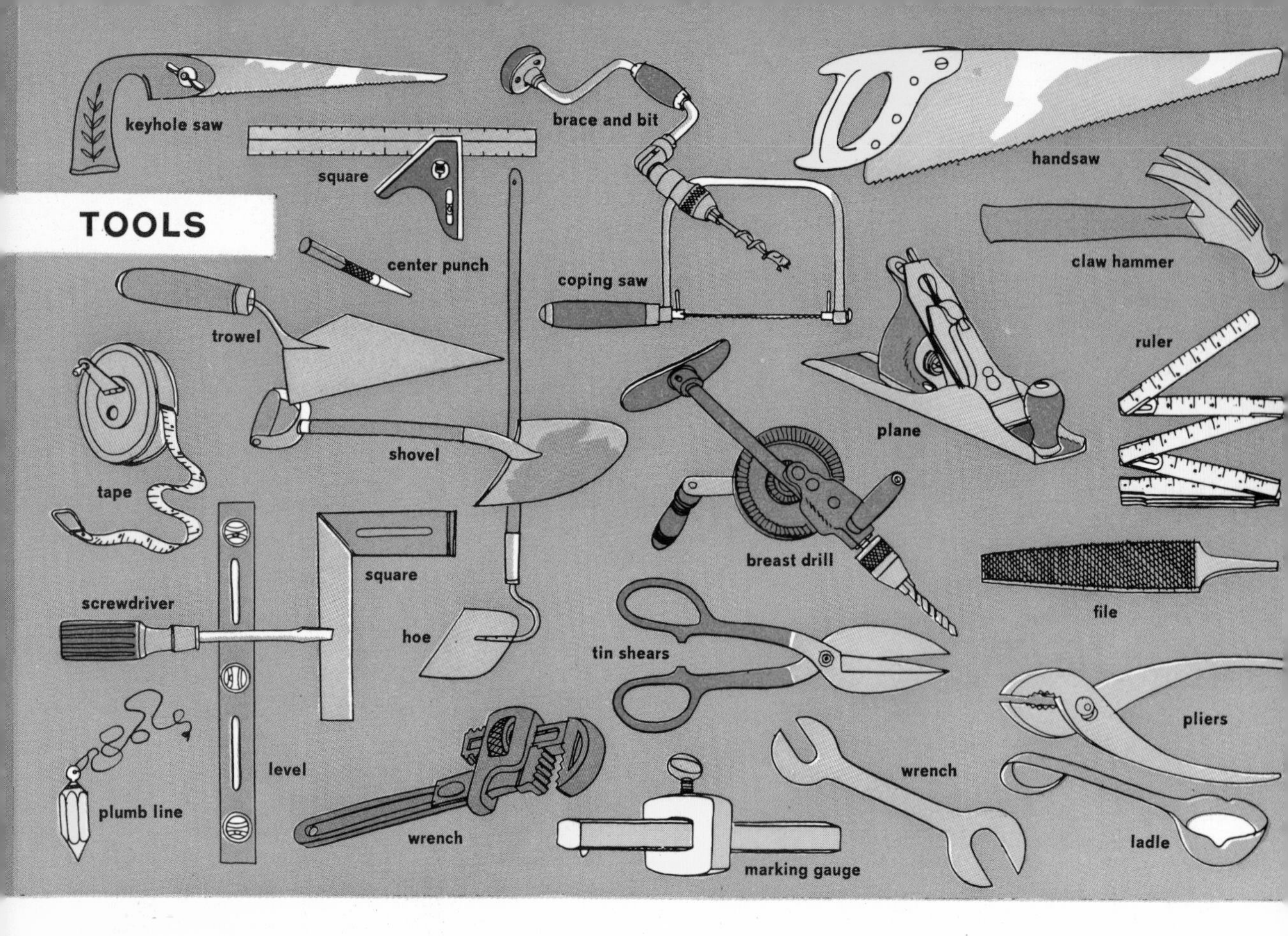

tom-tom (TAHM-tahm) *n. tom-toms.* A kind of drum originally used by primitive peoples. It is beaten with the hands or with sticks.

ton (TUN) *n. tons.* A unit of measure of weight. We measure hay, steel, coal, etc., by the *ton.* In the United States and Canada 2,000 pounds make 1 *ton.* In some other countries 2,240 pounds make 1 *ton.*

tone (TOHN) *n. tones.* 1. A sound; a note.–The shrill *tone* of the whistle frightened us.–The sweet *tones* of the organ echoed in the empty church.
2. Manner of speaking; quality of voice; accent.–Mother's soft *tones* soothe Baby.–Jack spoke in an angry *tone.*
3. A shade.–The picture has many *tones* of blue in it.

tongs (TAWNGZ *or* TAHNGZ) *n. pl.* Scissorslike tools used for lifting and holding, as ice *tongs,* sugar *tongs,* wood *tongs.*–Mother used sugar *tongs* to pick up the sugar cubes and drop them into her cup.

tongue (TUNG) *n. tongues.* 1. The flexible and movable organ in the mouth with which one tastes. We also use our *tongues* in speaking.
2. A language.–The Frenchman spoke in his native *tongue.* He spoke French.
3. A thing shaped or used like a tongue.–The *tongue* of a shoe is the leather piece under the laces of the shoe. – The *tongue* of a wagon is the long pole at the front.

ton•ic (TAHN-ik) *n. tonics.* A medicine or treatment to make one strong and give one an appetite.–The doctor gave Grandmother a *tonic.*–Sunshine and fresh air are *tonics.*

to•night (tə-NYT) *adv.* 1. The night following this day.–We are going to a show *tonight.*
2. This night; the night we are in.–The children seem happy *tonight.*

ton•sil (TAHN-səl) *n. tonsils.* One of two small organs on the sides of the throat at the back of the mouth.

too (TOO) *adv.* 1. Also.–We have a dog, and a kitten, *too.*–I should like to go *too.*
2. More than enough; more than is good.–Tommy ate *too* much candy.
3. Very.–The boy was only *too* glad to come to the party.

took (TUHK) *v.* One form of the verb *take.*–I *took* my doll to school with me yesterday.

tool (TOOL) *n. tools.* Anything used for some kind of work, such as a hammer, a saw, a broom, a ruler.–A carpenter's *tools* are used for building.–Brushes, palettes, and paints are an artist's *tools.*

tooth (TOOTH) *n. teeth.* 1. One of the sharp, white, bony, pointed parts in the mouth with which we chew.–Baby opened her mouth to show her new *tooth.* She now has six *teeth.*
2. One of the points on a rake or a comb.

tooth•ache (TOOTH-ayk) *n. toothaches.* A pain in a tooth.–When food gets into a cavity or hole in a tooth, one may get a *toothache.*

tooth•brush (TOOTH-brush) *n. toothbrushes.* A brush for cleaning the teeth. – Bob uses his *toothbrush* twice a day.

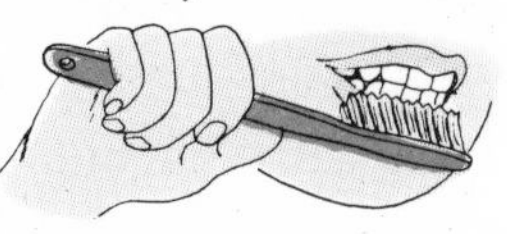

tooth•pick (TOOTH-pik) *n. toothpicks.* A small, pointed piece of wood used for removing food from between the teeth.–It is not polite to use a *toothpick* at the table.

top (TAHP) *n. tops.* 1. Highest point or part.–We walked up to the *top* of the hill.–The weather vane on *top* of Grandfather's barn pointed east.
2. The upper edge or side.–The snow came up to the *tops* of our shoes.–Mother wiped off the table *top.*
3. The head.–Bob is usually at the *top* of his class.

4. A leafy part that grows above the ground on vegetables such as carrots and beets. – Beet *tops* are good to eat.
5. A round toy made with a pointed tip on which it can be spun. –Tommy likes to spin his *top.*
–*v. tops, topped, topping.* Cover. – Mother *topped* the birthday cake with marshmallow frosting.

top•ic (TAHP-ik) *n. topics.* A subject one is talking about, thinking about, or writing about.–The *topic* we were discussing was the ball game. Mary doesn't like baseball and she tried to change the *topic* of conversation.

top•ple (TAHP-əl) *v. topples, toppled, toppling.* Fall forward; tumble.–The tower of blocks *toppled* over because it was too heavy at the top.

top•sy-tur•vy (TAHP-see-TER-vee) *adj.* and *adv.* Upset; upside down.–The playroom was *topsy-turvy* after the party. Nothing was in order.

torch (TORCH) *n. torches.* 1. A light made of something that burns easily and can be carried in the hand, like a stick of wood. – The man carried a *torch.*
2. A flashlight.

tore (TOR) *v.* One form of the verb *tear.*–Yesterday Mother *tore* up two old sheets for dust cloths.

tor•ment (TOR-ment) *n. torments.* Suffering; torture.–The boy's feeling of guilt filled him with *torment.*
–(tor-MENT) *v. torments, tormented, tormenting.* 1. Tease; annoy.–The dog *torments* the cat. He chases her, steals her food, and barks at her.
2. Give pain to.–The sore throat *tormented* the boy all night.

torn (TORN) *v.* One form of the verb *tear.*–The high wind had *torn* the leaves from the trees.

tor•na•do (tor-NAY-doh) *n. tornadoes.* A strong, whirling windstorm that often destroys trees and buildings.

tor•pe•do (tor-PEE-doh) *n. torpedoes.* 1. A large metal shell filled with material that explodes when it hits something. It has a propeller and machinery to drive it forward under water. *Torpedoes* are used to blow up ships.
2. A small firework that makes a loud noise when hit against something hard. – On the Fourth of July we had fun with *torpedoes.*
–*v. torpedoes, torpedoed, torpedoing.* Destroy or blow up with torpedoes. – The airplane *torpedoed* the enemy cruiser.

tor•rent (TOR- *or* TAHR-ənt) *n. torrents.* A rushing stream of water. – The boat was caught in the *torrent* and carried down the river.–It was raining in *torrents.*

tor•rid (TOR- *or* TAHR-id) *adj.* Very hot. – The jungles of Africa are in the *Torrid* Zone.

tor•til•la (tor-TEE-yah) *n. tortillas.* A thin, flat cake of corn meal. *Tortillas* are baked on a hot iron plate or stone.

tor•toise (TOR-təss) *n. tortoises.* A turtle, especially one that lives on land or in fresh water.

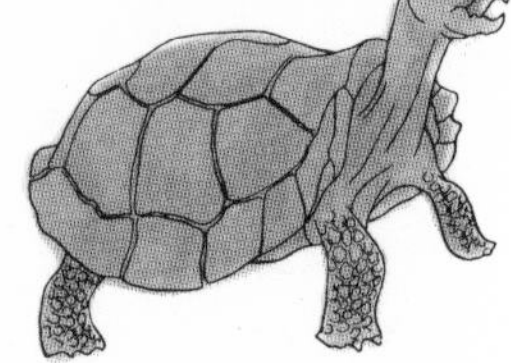

tor•ture (TOR-cher) *n. tortures.* 1. Great pain. – The victims of the fire suffered much *torture* from their severe burns.
2. The inflicting of great pain.–Flogging is a form of *torture.*
–*v. tortures, tortured, torturing.* Cause (a person or animal) to suffer greatly.–The enemy *tortured* the thirsty prisoners by not giving them water.

toss (TAWSS) *v. tosses, tossed, tossing.* 1. Throw lightly with an upward movement.–Jack *tossed* the ball to Bob.
2. Cause to move up and down, and to and fro.–The wind *tossed* the kites in the sky.
3. Roll back and forth.–The heat made Baby *toss* in her crib.
4. Throw back proudly. – Mary *tossed* her head as she went past Jack.

tot (TAHT) *n. tots.* A wee, tiny child.–Baby is still just a *tot.*

to•tal (TOHT-l) *n. totals.* Entire amount. – Jim's savings reached a *total* of twenty dollars.–If you add 4 + 5 + 2, the *total* is 11.
–*v. totals, totaled, totaling.* 1. Add. – *Total* 4 + 5 + 2, and you get 11.
2. Amount to; add up to.–Our expenses for our vacation *totaled* seventy-five dollars apiece.
–*adj.* 1. Whole; complete.–Father said Bob could buy the ball if two dollars was the *total* cost.
2. Complete; absolute. – There was *total* silence when our teacher came into the room. No one said a word.

to•tem pole (TOH-təm pohl) *totem poles.* A pole erected by primitive people, with animals or other figures carved or painted on it. The token or symbol of the family or tribe was always included.

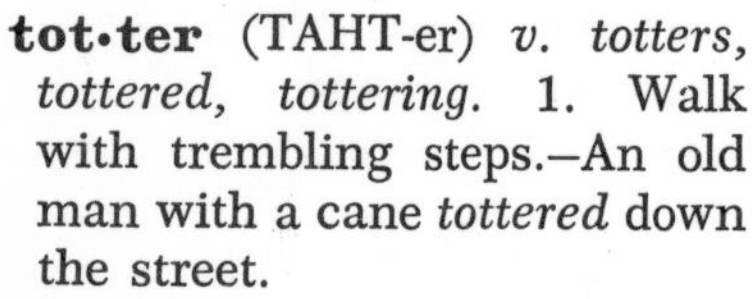

tot•ter (TAHT-er) *v. totters, tottered, tottering.* 1. Walk with trembling steps.–An old man with a cane *tottered* down the street.
2. Shake as if about to fall.–A sick person often *totters* when he tries to walk.

tou•can (TOO-kan *or* -kahn) *n. toucans.* A brilliantly colored bird of tropical America. The *toucan* has a huge colorful beak. The beak is light and thin in spite of its size. The *toucan* is a fruit-eating bird.

touch (TUCH) *n. touches.* 1. One of the senses of the body.–*Touch* makes us able to learn about things by feeling them.
2. A slight or mild trace.–Bob put a *touch* of salt on his egg.
3. A stroke of a brush or pencil.–The painter gave the picture a few *touches* and it was done.
–*v. touches, touched, touching.* 1. Feel something by placing the fingers or any other part of the body against it.–The blind man *touched* the raised letters of the sign.
2. Be or come together or in contact with.–Put the books on the table so that they *touch* each other.
3. Reach. – Mother's housecoat *touches* the floor.
4. Strike lightly.–Bob just *touched* the ball. He hit it lightly.
5. Lay hands on.–Do not *touch* the kitten.
6. Cause a feeling of kindness, sadness, or pity.–My parents were greatly *touched* by the stranger's story of his troubles.
–*Touch up* means to make small improvements in.–The picture needs *touching up.*
–*In touch* means in communication.–Father keeps *in touch* with us by letters and telephone when he is away.

touch•down (TUCH-down) *n. touchdowns.* Score made in football by taking the ball across the goal line of the opposite team.

tough (TUF) *adj. tougher, toughest.* 1. Not easily chewed or cut.–Some meat is tender; some is *tough.*
2. Able to stand much use or strain without breaking.–The ropes used to tie a ship to the dock must be *tough.*
3. Not pleasant; difficult.–This has been a *tough* winter for the poor family whose home burned down.
4. Sturdy and lasting. – Some plants are *tough;* others die with the first frost.
5. Stubborn and hard to manage.–The prisoner got *tough* when taken from his cell. It took two guards to handle him.
6. Rough and lawless.–The family moved from a *tough* part of the town to a better part.

tour (TUHR) *n. tours.* A journey for pleasure. –Frank is going to take a *tour* of Europe.
–*v. tours, toured, touring.* Travel about for pleasure.–We *toured* the United States during our vacation.

tour•ist (TUHR-ist) *n. tourists.* One who travels for pleasure.–Many *tourists* stop to see the Grand Canyon.

tour•na•ment (TUHR- *or* TER-nə-mənt) *n. tournaments.* 1. A contest or series of contests in which many players take part. – Stephen became the tennis champion by winning the tennis *tournament.*
2. A contest of skill and daring between knights on horseback. – The queen gave a prize to Sir Harold, the champion of the *tournament.*

tour•ni•quet (TUHR- *or* TER-nə-ket) *n. tourniquets.* Something that stops the flow of blood from a cut by pinching the bleeding blood vessel closed. A *tourniquet* can be made by twisting a handkerchief.

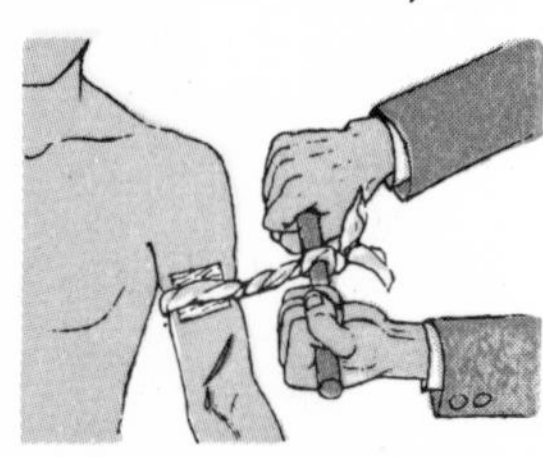

tow (TOH) *n. tows.* 1. Something being drawn along by a connecting rope, chain, or cable. –The bus being pulled is the *tow.*

2. A rope or chain used to pull something.
–*v. tows, towed, towing.* Pull or draw along by a connecting rope, chain, or cable.–The bus had a broken axle and had to be *towed* by a repair truck.
–*In tow* usually means being pulled.–While the bus was *in tow,* the tow rope broke.

to•ward or **to•wards** (TORD *or* TORDZ) *prep.* 1. In the direction of.–The dog ran *toward* the garage.
2. Near; close to.–It is getting *toward* the time to quit work.
3. For the purpose of; to help buy.–Mary gave some money *toward* the sick boy's flowers.–Bob has saved five dollars *toward* a new bicycle.
4. To.–The boy's behavior *toward* his classmates was not polite.

tow•el (TOW-əl) *n. towels.* A piece of cloth or paper used for wiping or drying.

tow•er (TOW-er) *n. towers.* A tall, slender part of a building, or a tall, slim building that stands alone. – The church bell is in the *tower.*
–*v. towers, towered, towering.* Be much taller or higher. – The tall boy *towers* above the rest of the class.– The chimney *towers* above the rest of the building.

town (TOWN) *n. towns.* 1. A place where many people live near each other, smaller than a city but larger than a village.
2. The people living in a town.–The whole *town* went to see the circus.

tox•ic (TAHK-sik) *adj.; toxin, n.* Having to do with poison; poisonous.–Many weed- and insect-killing agents are *toxic.* They will poison anyone who drinks them.

toy (TOI) *n. toys.* A thing for children to play with. – There were many *toys* under the Christmas tree.
–*v. toys, toyed, toying.* Play (with); amuse oneself (with).–Baby *toys* with her toes.

trace (TRAYSS) *n. traces.* 1. A sign; a mark; an indication.–He saw *traces* of deer in the woods.
2. A small bit.–The dog licked the plate so clean that not a *trace* of food was left.
–*v. traces, traced, tracing.* 1. Draw an outline of; sketch.–The man *traced* a plan of the playground.
2. Copy by drawing over the lines of.–Mary *traced* the picture by placing tissue paper over it and marking the lines of the picture on the tissue.
3. Follow.–The hunter *traced* the rabbit by its tracks in the snow.

tra•che•a (TRAY-kee-ə *or* trə-KEE-ə) *n. tracheae.* The windpipe. Air passes to and from the lungs through the *trachea.*

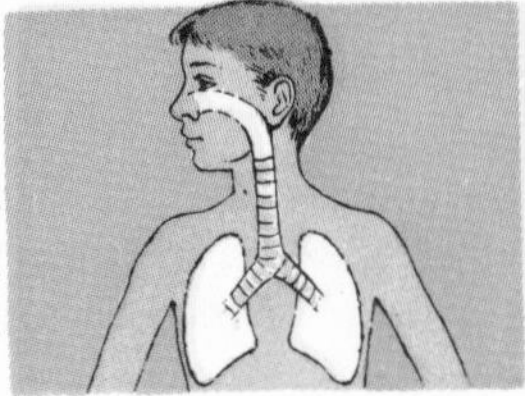

track (TRAK) *n. tracks.* 1. A mark left by the passing of something, as bicycle *tracks,* wagon *tracks,* rabbit *tracks.*–Judy left a *track* in the snow as she walked across the field to Grandmother's house.
2. A road or path.–The hunters followed the narrow *track* to their cabin.
3. A roadway or path, usually circular, built for racing. – The racers roared around the *track.*

4. A line of steel rails.–Trains run on *tracks.*
–*v. tracks, tracked, tracking.* Trace; follow from clues.–The dog *tracked* the rabbit to the old log.–The policeman *tracked* the robber to his hideout.

tract (TRAKT) *n. tracts.* 1. A region; an area. –The farmer is plowing a large *tract* of land.
2. An area of the body containing related organs or parts.–The nose, windpipe, and lungs are parts of the respiratory, or breathing, *tract.*
3. A pamphlet or little book.–*Tracts* usually are written about religious topics.

trac•tor (TRAK-ter) *n. tractors.* A heavy machine with a motor, used for pulling a plow or some other machine.–Many farmers use *tractors* instead of horses.

trade (TRAYD) *n. trades.* 1. The work one does to make a living.–Father's *trade* is toolmaking.
2. An exchange.–Bob exchanged his knife for Tom's kite. Bob thought it was a good *trade.*
–*v. trades, traded, trading.* 1. Do business.–We *trade* at the corner store.
2. Exchange.–Mary *traded* geography books with Ruth.

trade•mark (TRAYD-mahrk) *n. trademarks.* A name, mark, or picture put on goods by a manufacturer so that one can tell his goods from those made by someone else.

trad•er (TRAY-der) *n. traders.* A person who buys, sells, or exchanges goods.–That man is a horse *trader.* He buys and sells horses.

trade wind (TRAYD wind) *trade winds.* A steady wind blowing over the oceans toward the equator. North of the equator the *trade winds* blow from the Northeast to the Southwest. South of the equator they blow from the Southeast to the Northwest.

tra•di•tion (trə-DISH-ən) *n. traditions; traditional, adj.; traditionally, adv.* 1. Something that has been done for a long time, over and over again, without any written reason. –The Easter Parade on Fifth Avenue is a *tradition* in New York City.
2. A practice, custom, or belief handed down from the past.–John went to the same college from which his father and grandfather had graduated. It was a family *tradition* for all the boys to do so.

traf•fic (TRAF-ik) *n.* Movement of people or of cars, trucks, or other vehicles.–*Traffic* is very heavy on Sundays. Many cars are on the roads.
–*adj.* Having to do with the movement of people or vehicles.–There are many *traffic* accidents on holidays.

trag•e•dy (TRAJ-ə-dee) *n. tragedies.* 1. A play that has a sad ending.
2. A sad happening.–The death of the fireman in the burning house was a *tragedy.*

trail (TRAYL) *n. trails.* A path worn through the woods.–An old Indian *trail* led to the brook.

–*v. trails, trailed, trailing.* 1. Drag something along behind.–The runaway horse ran home *trailing* the broken rope.
2. Follow.–The dog *trailed* Jack across the field and into the woods.
3. Track; trace; follow the tracks of. – We *trailed* the rabbit to the hollow log.
4. Fall behind, come after, or follow the others.–Our favorite horse *trailed* in the race.

trail•er (TRAY-ler) *n. trailers.* 1. A vehicle used for living quarters that is drawn by an automobile.–We lived in a *trailer* during our vacation.

2. Any wheeled vehicle, such as the body of a truck, designed to be pulled by another vehicle with a motor.
3. A plant that crawls along the ground. – Arbutus, a spring flower, is a *trailer.*

train (TRAYN) *n. trains.* 1. A string of railway cars that are joined together and pulled by an engine or locomotive.

2. A part of a skirt that drags on the floor behind the wearer.–The bride's dress had a long *train.*
–*v. trains, trained, training.* 1. Bring up; teach.–The children's good manners showed that they were well *trained* at home.
2. Practice; prepare. – Our runners *trained* for the track meet. They made themselves fit and ready by exercising, by eating properly, and by getting enough rest.
3. Coax or fix in a certain way, till it becomes natural.–Grandmother *trained* the morning-glories over the fence.
4. Aim; point.–The sailors *trained* the ship's guns on the pirate vessel.

train•ing (TRAYN-ing) *n.* Study and practice.–It takes *training* to learn to be a carpenter or a mechanic.–The prize fighter went to bed at nine o'clock while he was in *training.*

trait (TRAYT) *n. traits.* A special feature, quality, or characteristic. – John's honesty, quick wit, and good manners are his outstanding *traits.*

trai•tor (TRAY-ter) *n. traitors.* A person who is not true to his country; one who helps the enemies of his country.

tramp (TRAMP) *n. tramps.* 1. A homeless man who goes from place to place.–A *tramp* came to the farm for food and water.
2. A steamship that goes from one port to another, picking up what freight it can.
3. A walk; a hike.–Bob and Father went for a long *tramp.*
–*v. tramps, tramped, tramping.* 1. Walk; march.–The children *tramped* through the halls.–Policemen *tramp* miles each day.
2. Walk (on) heavily. – The cows *tramped* on the new plants in the garden.

tram•ple (TRAM-pəl) *v. tramples, trampled, trampling.* Step on and crush.–The cows got into the cornfield and *trampled* the corn.

tran•quil (TRANG-kwəl) *adj.; tranquility, n.* Free from disturbance; quiet; peaceful; calm.–Nuns and monks lead *tranquil* lives.–The water on the lake is *tranquil.* There is not a ripple on it.

trans•act (tranz-AKT) *v. transacts, transacted, transacting.* Carry on; attend to; conduct; manage.–The company has been *transacting* business since 1905.–Although he is not feeling well, he can still *transact* his affairs.

trans•at•lan•tic (tranz-ət-LAN-tik) *adj.* Crossing the Atlantic Ocean.–The huge ship is a *transatlantic* liner. It is a ship that travels across the Atlantic Ocean.

trans•con•ti•nen•tal (transs-kahn-tə-NEN-tl) *adj.* Crossing or extending across a continent.–The radio broadcast was heard over a *transcontinental* network. It could be heard from New York to California.

trans•fer (TRANSS-fer) *n. transfers.* A ticket used to ride on another bus or car without paying the whole fare again.–The conductor gave us a *transfer* to another bus.
–(transs-FER) *v. transfers, transferred, transferring.* 1. Move; put in a different place.–Mr. Jones was *transferred* to a different department.
2. Change from one car or bus to another.–We *transfer* at the corner of Main Street and First Avenue.
3. Copy; trace; reproduce. – Mary used tracing paper to *transfer* the picture in the book to her notebook.

trans•form (transs-FORM) *v. transforms, transformed, transforming.* Change from one thing to another.–Cream is *transformed* into butter by churning. – The fairy godmother *transformed* the pumpkin into a splendid coach.

trans•fu•sion (transs-FYOO-zhən) *n. transfusions.* The transfer of blood from one person to another person.

tran•sis•tor (tran-ZISS-ter) *n. transistors.* A tiny device which takes the place of a vacuum tube. *Transistors* are used in scientific and electrical instruments and in pocket-size radios.

trans•late (transs-LAYT) *v. translates, translated, translating.* Change into a different language.–Father *translated* the French letter into English.
–*translation, n. translations.*

trans•lu•cent (transs-LOO-sənt) *adj.* Allowing light to pass through, but not letting objects be seen clearly. Frosted-glass windows and some stained-glass windows are *translucent.*

trans•mit (transs-MIT) *v. transmits, transmitted, transmitting.* 1. Send along; pass on; transfer; forward.–Please *transmit* the information as soon as you receive it.
2. Send out signals by such means as radio, television, and telegraph.–The radio station *transmits* only to a local area.

trans•mit•ter (transs-MIT-er) *n. transmitters.* An instrument by which messages are sent by telephone, telegraph, radio.

tran•som (TRAN-səm) *n. transoms.* A narrow window over a door.–The teacher opened the *transom* to let in some fresh air.

trans•par•ent (transs-PAIR-ənt) *adj.* Able to be seen through.–Most window glass is *transparent.*

trans•plant (transs-PLANT) *v. transplants, transplanted, transplanting.* Move; plant again somewhere else.–We planted tomato seeds in a box in the house. When the plants were large enough, we *transplanted* them into the garden.

trans•port (TRANSS-port) *n. transports.* 1. A ship, a train, a bus, or a truck that carries soldiers and sailors from one place to another.
2. An airplane that carries people and things from one place to another.
–(transs-PORT) *v. transports, transported, transporting.* Carry or take from place to place.

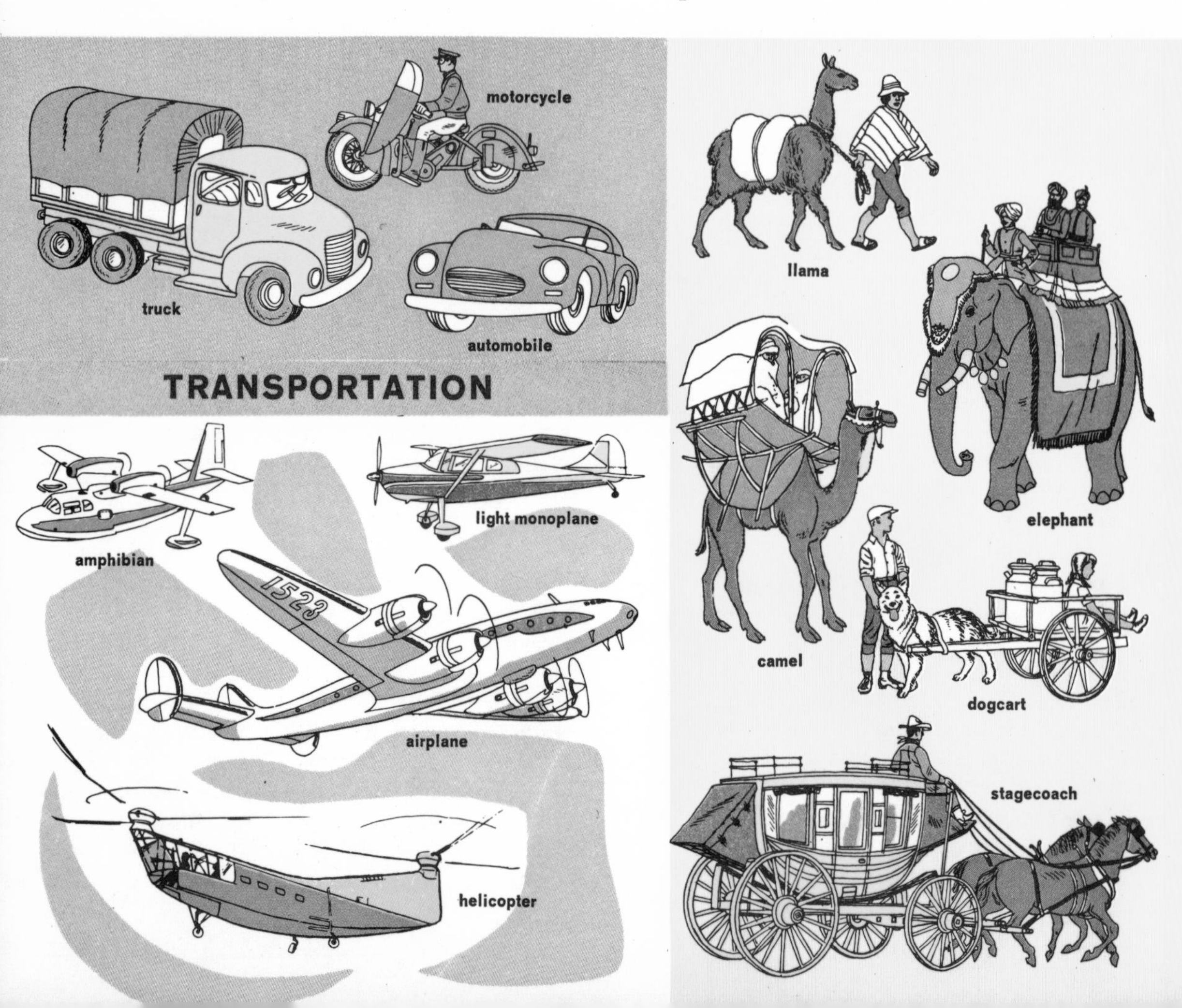

trans•por•ta•tion (transs-per-TAY-shən) *n.* The carrying of goods or passengers from one place to another.–*Transportation* is important to business.

trap (TRAP) *n. traps.* 1. A device to catch animals.–Father caught a rat in a *trap.*

2. A U-shaped pipe in a drainpipe that allows water to pass out but keeps sewer gas from coming back through it.–The plumber repaired the *trap* in the drainpipe.
–*v. traps, trapped, trapping.* Catch in a trap.–The hunter *trapped* the fox.

trap door (TRAP dor) *trap doors.* A door in a floor or ceiling or on a roof. – The man found a *trap door* in the floor.

tra•peze (tra-PEEZ) *n. trapezes.* A swing high above the ground.–The acrobats performed on a *trapeze.*

trap•per (TRAP-er) *n. trappers.* A person who traps wild animals to sell their furs.

trash (TRASH) *n.; trashy, adj.* Rubbish; broken and used-up things.–The barrel in the alley is filled with *trash.*

trav•el (TRAV-əl) *v. travels, traveled* or *travelled, traveling* or *travelling.* Go from place to place. – Mary wants to *travel* around the world when she grows up.

trav•el•er (TRAV-əl-er) *n. travelers.* A person who is going from one place to another.

tray (TRAY) *n. trays.* A large, flat piece of metal, wood, or other material, often with a shallow rim around the edge. Food, dishes, glasses, and so on, are often carried on a *tray.*–Mary served Mother her breakfast in bed on a *tray.*

treach•er•ous (TRECH-er-əss) *adj.; treacherously, adv.* 1. Not trustworthy; not reliable; deceiving; not loyal.
2. Having a false appearance of dependability or strength.–The floors of the old building are *treacherous.* The boards look solid but they are rotten in many places and will not hold a person safely.

tread (TRED) *n. treads.* 1. Walking; steps.–We heard the heavy *tread* of marching feet.
2. The part of a rubber tire that touches the ground.
3. The part of a stair step that one puts his foot on. If the *treads* are narrow, it makes the stairs steep.
–*v. treads, trod, treading.* 1. Step; walk; step on.–Do not *tread* on my toes.
2. Trample; beat down.–The hordes of buffaloes *trod* down the grass with their feet.

trea•son (TREE-zən) *n.* Being untrue to one's country; secretly helping the enemies of one's country. – The man was found guilty of *treason.* He had sold supplies to the enemy.

treas•ure (TREZH-er) *n. treasures.* Money, jewels, or any things of value that have been collected or saved up.–The boys were digging in the cave for *treasure.*
–*v. treasures, treasured, treasuring.* Value dearly.–Mother *treasures* the old picture of Grandmother and Grandfather.

treas•ur•er (TREZH-er-er) *n. treasurers.* A person chosen or elected to take care of money that is taken in and paid out.–As club *treasurer,* Mary collects the dues and records how much the club spends.

treas•ur•y (TREZH-ər-ee) *n. treasuries.* A place where money is received or paid out.–Long ago in England, when the funds in the king's *treasury* were low, the king would simply ask his nobles for more money.

treat (TREET) *n. treats.* An unusual pleasure.–It was a *treat* to get a chance to swim in the ocean.
–*v. treats, treated, treating.* 1. Act towards.–Bob *treats* his friends well.
2. Take care of; give medical attention to.–The doctor *treated* Father for a strained back.
3. Pay for a pleasure for someone.–Uncle Pete *treated* Betty to an ice-cream soda.

treat•ment (TREET-mənt) *n. treatments.* 1. A cure or remedy; care.–The doctor is giving Father heat *treatments.*
2. A way of acting towards, or dealing with. –Grandfather's *treatment* of his animals is always gentle and thoughtful.–Jack felt he had received unfair *treatment* from his teacher.

trea•ty (TREE-tee) *n. treaties.* A written agreement among countries. – The nations that were at war have signed a peace *treaty.*

tree (TREE) *n. trees.* A very large, woody, leafy plant with a stem called a trunk. Some *trees* have fruit or nuts on them. Wood for building houses and furniture comes from the trunks and branches of *trees.*

trem•ble (TREM-bəl) *n. trembles.* Shaking. –We could feel the *tremble* of the house after the explosion.
–*v. trembles, trembled, trembling.* 1. To shake slightly from a strong feeling such as fright, cold, or nervousness. – Jack *trembled* with eagerness as he unwrapped his present.
2. Shake slightly.–The wind made the leaves *tremble.*

tre•men•dous (tri-MEN-dəss) *adj.; tremendously, adv.* Very great.–The fire caused a *tremendous* loss for the owners of the house.

trench (TRENCH) *n. trenches.* 1. A ditch.–The farmer dug a *trench* at the side of the barn to drain the water off.
2. A ditch with a bank of dirt in front for protection.–The soldiers shot from *trenches.*

tres•pass (TRESS-pəss) *v. trespasses, trespassed, trespassing.* Go onto the property or land of someone else without their permission to do so.–Hunters sometimes *trespass* on the farmer's land.

tres•tle (TRESS-əl) *n. trestles.* A strong framework that holds something up. – The bridge was built on *trestles.*

tri•al (TRY-əl) *n. trials.* 1. A test. – Father took the new car out for a *trial;* he wanted to see how it would run.
2. A hearing before a judge in court.–The thief was given a *trial* and found guilty.

tri•an•gle (TRY-ang-gəl) *n. triangles.* 1. A flat figure or shape with three sides and three corners.
2. A musical instrument made of a steel rod shaped like a triangle and played with a small straight steel rod.

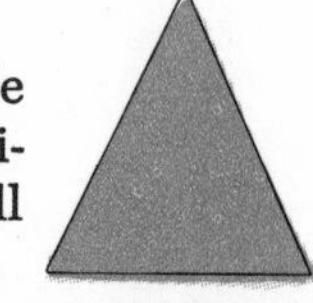

tribe (TRYB) *n. tribes.* A group of people, especially nomadic or primitive, who have the same beliefs or customs, and who live together under the same leaders.–American Indians once lived in *tribes.*

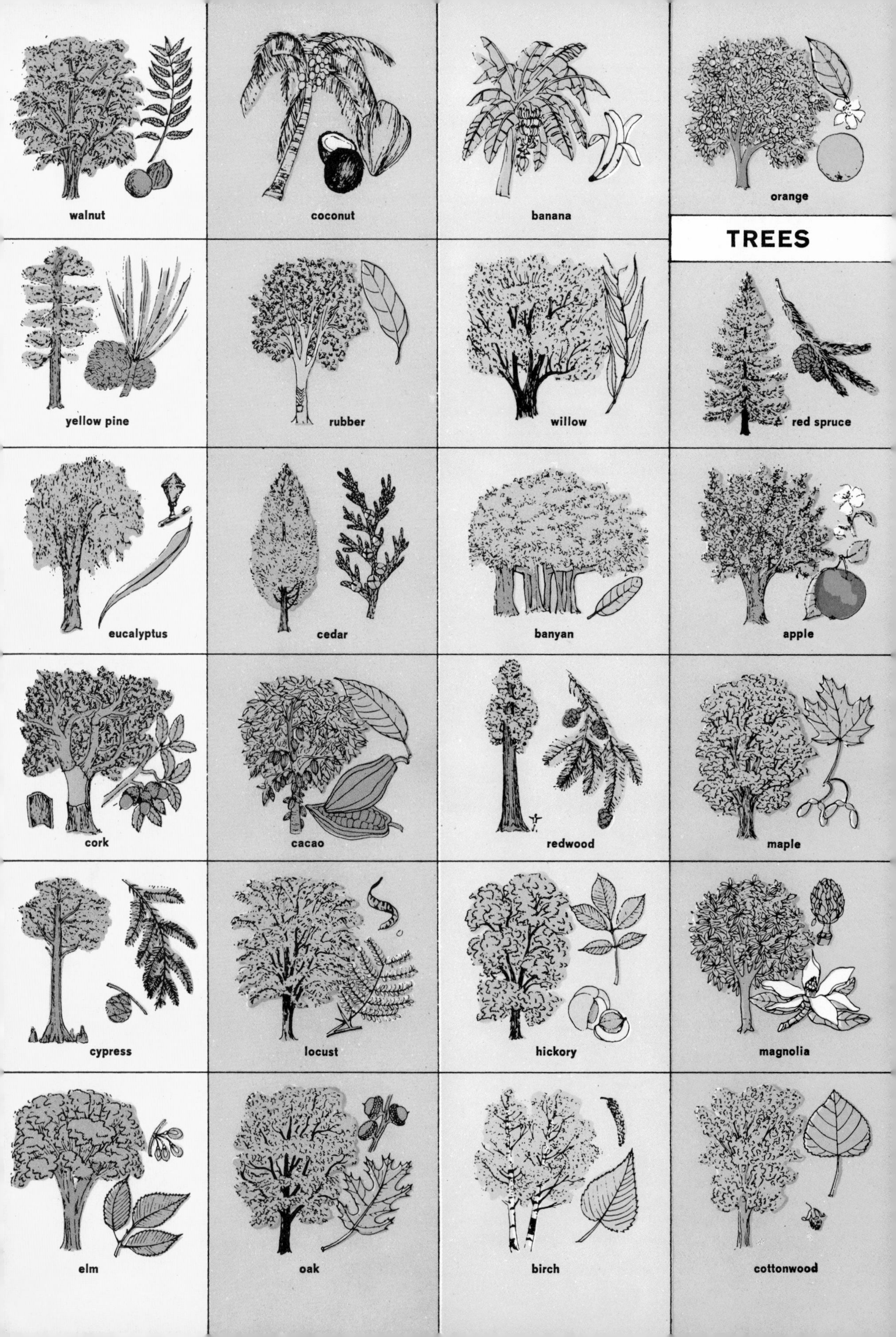
TREES
walnut
coconut
banana
orange
yellow pine
rubber
willow
red spruce
eucalyptus
cedar
banyan
apple
cork
cacao
redwood
maple
cypress
locust
hickory
magnolia
elm
oak
birch
cottonwood

trib•u•tar•y (TRIB-yə-tair-ee) *n. tributaries.* 1. A stream flowing into a body of water larger than itself.–The Ohio and Arkansas Rivers are *tributaries* of the Mississippi River.
2. A person, state, or nation that pays tribute.–The defeated nation became a *tributary* of its conqueror.

trib•ute (TRIB-yoot) *n. tributes.* Thanks; respect; praise. – On Memorial Day we pay *tribute* to the soldiers who gave their lives for their country.

trick (TRIK) *n. tricks; tricky, adj.* 1. A clever act or stunt which amuses people.–The magician's best *trick* was pulling rabbits out of a hat that seemed to be empty.
2. A joke; a prank.–Bill played a *trick* on Mother by filling the salt shaker with sugar.
–*v. tricks, tricked, tricking.* Cheat; deceive. – The man tried to *trick* Uncle Henry into buying an inferior watch.

trick•le (TRIK-əl) *n. trickles.* A thin stream. –A *trickle* of water leaked from the pipe.
–*v. trickles, trickled, trickling.* Run in a fine stream; fall in drops.–It was so hot that perspiration *trickled* down the man's forehead. –Water *trickled* from the leak in the pipe.

tri•cy•cle (TRY-sik-əl) *n. tricycles.* A small, three-wheeled vehicle that is run by pedals and steered by handle bars.

tried (TRYD) *v.* One form of the verb *try.* –I try each day to do a kind deed. Yesterday I *tried* hard.
–*adj.* Proved; sure.–Joe is Jack's *tried* and true friend.

tri•fle (TRYF-əl) *n. trifles.* 1. A little thing that is not important.–Don't fret over *trifles.*
2. A very small amount of money. – We bought this knife for a *trifle;* it cost only ten cents.

trig•ger (TRIG-er) *n. triggers.* The small, movable piece on the underside of a gun that is pulled back to fire the gun.

tril•li•um (TRIL-ee-əm) *n. trilliums.* A plant that has a large, white or pinkish flower with three petals and three green leaves. The flower which grows on the plant is also called a *trillium.*

trim (TRIM) *n.* Good condition.–Our baseball team is in *trim* for the game. All the players are in good shape.
–*v. trims, trimmed, trimming.* 1. Make neat and orderly by cutting some away. – Bob *trims* the rose bushes.–Mother *trims* her fingernails.
2. Decorate; add decoration to. – Mother *trimmed* the birthday cake with pink flowers.
–*adj.* Neat and orderly.–The room is *trim.* Everything is in place.

trin•ket (TRING-kit) *n. trinkets.* A small or cheap toy or piece of jewelry.–The children bought some *trinkets* at the fair.

tri•o (TREE-oh) *n. trios.* 1. A group of three persons or things.–A *trio* of girls sang the song.

2. Music written for three people to sing or play.–The *trio* was played by a violin, a cello, and a piano.

trip (TRIP) *n. trips.* A journey.–We are going for a *trip* in the automobile soon.
–*v. trips, tripped, tripping.* 1. Step lightly and quickly.–The children *tripped* along after the Pied Piper.
2. Catch one's foot; stumble.–Grandfather *tripped* on the edge of the rug and fell.
3. Cause to stumble.–The boy put his foot out and *tripped* the fleeing bandit.

tri•ple (TRIP-əl) *n. triples.* In baseball, a three-base hit.–The batter got a *triple.*
–*v. triples, tripled, tripling.* Make three times as great.–Jack *tripled* his income from his paper route. Last year he made five dollars a week; this year he makes fifteen dollars a week.
–*adj.* 1. Three times as great.–Jack's income this year is *triple* what it was last year.
2. Of three parts. – Some forks are *triple*-pronged. They have three prongs.

tri•plet (TRIP-lət) *n. triplets.* 1. A group of three things that are alike or related; a trio.
2. One of three children born at one birth to the same mother.

tri•pod (TRY-pahd) *n. tripods.* Anything having three feet or legs, like a stool, or a stand. –The photographer mounted his camera on a *tripod.* He set it on a three-legged stand.

tri•umph (TRY-əmf) *n. triumphs.* A victory; a success.–Our ball team celebrated its *triumph* by marching through the streets and singing.
–*v. triumphs, triumphed, triumphing.* Be victorious; win. – We have always *triumphed* over our opponents.

trod•den (TRAHD-n) *v.* One form of the verb *tread.*–The path had been *trodden* by the cows until it was packed hard.

troll (TROHL) *n. trolls.* An ugly fairy dwarf that lives in caves. – A *troll* waited on the bridge for the goat.

trol•ley (TRAHL-ee) *n. trolleys.* 1. An electric bus or streetcar.–We went to town on the *trolley.*
2. The wheel that runs along an electric wire and carries electricity to the streetcar.–The *trolley* came off the wire and the car stopped.

trom•bone (TRAHM-bohn *or* trahm-BOHN) *n. trombones.* A musical instrument made of a bent brass tube, with a section which slides in and out to make different tones.

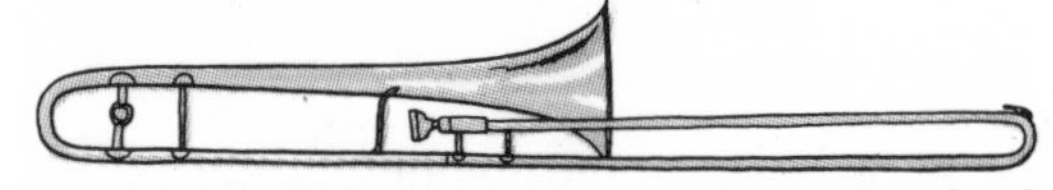

troop (TROOP) *n. troops.* 1. A group of soldiers, or other united group. – A Boy Scout *troop* is camping at the lake.
2. Soldiers. – The general said there were ten thousand *troops* in his army. There were ten thousand men.
–*v. troops, trooped, trooping.* March together. – The children following the Pied Piper *trooped* into the opening in the hillside.

tro•phy (TROH-fee) *n. trophies.* Something given as a sign of victory; something won.–The winner of the race won a silver cup as a *trophy.*

trop•ic (TRAHP-ik) *n. tropics.* 1. A line of latitude lying about 32½ degrees either north or south of the equator. The northern line is called the *Tropic* of Cancer. The southern line is called the *Tropic* of Capricorn. The area that lies between the *tropics* is called the Torrid Zone.
2. (In the plural and usually spelled with a capital "T.") The land that lies in the Torrid Zone.–The weather in the *Tropics* is usually very hot.

trop•o•sphere (TRAHP-əss-feer) *n.* The lowest layer of the atmosphere; the part in which we live. Temperature varies with altitude in the *troposphere;* the higher the altitude, the lower the temperature. Almost all clouds are formed in the *troposphere.*

trot (TRAHT) *n. trots.* A gait of a horse in which a front foot and the opposite hind foot move together.
–*v. trots, trotted, trotting.* 1. Move at a trot.–The cowboy's horse *trotted* slowly along.
2. Run slowly.–The dog *trots* along after its master.

trou•ble (TRUB-əl) *n. troubles.* 1. A worry; a concern; a disturbance.–The girl's mischievous pranks at school make *trouble* for her family.
2. A nuisance; additional work. – We will stay for lunch, if it isn't too much *trouble* for you.
3. A difficulty; something that causes worry, unhappiness, unpleasantness, and so on; misfortune. – That family has had many *troubles.*
–*v. troubles, troubled, troubling.* Worry. – Baby's sickness *troubles* Mother.

trou•ble•some (TRUB-əl-səm) *adj.* Causing trouble, difficulty, disturbance, and so on.

trough (TRAWF *or* TRAHF) *n. troughs.* 1. A narrow box or holder for animal food. – Horses, cattle, pigs, and other animals eat and drink from *troughs.*

2. A gutter or drain.–*Troughs* carry water from the roofs of buildings into drainpipes.

trou•sers (TROW-zerz) *n. pl.* The part of a man's or boy's clothing which covers the body from the waist down.

trous•seau (TROO-soh *or* troo-SOH) *n. trousseaux* or *trousseaus.* A set of clothes and other things, such as bed linen and table linen, that a bride has when she marries.–My sister is going to get married next month, so she is shopping for her *trousseau.*

trout (TROWT) *n. trouts.* 1. A kind of fish that is found in fresh water and used for food.

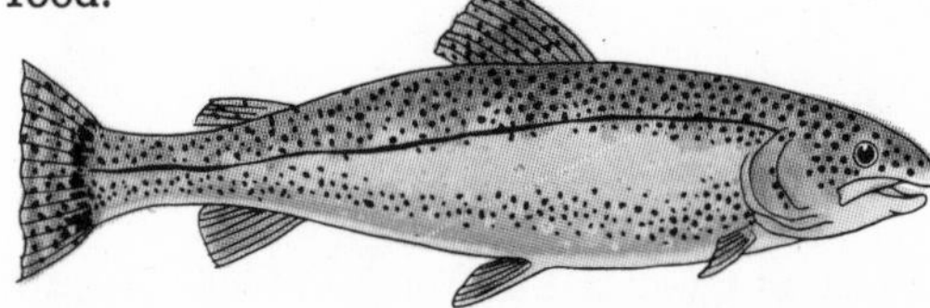

2. A salt-water fish that is something like the salmon.

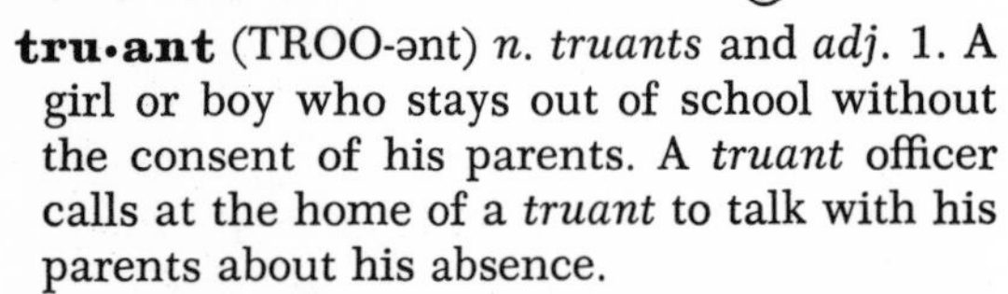

trow•el (TROW-əl) *n. trowels.* 1. A hand tool with a broad, flat blade used to smooth plaster and cement. –A bricklayer uses a *trowel* for putting mortar between bricks.
2. A small digging tool.–Mother uses a garden *trowel* for digging up plants.

tru•ant (TROO-ənt) *n. truants* and *adj.* 1. A girl or boy who stays out of school without the consent of his parents. A *truant* officer calls at the home of a *truant* to talk with his parents about his absence.
2. Absent without permission.–Bob was *truant* from school once when he went fishing.

truce (TROOSS) *n. truces.* A pause or short stop in fighting.–The two armies called for a *truce.* During the *truce* the leaders talked about peace.

truck (TRUK) *n. trucks.* 1. A big, powerful vehicle for carrying loads.
2. A group of wheels that holds up one end of a railroad car and let it turn easily.
3. A small platform on wheels that is pushed by hand.–Cases of food are moved about the grocery store on a hand *truck.*
4. Worthless rubbish.–Bob's room was littered with *truck.*
5. Vegetables.–Grandfather sells his garden *truck* to the market in town.
–*v. trucks, trucked, trucking.* Transport or carry on a truck.–The goods were *trucked* to us by the manufacturer.
–*adj.* Vegetable. – Grandfather has a *truck* garden.

true (TROO) *adj.* 1. Correct; real.–This is *true:* the sun shines here in the daytime. This is false: the sun shines here at night.–Mary likes imaginary stories, but Bob likes *true* stories.
2. Sincere; faithful.–Sally is a *true* friend to Mary and Jane.
3. Rightful; actual; real.–The teacher asked us who the *true* owner of the ball was.

tru•ly (TROO-lee) *adv.* 1. Sincerely; faithfully.–The letter ended, "Very *truly* yours."
2. Really.–I am *truly* coming to see you.

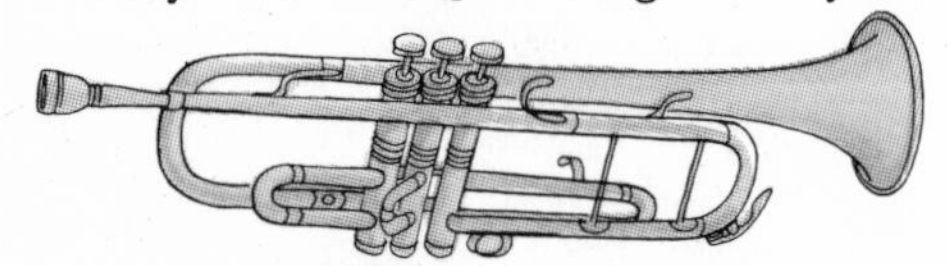

trum•pet (TRUM-pət) *n. trumpets.* A musical instrument sounded by blowing. – The *trumpet* is a wind instrument.

trunk (TRUNGK) *n. trunks.* 1. The main stem of a tree.–The owl lived in the hollow *trunk* of an old oak.
2. The body of a person or animal, not including the legs, arms, or head.
3. The snout of an elephant.–The elephant can pour water over his head with his *trunk.*

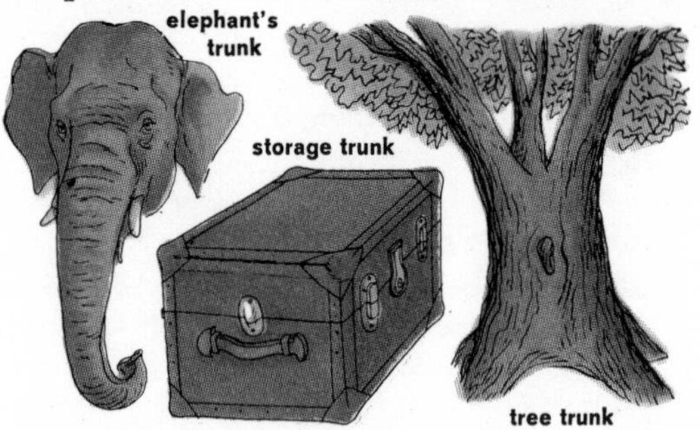

4. A large covered chest for storing or moving clothing or other belongings. – When traveling, we send our clothes in a *trunk.*

trunks (TRUNGKS) *n. pl.* Short, tight pants. –Men wear *trunks* when they swim.

trust (TRUST) *n. trusts.* 1. A duty; something one promises to do.–Bob lived up to his *trust* to take care of the garden.
2. Faith.–The children have complete *trust* in what their teacher tells them.
–*v. trusts, trusted, trusting.* 1. Have faith in; believe in; depend upon. – Children *trust* their parents.–The teacher knew she could *trust* Jack to bring back the book.–We did not have enough money with us to pay for the groceries, but the storekeeper *trusted* us.
2. Hope; expect.–I *trust* you will be coming home soon.

trust•wor•thy (TRUST-wer-thee) *adj.; trustworthily, adv.; trustworthiness, n.* Dependable; true to one's word or duty.–The teacher found the boy to be *trustworthy.*

trust•y (TRUSS-tee) *n. trusties.* In a prison, one who has earned special privileges by his good behavior.
–*adj. trustier, trustiest.* Dependable; not failing.–Robin Hood bent his *trusty* bow and shot his arrow right into the bull's-eye.

truth (TROOTH) *n. truths.* What is true or real; exactly what happened.–Mother taught us to tell the *truth.*–It would not be telling the *truth* to say that the children are perfect.

truth•ful (TROOTH-fuhl) *adj.; truthfully, adv.; truthfulness, n.* Honest; telling what really is so.–It pays to be *truthful.*–In the story, George Washington was *truthful* about what happened to the cherry tree.

try (TRY) *n. tries.* A test or trial.–Mother is giving the new soap a *try* today.
–*v. tries, tried, trying.* 1. Use or test; give a trial to.–If you cannot work out the problem this way, *try* another way.–*Try* one of these candies.
2. Attempt; make an effort. – At first Bob could not work out the puzzle. He *tried* again and finally solved it.
3. Give a court hearing to, before a judge.–The man was *tried* for stealing.

try•out (TRY-owt) *n. tryouts.* A test or trial to determine one's fitness for a particular purpose. *Tryouts* may be held for membership on a team or for parts in a play.

tub (TUB) *n. tubs.* 1. A large, open vessel that holds water in which to wash clothes or bathe. – Bob takes showers, but Jack bathes in the *tub*.

2. A low, wooden, barrel-like vessel. – The grocer had a *tub* half full of butter.

tu•ba (TOO- *or* TYOO-bə) *n. tubas.* A large, low-toned horn.

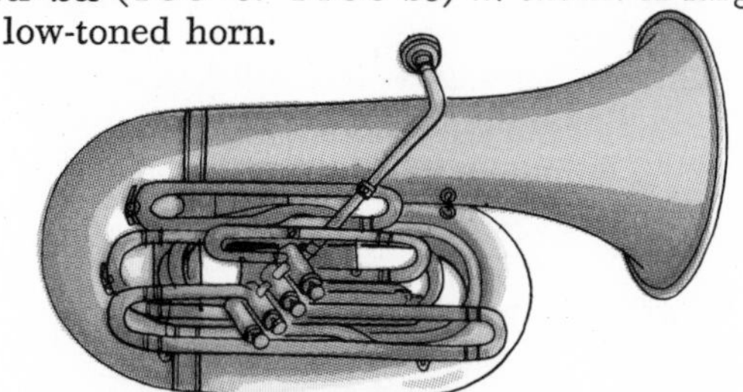

tube (TOOB *or* TYOOB) *n. tubes.* 1. A pipe; a long, hollow piece of rubber, metal, glass, etc.
2. Any hollow stem.–We drink sodas and lemonade through paper *tubes* called straws.
3. A part of a radio that looks something like an electric light bulb.

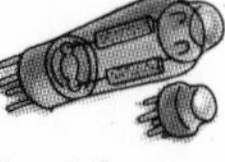

4. A round container of thin metal with a top that screws on.–Medicines, shaving creams, and toothpastes often come in *tubes*.
5. A tunnel for trains. – Many people travel under the Hudson River through *tubes*.

tu•ber•cu•lo•sis (too- *or* tyoo-ber-kyə-LOH-səss) *n.* A disease, usually of the lungs. When a person has *tuberculosis,* he is often sent to a hospital for treatment and rest.

tuck (TUK) *n. tucks.* A stitched fold. – The sleeves of Father's shirt were too long, so Mother put a *tuck* in them.
–*v. tucks, tucked, tucking.* Place, fit, or squeeze in neatly.–Mother *tucked* Baby's curls into the bonnet.–Mary *tucked* the blankets in.

Tues•day (TOOZ- *or* TYOOZ-dee) *n. Tuesdays.* The day after Monday. *Tuesday* is the third day of the week.

tuft (TUFT) *n. tufts.* 1. A group of threads, hair, feathers, or anything of the kind, fastened together at one end and loose at the other. – The bluejay has a *tuft* of feathers on his head.
2. A bunch of yarn. – The bedspread was white with blue *tufts*.

tug (TUG) *n. tugs.* 1. A small boat that can pull or tow other boats, even those much larger than the *tug* is.

2. A hard pull. – Bob gave just one *tug* and the box opened.
–*v. tugs, tugged, tugging.* Pull hard.–The boys *tugged* at the wagon to get it out of the pool of mud at the bottom of the hill.

tu•i•tion (too- *or* tyoo-ISH-ən) *n.* 1. Instruction or teaching.–Fine *tuition* is available at a great many schools, colleges, and universities.
2. The fee or money paid for instruction.–*Tuition* is payable in advance in many schools.

tu•lip (TOO- *or* TYOO-lip) *n. tulips.* A bright-colored, cup-shaped flower that grows from a bulb. The bulbs are put into the ground in the fall. The flowers blossom in the spring.–Many *tulips* grow in Holland.

tum•ble (TUM-bəl) *v. tumbles, tumbled, tumbling.* 1. Fall.–Baby *tumbled* out of bed. –The books *tumbled* off the shelf.
2. Roll or toss.–The apples *tumbled* about in the basket when Bob ran.
3. Turn handsprings, somersaults, and the like.–Bob is learning how to *tumble* in the hope that he may someday be able to join a circus as an acrobat.

tum•bler (TUM-bler) *n. tumblers.* 1. A person who can turn somersaults, handsprings, and the like; an acrobat.
2. A drinking glass.–Mary dropped the water *tumbler,* and it broke.

tu•na (TOO-nə) *n. tuna* or *tunas.* A large fish that is good to eat. The meat of *tuna* is canned and sold in stores.

tune (TOON *or* TYOON) *n. tunes.* 1. A melody.–I know the *tune* of "America."
2. A piece of music; a song.–Play a *tune* for us.
–*v. tunes, tuned, tuning.* Bring to the proper pitch or tone.–Mary *tuned* her violin.–Mother had the piano *tuned.*

tung·sten (TUNG-stən) *n.* A rare heavy metal. *Tungsten* has the highest melting point of all metals. It is used for filaments in electric lamps and for hardening other metals against easy melting.

tun·nel (TUN-əl) *n. tunnels.* A passageway made underground.–Trains and automobiles go through a *tunnel* to get through a mountain or under a river.

–*v. tunnels, tunneled, tunneling.* Dig an underground passage.–The mole *tunneled* under the vegetable garden and made the row of radishes sink.

tur·ban (TER-bən) *n. turbans.* 1. A cap with a scarf wound around it.–The man is wearing a *turban.*

2. A scarf wound around the head.–The woman is wearing a *turban.*
3. A kind of small, close-fitting hat without a brim, resembling a wound scarf.

tur·bine (TER-bin *or* -byn) *n. turbines.* An engine in which the motion is produced by the push of water, gas, or steam against a series of curved blades set into a shaft or wheel. As the water, gas, or steam pushes each successive blade, the shaft or wheel rotates.–*Turbines* are often used to provide the power to run ships.

Steam Turbine

turf (TERF) *n.* Sod; grass with its tangled roots.–Men playing golf often dig up *turf* with their clubs.

tur·key (TER-kee) *n. turkeys.* 1. A kind of large bird with wrinkled, red skin on its head and neck. Some *turkeys* are wild.
2. The meat of a turkey.–We eat *turkey* on Thanksgiving.

tur·moil (TER-moil) *n.* Confusion, as of movements, sounds, ideas, etc.; a disturbance.–The barking dog put the barnyard in a *turmoil.*

turn (TERN) *n. turns.* 1. A chance; an opportunity; a time.–We took *turns* batting.–The children formed a line, and each waited his *turn* to get a drink.
2. A deed; an act.–If you will help me now, sometime I will do you a good *turn.*
3. A sudden change.–Bill's behavior takes a *turn* for the better just before Christmas.
4. A complete circular movement.–If you give the clock stem too many *turns* when winding it, it will break.–Father unlocks his safe with two *turns* to the right, and three to the left.
–*v. turns, turned, turning.* 1. Change direction; go a different way.–We were driving west. Then we *turned* a corner and drove south.–Bob *turned* when I called to him.
2. Move in a circle.–The hands of the clock *turn.*–A top *turns.*
3. Change; become.–Ice *turns* to liquid when it gets warm.
4. Transform; change.–The witch *turned* the little girl into a toad in the fairy story.–Caterpillars *turn* into butterflies.
5. Upset.–The sight of a mouse *turns* Mother's stomach.

tur·nip (TER-nəp) *n. turnips.* A kind of plant with a root that is often eaten; the root of this plant.–*Turnips* are sometimes cooked as table vegetables, and sometimes they are eaten raw.

turn•stile (TERN-styl) *n. turnstiles.* A turning gate with crossed bars at the top. Some *turnstiles* register the number of persons passing through. – When going from the depot to the train, we passed through a *turnstile.*–We put our fare in a slot in a subway *turnstile* before we pass through.

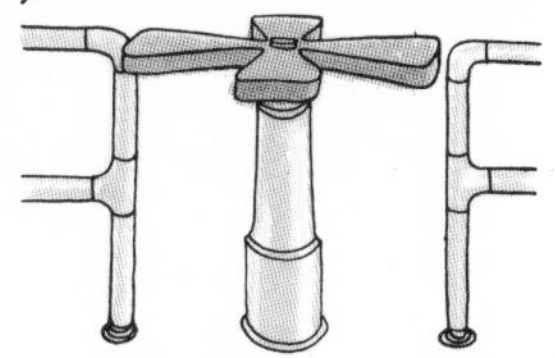

tur•pen•tine (TER-pən-tyn) *n.* An oily substance that comes from trees that have cones. –Father thinned the paint with *turpentine.* –*Turpentine* is sometimes used in medicine.

tur•quoise (TER-koiz *or* -kwoiz) *n. turquoises* and *adj.* 1. A greenish-blue stone.– Hannah's pretty new ring is set with a *turquoise.*
2. Greenish-blue. – Mother has a *turquoise* silk dress.

tur•tle (TER-tl) *n. turtles.* An animal with a hard shell over its back. *Turtles* live both in the water and on the land.

tusk (TUSK) *n. tusks.* A long, pointed tooth. – Elephants have a *tusk* on each side of the head. – Walruses and some other animals also have *tusks.*

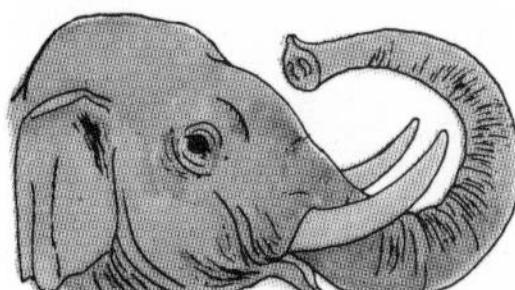

tu•tor (TOO- *or* TYOO-ter) *n. tutors.* A teacher who gives private lessons.–The sick boy could not go to school, so he had a *tutor* instruct him at home.
–*v. tutors, tutored, tutoring.* Teach privately. –Father *tutored* the boy in arithmetic.

tux•e•do (tuk-SEE-doh) *n. tuxedos.* A suit worn by men on semi-formal occasions. The coat of a formal suit is long and has tails. The coat of a *tuxedo* is suit length and has no tails.

tweed (TWEED) *n.* A kind of wool cloth with rough threads woven into it.–Father's suit is made of *tweed.*

tweez•ers (TWEE-zerz) *n. pl.* A small implement for pulling, grasping, or picking up objects; a small pinchers.–*Tweezers* are used by jewelers, watchmakers, printers, and doctors.

twelfth (TWELFTH) *n. twelfths.* One of 12 equal parts. If you divide anything into twelve parts all the same size, each part is one *twelfth.* It may be written 1/12.
–*adj.* Coming as number 12 in a series. – Carrie's name was *twelfth* on the list.

twelve (TWELV) *n. twelves* and *adj.* The number [12] coming after 11 and before 13. –Ten and two make *twelve.–Twelve* eggs are a dozen eggs.

twen•ti•eth (TWEN-tee-ith) *n. twentieths.* One of 20 equal parts. If you divide anything into twenty parts all the same size, each part is one *twentieth.* It may be written 1/20.
–*adj.* Coming as number 20 in a series.–Albert's name was *twentieth* on the list.

twen•ty (TWEN-tee) *n. twenties* and *adj.* The number [20] coming after 19 and before 21.–Ten and ten make *twenty.*

twice (TWYSS) *adv.* Two times.–The teacher told us *twice* how to spell the word.

twig (TWIG) *n. twigs.* A tiny branch of a tree.–The sparrow sat on a *twig* of the tree.

twi•light (TWY-lyt) *n. twilights.* Dusk; the half-light just after the sun sets in the evening, or just before it rises in the morning.

twin (TWIN) *n. twins.* 1. One of two children or animals born to the same mother at the same birth. *Twins* often look alike.

2. One of two things that are just alike or nearly alike.–The airplane has *twin* engines.

twine (TWYN) *n. twines.* Heavy cord or string.–We put *twine* around the package before we mailed it.
–*v. twines, twined, twining.* Twist and wind. –The ivy *twines* around the fence.

twinge (TWINJ) *n. twinges.* A sharp, sudden pain.–Jack felt a *twinge* in his leg when he fell down.

twin•kle (TWING-kəl) *v. twinkles, twinkled, twinkling.* Sparkle. – Baby's eyes *twinkle* when she sees something good to eat.–The reflection of the stars *twinkled* in the lake.

twirl (TWERL) *v. twirls, twirled, twirling.* Spin; whirl; go or make go round and round. –Bob *twirls* his key chain when he thinks.

twist (TWIST) *n. twists.* A special thread made by twisting two strands of thread together.–Mother mended the buttonholes in Bob's old coat with *twist.*
–*v. twists, twisted, twisting.* 1. Wind.–The girl stood *twisting* her handkerchief around in her hands.
2. Move restlessly.–The children *twist* and turn in their seats when they are too tired to sit still.
3. Bend around; bend out of shape.–The rim of Bob's bicycle was *twisted* where it had hit the curb.

two (TOO) *n. twos* and *adj.* The number [2] coming after 1 and before 3.–One and one make *two.*

ty•ing (TY-ing) *v.* One form of the verb *tie.* –Baby can't tie her shoe strings, so Mary is *tying* them for her.

type (TYP) *n. types.* 1. A kind; sort.–Children like books of different *types.* Fairy stories are the *type* that Mary likes.
2. Metal blocks with letters on them, used in printing.–Books and papers are printed with *type.*
–*v. types, typed, typing.* Write on a typewriter. –Mother can *type.*

type•write (TYP-ryt) *v. typewrites, typewrote, typewriting.* Write with a typewriter. –Mother *typewrites* all of Father's letters for him.

type•writ•er (TYP-ryt-er) *n. typewriters.* A machine which prints letters and figures by an arrangement of keys which are struck by hand.

ty•phoid fe•ver (TY-foid FEE-ver). An illness caused by a germ usually found in impure water.

ty•phoon (ty-FOON) *n. typhoons.* A very strong or severe whirling windstorm. – The ship was blown ashore by the *typhoon.*

typ•i•cal (TIP-ə-kəl) *adj.; typically, adv.* Showing the regular traits or qualities of a particular type, as: a *typical* teacher, a *typical* day, a *typical* party.–A *typical* student is one who is just about the same in ability and behavior as most other students.

typ•ist (TYP-ist) *n. typists.* A person whose work is writing on a typewriter.–There are many *typists* in the office where Father works.

ty•rant (TY-rənt) *n. tyrants.* 1. A cruel king; an unjust ruler.–The people overthrew the *tyrant* and formed a new government.
2. Any unjust or cruel person with power.– Harry's boss is a *tyrant.* He makes Harry work very hard and pays him very little money.

U u

U, u (YOO) *n. U's, u's.* The twenty-first letter of the alphabet.

ud·der (UD-er) *n. udders.* The large, baggy-looking milk gland from which cows give milk. Some other female animals, such as goats, have *udders,* too.

ug·ly (UG-lee) *adj. uglier, ugliest; ugliness, n.* 1. Not at all pretty; not pleasing to see.–The monster's face was *ugly.*
2. Unpleasant; cross; bad-tempered.–Sometimes Baby is *ugly* when she first wakes up from her nap.
3. Very severe and causing ruin.–A very *ugly* accident happened at the corner of Main and Broadway this morning.

u·ku·le·le (yoo-kə-LAY-lee) *n. ukuleles.* A small musical instrument with four strings, played by picking the strings.

ul·cer (UL-ser) *n. ulcers.* An open sore discharging pus.–A person with stomach *ulcers* must eat very simple foods.

ul·ti·mate (UL-tə-mət) *adj.; ultimately, adv.* 1. Final; last.–Everyone knows that Tom is going to the city, but no one knows where he is going after that. He is keeping his *ultimate* destination a secret.
2. Basic; not capable of further examination or division; elementary.–The *ultimate* necessity of kindness is recognized by all good men.

ul·ti·ma·tum (ul-tə-MAY-təm) *n. ultimatums* or *ultimata.* A last or final proposition; a set of final terms or conditions.–Mother gave Sally her *ultimatum:* finish her homework, or not watch television.

ul·tra·vi·o·let (ul-trə-VY-ə-lit) *adj.* Having to do with the invisible light lying beyond violet in the spectrum.–*Ultraviolet* rays are used in the treatment of various skin diseases, rickets, tuberculosis, and other disorders.

um·brel·la (um-BREL-ə) *n. umbrellas.* A collapsible frame with a cloth covering that is used to keep off the rain or sun.

um·pire (UM-pyr) *n. umpires.* A person who decides who is right and who is wrong in games like baseball.

–*v. umpires, umpired, umpiring.* Make decisions as an umpire.–The principal of our school *umpired* our ball game.

un·a·ble (un-AY-bəl) *adj.* Not able; not strong or capable enough.–Mary has been sick and is still *unable* to go to school.

un·ac·count·a·ble (un-ə-KOWN-tə-bəl) *adj.* Not accountable; not responsible; not to be explained; mysterious; without reason. –The man apologized for his dog's *unaccountable* behavior. He said his dog had never growled at anyone before and he didn't know why it was growling now.–An *unaccountable* light was seen in the sky. There didn't seem to be any reason for its sudden appearance.

u·nan·i·mous (yoo-NAN-ə-məss) *adj.; unanimously, adv.* In complete agreement; of a single mind or opinion. – The members were *unanimous* in their choice of a new club location.–The judges handed down a *unanimous* decision. They all agreed that Mary should win the essay contest.

un·a·ware (un-ə-WAIR) *adj.* Not aware; without knowledge. – We were *unaware* of your sickness. We didn't know that you were sick.

un·bal·anced (un-BAL-ənst) *adj.* 1. Not in balance.–The scales are *unbalanced.* They showed my weight as 65 pounds, and I really weigh 72 pounds.
2. Insane; mentally ill.–The poor woman is *unbalanced.*

un·bear·a·ble (un-BAIR-ə-bəl) *adj.* Not bearable; not to be endured or tolerated.–The heat was *unbearable.* It was so great that I couldn't stay in the room.

un•be•liev•a•ble (un-bə-LEEV-ə-bəl) *adj.; unbelievably, adv.* Not to be believed.–The strange tale of witches, monsters, and giants is *unbelievable.* Witches, monsters, and giants don't exist.

un•buck•le (un-BUK-əl) *v. unbuckles, unbuckled, unbuckling.* Undo a buckle; loosen a buckle.–*Unbuckle* your belt.

un•but•ton (un-BUT-n) *v. unbuttons, unbuttoned, unbuttoning.* Loosen or undo the buttons of; remove buttons from their buttonholes.

un•cer•tain (un-SER-tən) *adj.* Not certain; not sure.–I am *uncertain* about my answer. I am not sure it is right.

un•changed (un-CHAYNJD) *adj.* Not changed; remaining the same.–The time for the party is *unchanged.*

un•civ•i•lized (un-SIV-ə-lyzd) *adj.* Not civilized; savage; barbarian.–There still are *uncivilized* people living in parts of the world. Their tools are crude; they have no written language; they have many superstitions.

un•cle (UNG-kəl) *n. uncles.* The brother of one's mother or father, or the husband of one's aunt.–My mother's brother is my *uncle.* –Aunt Sally is my mother's sister; she is married to *Uncle* Joe.

un•clean (un-KLEEN) *adj.* 1. Filthy; dirty. –My shirt was *unclean,* so Mother washed it.
2. Impure; evil.–Boy Scouts are taught to avoid *unclean* thoughts.

un•com•fort•a•ble (un-KUM-fer-tə-bəl) *adj.* Not comfortable; causing or feeling discomfort.–This chair is *uncomfortable.* Bob is *uncomfortable* when he sits in it.

un•com•mon (un-KAHM-ən) *adj.; uncommonly, adv.* Not common; remarkable; unusual; rare.–An eclipse of the sun is *uncommon.* It doesn't happen very often.

un•con•cerned (un-kən-SERND) *adj.; unconcernedly, adv.* Not concerned; not worried; free from care or interest.–Tom was *unconcerned* about the test. He had studied hard and knew he would do well.

un•con•di•tion•al (un-kən-DISH-ən-əl) *adj.; unconditionally, adv.* Without conditions or reservations; absolute.–The general demanded *unconditional* surrender of the enemy.

un•con•scious (un-KAHN-shəss) *adj.* Not conscious; not aware of things about one.– The man was *unconscious* after the accident.

un•con•sti•tu•tion•al (un-kahn-stə-TOO-shən-əl *or* un-kahn-stə-TYOO-shən-əl) *adj.; unconstitutionally, adv.* Not constitutional; not in agreement with, or contrary to, the constitution.–The Supreme Court declared the law *unconstitutional.*

un•cov•er (un-KUV-er) *v. uncovers, uncovered, uncovering.* 1. Take the cover off.–*Uncover* the butter dish, please.
2. Make known; find out.–A big secret was *uncovered.*
3. Take off one's hat. – The boys *uncover* when the flag goes by.

un•der (UN-der) *prep.* The opposite of on or over; beneath; below.–Put your hands on your desk and your feet *under* it.–Miners go *under* the surface of the earth to work.

un•der•brush (UN-der-brush) *n.* Shrubs, small trees, and bushes that grow under larger trees.–The rabbit ran into the *underbrush.*

un•der•clothes (UN-der-klohthz) *n. pl.* Clothes worn next to the body, under other clothes.

un•der•foot (un-der-FUHT) *adj.* and *adv.* Under one's feet; on the ground.–It is often wet and slushy *underfoot* in the winter, especially during a thaw.–Be careful not to fall. It is slippery *underfoot.*

un•der•go (un-der-GOH) *v. undergoes, underwent, undergoing.* 1. Suffer; bear; endure. –The actor *underwent* many hardships before he finally won success and became a television star.
2. Experience; go or pass through.–The big city is constantly *undergoing* changes. Old buildings are being torn down, and new ones are being built.–Aunt Jane entered the hospital to *undergo* an operation.

un•der•ground (un-der-GROWND) *adj.* and *adv.* Under the ground or under the surface of the earth.–Henry's uncle was a coal miner who worked *underground.*

un•der•line (un-der-LYN *or* UN-der-lyn) *v. underlines, underlined, underlining.* Put a line under.–*Underline* the title of the book that you enjoyed most and then *underline* the author's name.

un•der•neath (un-der-NEETH) *prep.* Under; below; beneath.–We found a small snail *underneath* the log.

un•der•pass (UN-der-pass) *n. underpasses.* A place where a road or railroad track goes under another road or railroad track. – We drove through the *underpass* at the same time that a train was going over it.

un•der•rate (un-der-RAYT) *v. underrates, underrated, underrating.* Rate too low; set too low a value on; underestimate.–Never *underrate* the strength of your opponent.

un•der•shirt (UN-der-shert) *n. undershirts.* A shirt worn next to the skin, under one's outer clothing.

un•der•stand (un-der-STAND) *v. understands, understood, understanding.* 1. Get the meaning of. – Mary *understands* the directions for making the box.
2. Know the meaning of. – Father *understands* French.
3. Have heard; have learned that.–I *understand* that you have a new car.

un•der•stand•ing (un-der-STAND-ing) *n. understandings.* 1. An agreement.–Bob and his father have an *understanding* about the work to be done.
2. The ability to know what things mean.–How Mother can do so many things at once is beyond my *understanding.*

un•der•take (un-der-TAYK) *v. undertakes, undertook, undertaking.* Try to do; agree to do.–Mother has so much work to do that she can not *undertake* any more.–Bob *undertook* to find the missing books.

un•der•tak•er (UN-der-tayk-er) *n. undertakers.* A person whose business is getting dead persons ready to be buried and taking charge of funerals.

un•der•tow (UN-der-toh) *n.* 1. An underwater current moving towards the sea.–You shouldn't swim in the ocean when there is a strong *undertow.* It can sweep you out to sea.
2. Any strong current below the surface of an ocean, river, or lake that moves in a different direction from water at the surface.

un•der•wear (UN-der-wair) *n.* Underclothing; clothing worn under one's outer clothes. –Woolen *underwear* helps keep one warm.

un•de•sir•a•ble (un-di-ZYR-ə-bəl) *adj.; undesirably, adv.* Not desirable; objectionable; not to one's liking.–A dirty city is an *undesirable* place to live in.

un•de•ter•mined (un-di-TER-mənd) *adj.* Not settled or decided upon; not fixed.–An *undetermined* number of guests will be invited to the party. The exact number will have to be decided upon later.–The boundary between Mr. Jones' farm and ours is *undetermined.* We don't know the exact point where our farm ends and his begins.

un•do (un-DOO) *v. undoes, undid, undoing.* Loosen; unfasten. – Baby pulled her shoestring into a knot, and Mary tried to *undo* it.

un•done (un-DUN) *adj.* Not accomplished; not finished.–The work was still *undone* at six o'clock.
–*v.* One form of the verb *undo.*–Jack found that Baby had *undone* the knot.

un•dress (un-DRESS) *v. undresses, undressed, undressing.* Take off the clothes. – Mother has to *undress* Baby and bathe her. –*Undress* quickly and go to bed, for it is late.

un•earth (un-ERTH) *v. unearths, unearthed, unearthing.* 1. Dig up from beneath the earth. –The explorers *unearthed* a buried temple.
2. Bring to light; discover; uncover. – The guards have *unearthed* a plot to kill the king.

un•eas•y (un-EE-zee) *adj.; uneasily, adv.* Restless; nervous.–The dog is *uneasy* when his master is away.

un•em•ployed (un-em-PLOID) *adj.* Out of work; without a job.–When times are hard, many people are *unemployed.*

un•e•qual (un-EE-kwəl) *adj.; unequally, adv.* 1. Not equal; not of the same number, size, or value.–A diamond and a piece of glass are *unequal* in value. A diamond has much more value than a piece of glass.
2. Unfair; poorly matched; one-sided.–The tennis match was *unequal* because one of the players had a sore back and couldn't play well.

un•e•ven (un-EE-vən) *adj.; unevenly, adv.; unevenness, n.* 1. Not straight and flat; not level.–The table rocks because the floor is *uneven.*
2. Not the same size.–The pickets in the fence are *uneven.*
3. Odd (of numbers).–The houses are numbered so that the even numbers are on one side of the street and the *uneven* numbers (numbers ending in 1, 3, 5, 7, 9) are on the other side.

un•ex•pect•ed (un-iks-PEK-təd) *adj.; unexpectedly, adv.; unexpectedness, n.* Not looked for; not waited for.–I received an *unexpected* gift from Uncle Jim.

un•fair (un-FAIR) *adj.; unfairly, adv.; unfairness, n.* Not just.–Jack felt it was *unfair* of the teacher to expect him to know the answer to the question when none of the others knew it.

un•faith•ful (un-FAYTH-fuhl) *adj.; unfaithfully, adv.; unfaithfulness, n.* Not true; not loyal.–Do not be *unfaithful* to your old friends. Do not desert them.

un•fa•mil•iar (un-fə-MIL-yer) *adj.* Not known; not seen before.–The man's face is *unfamiliar* to me.

un•fas•ten (un-FASS-ən) *v. unfastens, unfastened, unfastening.* Undo; loosen (as to untie, unlock, unbutton).–Can you *unfasten* this suitcase for me?

un•fa•vor•a•ble (un-FAY-ver-ə-bəl) *adj.; unfavorably, adv.* Not favorable; not to one's advantage; bad.–Bill received an *unfavorable* report card. His conduct and marks were unsatisfactory.–The weather seemed *unfavorable* for a picnic. It looked as if it were going to rain.

un•fin•ished (un-FIN-isht) *adj.* 1. Not all done; not completed.–The model plane is *unfinished;* it hasn't been painted yet.
2. Without paint, varnish, or other finish.–We bought *unfinished* furniture and painted it ourselves.

un•fit (un-FIT) *adj.* Not good; not suitable.–The meat is spoiled and is *unfit* to eat.–Your white dress is *unfit* for traveling on the dusty train.

un•fold (un-FOHLD) *v. unfolds, unfolded, unfolding.* 1. Open the folds of; spread out; open up.–*Unfold* your handkerchief quickly when you feel you may be going to sneeze.
2. Open.–A bud *unfolds* as it becomes a flower.

un•fore•seen (un-for-SEEN) *adj.* Not expected; not looked for. – We shall come if nothing *unforeseen* happens.

un•for•tu•nate (un-FOR-chə-nit) *adj.; unfortunately, adv.* Unlucky; unsuccessful. – The lady is a very *unfortunate* person. She lost her new watch.

un•found•ed (un-FOWND-əd) *adj.* Without foundation; without reason; without basis; groundless.–The rumors are completely *unfounded.* There is no truth in them at all.

un•friend•ly (un-FREND-lee) *adj.* Not liking other people; not wanting to get to know others. – The boy is so shy that he seems *unfriendly.*

un•furl (un-FERL) *v. unfurls, unfurled, unfurling.* Unfold; unroll; spread.–The soldiers stood at attention as the flag was *unfurled.*–The sailors are *unfurling* the sails.

un•grate•ful (un-GRAYT-fuhl) *adj.; ungratefully, adv.; ungratefulness, n.* Not thankful. – The boy is *ungrateful* for the many things you have done for him.

un•hap•py (un-HAP-ee) *adj. unhappier, unhappiest; unhappily, adv.; unhappiness, n.* 1. Without cheer; sad.–Cinderella was *unhappy* because she couldn't go to the ball.
2. Unlucky; unfortunate. – By an *unhappy* chance, Jack had a bad fall the first day he rode his new bicycle.

u•ni•corn (YOO-nə-korn) *n. unicorns.* An imaginary animal that has a single horn in the center of its forehead. The *unicorn* is usually represented as having the head and body of a horse, the tail of a lion, and, at times, the beard of a goat.

u•ni•form (YOO-nə-form) *n. uniforms.* Clothes that are made to show the wearer's occupation or rank, and are exactly like those of other people of the same occupation or rank. – Soldiers, sailors, nurses, policemen, and firemen wear *uniforms.*
–*adj; uniformly, adv.* 1. Alike in size, shape, speed or the like.–The telephone poles along the highway are all of *uniform* size.
2. Consistent; even; steady; regular. – The driver drives his car at a *uniform* speed.

u•ni•fy (YOO-nə-fy) *v. unifies, unified, unifying.* Unite; become or make into one; bring together.–After the Civil War, the nation was *unified* once again.

un•in•hab•it•ed (un-in-HAB-ə-təd) *adj.* Not inhabited; not lived in; having no inhabitants.–The old house is *uninhabited.* No one lives in it.

un•ion (YOON-yən) *n. unions.* 1. A joining together of things into one, or the things that have been joined together. – The United States is a *union* of states.
2. A group of workers who are joined together to bring about better working conditions and better wages.

UNIFORMS
Roman Empire A.D. 400
England 1415
Germany 1520
France 1630
Spain 1710
France 1743
England 1758
United Colonies 1775
Sweden 1779
France 1796
Prussia 1813
United States 1862
Confederate States 1864
Canada 1885
Belgium 1914
Vatican City 1930
Germany 1943
Russia 1948
Argentina 1950
United States 1960

u•nique (yoo-NEEK) *adj.; uniquely, adv.* Standing alone; being without comparison; unmatched; without equal; rare.–This is a *unique* fossil. It is the only one of its kind.

u•nit (YOO-nit) *n. units.* One person or thing, or a group of persons or things considered as one.–We are working on the first *unit* of a number of lessons grouped together to make a course of study.

u•nite (yoo-NYT) *v. unites, united, uniting.* Join together as one.–The children *united* in reciting the poem.

U•nit•ed Na•tions (yoo-NY-təd NAY-shənz). An organization of nations formed in San Francisco in 1945. The *United Nations* has

its headquarters in New York City. The members of the *United Nations* have pledged themselves to work for international peace and social progress.

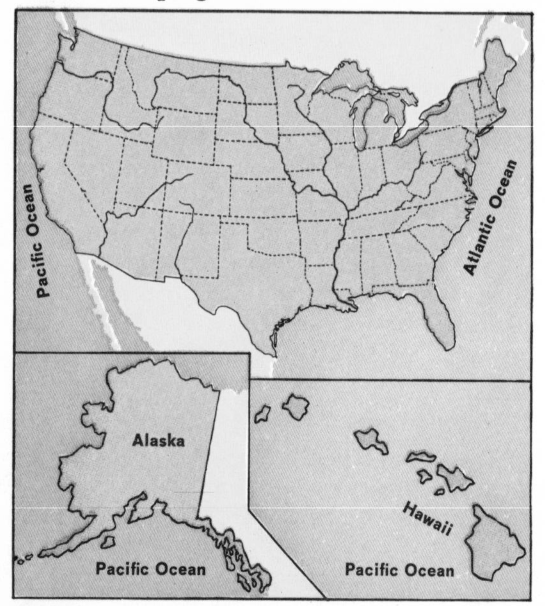

U•nit•ed States (yoo-NY-təd STAYTSS). One of the largest countries in the Western Hemisphere, and the one with the most inhabitants; 179,500,000 people live in the *United States.* It consists of fifty states and the District of Columbia.

u•ni•ty (YOO-nə-tee) *n. unities.* 1. The state of being a single undivided unit; oneness; wholeness.–The United States is proud of its *unity.* Although there are fifty separate states, the country acts as one.
2. Harmony; accord. – The children are playing together in *unity.* They are playing quietly, peacefully, and happily, without argument or disagreement.

u•ni•ver•sal (yoo-nə-VER-səl) *adj.; universally, adv.* 1. Having to do with the universe; present or existing everywhere; to be found anywhere.–Arithmetic is a *universal* school subject. Every school teaches it.
2. Concerning everyone; used or done by all; general.–Eating and sleeping are *universal* needs. Everyone has to eat and sleep.

u•ni•verse (YOO-nə-verss) *n.* 1. The earth, sun, stars, and all other objects in space, considered together.
2. Everything that exists.

u•ni•ver•si•ty (yoo-nə-VER-sə-tee) *n. universities.* A large school made up of several colleges.–Students learn engineering, dentistry, medicine, teaching, law, and many other things at a *university.*

un•just (un-JUST) *adj.; unjustly, adv.* Not fair.–The man is *unjust* with his helpers. He does not pay them enough and he does not treat them well.

un•kind (un-KYND) *adj.; unkindly, adv.; unkindness, n.* Not gentle or considerate; cruel.–The *unkind* boy abused his little dog.

un•known (un-NOHN) *n. unknowns.* A person or thing that is not known; that which is not known.–Bill didn't want to go into the dark room because he was afraid of the *unknown.* But as soon as he turned on the lights, he saw that there was nothing to be afraid of.
–*adj.* Not familiar; not known; strange.–That girl is *unknown* in the neighborhood. She is a stranger.

un•lace (un-LAYSS) *v. unlaces, unlaced, unlacing.* Take out the strings; loosen the laces of.–Baby likes to *unlace* Mother's shoes.

un•less (un-LESS) *conj.* and *prep.* If not.–I can't go *unless* you wait for me.

un•like (un-LYK) *adj.* and *prep.* Not like; different from.–This fruit is *unlike* any I have ever eaten.

un•lim•it•ed (un-LIM-it-əd) *adj.* Not limited; without bounds; not restricted.–Ancient kings and rulers often had *unlimited* power over their subjects.

un•load (un-LOHD) *v. unloads, unloaded, unloading.* Remove the load from. – The farmer *unloaded* his truck.

un•lock (un-LAHK) *v. unlocks, unlocked, unlocking.* Unfasten the lock of.–The key would not *unlock* the door.

un•luck•y (un-LUK-ee) *adj. unluckier, unluckiest.* Unfortunate; having or bringing bad luck.–This is an *unlucky* day for the boy who lost his watch. He was *unlucky.*

un•nat•u•ral (un-NACH-ə-rəl) *adj.; unnaturally, adv.* 1. Not natural; contrary to the normal order of things; not normal; strange. –If a man were to grow wings and fly, it would be most *unnatural.*
2. Very cruel; evil; wicked. – The man trapped under the fallen tree was suffering *unnatural* pain.

un•nec•es•sar•y (un-NESS-ə-sair-ee) *adj.; unnecessarily, adv.* Not needed; useless. – The teacher told her pupils that their noise was *unnecessary.*

un•of•fi•cial (un-ə-FISH-əl) *adj.; unofficially, adv.* Not official; without authority.–The runner set an *unofficial* record in the 100-yard dash. There was no judge present to score his fast time.–The teacher gave the student some *unofficial* advice, not as a teacher, but as a friend.

un•pack (un-PAK) *v. unpacks, unpacked, unpacking.* Take out packed contents.–Mary helped Mother *unpack* the suitcase.–We *unpacked* our lunch and had a picnic.

un•pleas•ant (un-PLEZ-ənt) *adj.* Disagreeable; not pleasant or nice.–When the sun shines, it is a pleasant day. When it rains and is dark, the weather is *unpleasant.*

un•pop•u•lar (un-PAHP-yə-ler) *adj.* Not liked or sought after.–A boy who does not tell the truth is *unpopular.*

un•pre•pared (un-pri-PAIRD) *adj.* Not ready.–The teacher gave us a spelling test, and we were *unprepared* for it.

un•re•al (un-REE-əl) *adj.* Not true; not like actual things. – This is an *unreal* story. Things do not actually happen the way they do in this story.

un•rea•son•a•ble (un-REE-zən-ə-bəl) *adj.* 1. Foolish; not sensible.–The girl was *unreasonable* about spending her money. She paid an *unreasonable* price for the dress.
2. Not fair.–The man is *unreasonable* to his workers; he makes them work too hard and gets angry at them too easily.

un•re•lat•ed (un-ri-LAY-təd) *adj.* 1. Not related; untold.–The man left before he could tell his story. The story, therefore, remained *unrelated.*
2. Without connection; having no relationship.–The two events are completely *unrelated.* They have nothing to do with each other.
3. Not a relative or relation.–Mary is *unrelated* to me. She is not my sister; she is my friend.

un•rest (un-REST) *n.* 1. Lack of rest, peace, or quiet; uneasiness.–His mind is in a state of *unrest.* He is troubled by many problems.
2. Popular disturbance; lack of satisfaction among the people, with the possibility of rebellion.–The heavy taxes caused great *unrest* in the kingdom.

un•roll (un-ROHL) *v. unrolls, unrolled, unrolling.* Roll out or spread out something that has been rolled.–Someone *unrolled* the paper towels.–*Unroll* the ribbon from the spool.

un•rul•y (un-ROO-lee) *adj.* Not easy to rule; hard to control; causing disturbance; lawless.–The police broke up and scattered the *unruly* mob.–The cowboy finally made the *unruly* horse stop kicking.

un•safe (un-SAYF) *adj.* Dangerous; not safe. –The dirty water is *unsafe* for drinking.

un•sat•is•fac•to•ry (un-sat-əss-FAK-tə-ree) *adj.* Not good enough; not sufficient; not up to certain standards.–The teacher said Jack's work was *unsatisfactory.*

un•seen (un-SEEN) *adj.* Not seen; not visible to anyone.–The small child stood *unseen* behind the chair.

un•self•ish (un-SEL-fish) *adj.* Thoughtful; considerate of others; generous.–Selfish people think only of themselves. *Unselfish* people are kind and helpful to others.

un•set•tled (un-SET-əld) *adj.* 1. Upset; not in order.–Father is papering the walls, so our house is *unsettled.*
2. Not inhabited.–The family moved to an *unsettled* part of the country.
3. Uncertain; likely to change.–The weather is *unsettled.*

un•skilled (un-SKILD) *adj.* Without special ability; not trained.–The man wanted the job but he was *unskilled* in that kind of work.

un•stead•y (un-STED-ee) *adj.; unsteadily, adv.; unsteadiness, n.* Shaky; not firm or strong.–The sick man's knees were still a little *unsteady.*

un•think•a•ble (un-THINGK-ə-bəl) *adj.* Not to be thought of or imagined; not even to be dreamt of.–His sudden good fortune was almost *unthinkable.* He had never dreamed of possessing so much money.

un•ti•dy (un-TY-dee) *adj.* Not tidy; not orderly; not neat; sloppy.–Susan is very careful about things. Her room is rarely *untidy.*

un•tie (un-TY) *v. unties, untied, untying.* Unfasten; undo; loosen the knot of.–It is easier to *untie* one's shoestrings than it is to tie them.

un•til (un-TIL) *conj.* 1. Up to (a certain time). –Wait here *until* school is out.
2. Up to (a certain point).–We ate *until* we could eat no more.
–*prep.* 1. Till; to.–We had to wait from noon *until* after four o'clock for the doctor to come.
2. Before.–Bill won't get here *until* noon.

un•u•su•al (un-YOO-zhuh-əl) *adj.; unusually, adv.* Different from most; not ordinary; rare or outstanding.–Mary has *unusual* musical talent.

un•wel•come (un-WEL-kəm) *adj.* Not wanted.–The visitor felt *unwelcome* among so many strangers.

un•will•ing (un-WIL-ing) *adj.; unwillingly, adv.; unwillingness, n.* Not willing; not wanting or consenting.–The workman was *unwilling* to work after six o'clock at night.

un•wise (un-WYZ) *adj.; unwisely, adv.* Foolish.–It is *unwise* to eat too much.

un•wor•thy (un-WER-thee) *adj.; unworthily, adv.; unworthiness, n.* 1. Not deserving. –The bad boy is *unworthy* of your kindness.
2. Bad; not deserving praise.–Some of the early settlers had *unworthy* aims. They wanted to take land belonging to the Indians.
3. Not as good as one would expect; not fitting.–The mayor has done nothing *unworthy* of his position.

un•wrap (un-RAP) *v. unwraps, unwrapped, unwrapping.* Remove the wrappings from; undo or open (as a package). – Mark *unwrapped* his birthday present. He untied the ribbon, tore off the paper, and opened the box.

up (UP) *adv.* 1. To a higher place.–Bob tried to get his kite farther *up* in the sky.
2. Upright; straight; on one's feet. – We stood *up* to salute the flag.
3. To pieces.–Dynamite was used to blow *up* the rocks on the hill.
4. Over; at an end.–Our playtime is *up.*
5. Out of bed; awake.–The farmer gets *up* early each morning.
6. Tightly.–Close *up* your purse.
7. Out of the ground.–The children pulled the weeds *up.*
8. Above the ground. – The spring flowers will soon be *up.*
9. Higher than the horizon.–The sun is *up* in the daytime.
10. Completely; to the end or final point; until finished.–Eat your food *up!*–The house burned *up.*
11. Into sight or view.–My lost watch has finally turned *up.*
–*prep.* 1. To a higher place.–I went *up* to bed.
2. To or near the top of.–"Jack and Jill went *up* the hill to fetch a pail of water."
3. Along. – Our house is just *up* the road from school.
4. Toward the beginning of. – Albany is farther *up* the Hudson River than New York.
–*Bring up* means to improve, educate, or bring to an advanced state or condition.–Mother wants to *bring* us *up* in a small town.
–*Keep up* means to maintain or keep the same rate of speed or progress as another.–Bill tried to *keep up* with Jim in the race, but he couldn't. He was too slow.
–*Ups and downs* means to have a rise and fall in luck or fortune.–Our school's baseball team has many *ups and downs.* Sometimes it wins, and sometimes it loses.

up•hold (up-HOHLD) *v. upholds, upheld, upholding.* Agree to; back up with agreement. –The teacher *upheld* Jack's statement. She agreed that he was right.

up•hol•ster (up-HOHL-ster) *v. upholsters, upholstered, upholstering.* Make cushions and other padded parts of furniture, and cover them with heavy cloth.–The couch in the living room was *upholstered* in deep blue velvet.
–*upholstery, n.*

up•keep (UP-keep) *n.* 1. The act or process of maintaining in good working order, condition, or state of repair.—The *upkeep* of the farm is not difficult. Very few things need fixing.
2. The cost of keeping things in good working condition; general operating expenses. —Our house is large and comfortable, but the *upkeep* is high. It costs a lot to maintain it.

up•on (ə-PAHN *or* -PAWN) *prep.* On; on the top of.—Put the cup *upon* the table.

up•per (UP-er) *adj.* Higher; top.—The *upper* part of anything is the higher part. – The *upper* shelves of a cupboard are the ones near the top.

up•right (UP-ryt) *adj.* 1. Straight up and down; standing.—Two of the telephone poles were blown down in the storm, but the others were *upright.*—Baby can sit *upright* in her crib.
2. Honest.—The mayor is an *upright* man.

up•ris•ing (UP-ry-zing *or* up-RY-zing) *n. uprisings.* A rising up or revolt; a rebellion. – Troops were called to put down the *uprising.*

up•roar (UP-ror) *n. uproars.* A loud shouting; a noise or disturbance.—When the boy got a home run, an *uproar* rose from the crowd.

up•set (up-SET) *v. upsets, upset, upsetting.* Turn over; tip over.—The cat *upset* the can of fish so she could eat them.
—*adj.* Disturbed; worried.—Father was *upset* when Bob got home late from school.

up•side down (UP-syd DOWN). 1. With the upper part or the top side down.—Turn the clean glasses *upside down* on the shelves.
2. Topsy-turvy. – The boys, in searching for the lost key, turned the room *upside down.* They upset everything.

up•stairs (up-STAIRZ) *adv.* 1. On a floor above the first floor.—We cook and eat downstairs. We sleep *upstairs.*
2. Up the stairs; up a flight of stairs.—We go *upstairs* to our bedroom.

up•stream (up-STREEM) *adv.* In the direction from which the water in a stream or river is coming or flowing.—It is hard to row a boat *upstream.*

up-to-date (UP-tə-DAYT) *adj.* In the latest style or fashion.—Mary's suit is *up-to-date.*

up•ward or **up•wards** (UP-werd *or* -werdz) *adv.* To a higher place; away from the ground. – The elevator shot *upward.* – The smoke floated *upward.*

u•ra•ni•um (yuh-RAY-nee-əm) *n.* A hard, heavy, radioactive, metallic element. *Uranium* is found in pitchblende, a black lustrous mineral, and in several other minerals. In certain forms, it is used in making atomic bombs.

U•ra•nus (YUHR-ə-nəss) *n.* 1. In ancient Greek mythology, the imaginary person representing Heaven. *Uranus* was supposed to be the ruler of the world. He is shown in works of art as a bearded old man holding a robe above his head.
2. The seventh planet from the sun. It is the third largest planet and has five moons. *Uranus* takes eighty-four Earth years to complete its journey around the sun.

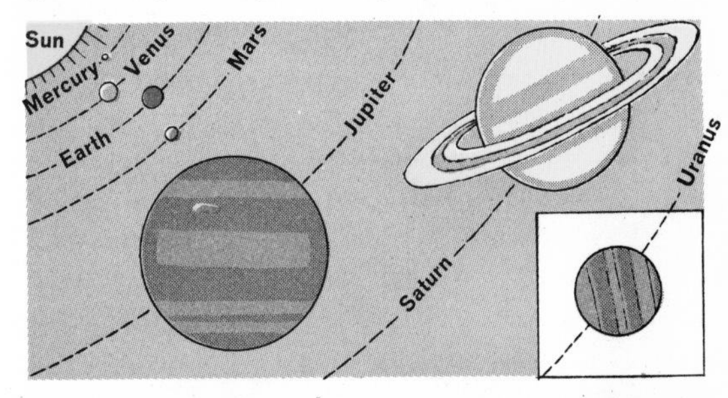

ur•ban (ER-bən) *adj.* Having to do with city life, a city, or cities.—Some people like rural, or farm, life. Others prefer *urban* living.

urge (ERJ) *n. urges.* An impulse; an involuntary or automatic desire.—As soon as she saw the flower, she had an *urge* to smell it. She had a sudden desire to smell it.
—*v. urges, urged, urging.* 1. Ask earnestly; coax.—Bob *urged* his mother to allow him to play football for the school team.
2. Drive; force.—The angry driver *urged* his horse to go faster by using a whip.

ur•gent (ER-jənt) *adj.; urgently, adv.; urgency, n.* Requiring immediate attention; pressing.—This is an *urgent* matter. It must be dealt with at once.

u•rine (YUHR-in) *n.* A watery fluid given off by the kidneys and stored in the bladder of the body. Later it is released from the body.

urn (ERN) *n. urns.* A kind of vessel, usually set on a base.—We have an *urn* for flowers.

us (USS) *pron.* The others and me. – This is our dog. Grandfather gave him to *us.*—Give *us* some books to read.

us•a•ble (YOO-zə-bəl) *adj.* In a condition to be used; fit for use.–Although the handle is broken, the coffee pot is still *usable.*

us•age (YOO-sij) *n.* 1. The way something has been used, said, or done over a long period; usual manner or custom; habit. – A dictionary is a record of language *usage.* It shows how words are used.
2. Handling; treatment.–The packages received rough *usage* before their delivery.

use (YOOSS) *n. uses.* 1. Getting help or work from.–Bob thanked Mary for the *use* of her pen.
2. A need.–We have no *use* for broken baseball bats.
3. A point; a value.–There is no *use* coaxing Father to let you go.
4. A way in which a thing is used or employed.–The teacher asked us to name some of the *uses* of rubber, and Jack mentioned automobile tires and heels for shoes.
5. State of being employed, occupied, acted upon, or put into service. – The book Jim wanted to read at the library was in *use.*
–*Of no use* means being of little or no help; of no service or advantage.–Jim's stamp collection was *of no use* to Bob. Bob had no interest in it. He liked to save coins.

use (YOOZ) *v. uses, used, using.* 1. Cause (something) to help to do certain work.–We *use* a pencil to write with.–We *use* our eyes to see things.
2. Treat.–Jack felt that the salesperson had *used* him badly.

used (YOOST) *v. Used* helps other verbs show repeated or prolonged action in the past.– Mary *used* to wear a hair ribbon. She wore a hair ribbon for many years but she does not any more.
–*adj.* Accustomed.–Grandfather is *used* to getting up early.

use•ful (YOOSS-fuhl) *adj.; usefully, adv.; usefulness, n.* 1. Helpful; of value or service. –The child makes himself *useful* around the house.
2. Of some use or help.–A watch is a *useful* gift, one that can be used by its owner.

ush•er (USH-er) *n. ushers.* A person who shows one to one's seat in a church, in a theater, at a ball game, etc.
–*v. ushers, ushered, ushering.* To lead or bring one to a place. – Mary *ushered* the guests into the living room.

u•su•al (YOO-zhuh-əl) *adj.; usually, adv.* Ordinary; accustomed; same.–We go to school this year at the *usual* time.–We met at the *usual* place.

U•tah (YOO-taw *or* -tah) *n.* A mountainous state in western United States, with rich fruit- and vegetable-growing valleys. Over half the land is usable only for pasturage. Many minerals, especially copper and silver, come from *Utah.* Great Salt Lake, which has water five times as salty as ocean water, is in *Utah.*

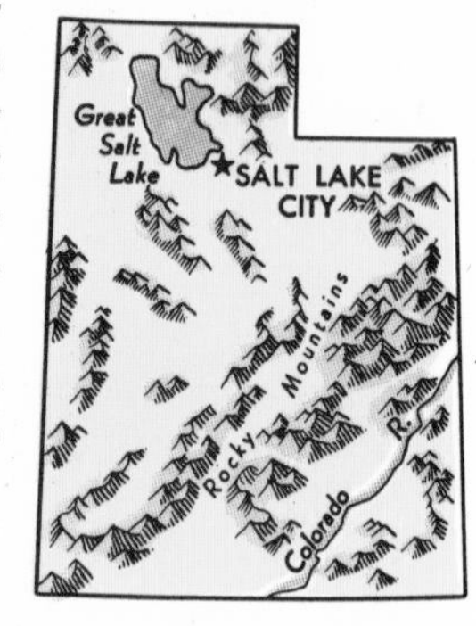

u•ten•sil (yoo-TEN-səl) *n. utensils.* A tool, an instrument, or anything that is used in doing some special kind of work.–Pots and pans, skillets and strainers are kitchen *utensils.* Mops, vacuum cleaners, brushes, and brooms are household *utensils.*

u•til•i•ty (yoo-TIL-ə-tee) *n. utilities.* Usefulness.–The *utility* of a safety pin is quite remarkable.
–A *public utility* is a business company, such as a gas or electric company, which performs a useful public service.
–A *utility room* is a room in which such things as mops and ironing boards are kept or stored.

ut•most (UT-mohst) *adj.* 1. Most distant; farthest.–Pluto is the *utmost* known planet in our solar system.
2. Of the highest sort, degree, quality; extreme; greatest.–The President accepted his adviser's resignation with the *utmost* regret.

ut•ter (UT-er) *v. utters, uttered, uttering.* Speak; say.–No one *uttered* a word.
–*adj.; utterly, adv.* Complete.–The bombed city is in *utter* ruin.

V v

V, v (VEE) *n. V's, v's.* The twenty-second letter of the alphabet.

va•can•cy (VAY-kən-see) *n. vacancies.* 1. An empty space; an empty office, house, or apartment.–The sign on the apartment building said that there were no *vacancies.*
2. An open job; a position waiting to be filled.–When Bob quit his job to go to school, he left a *vacancy* to be filled by someone else.

va•cant (VAY-kənt) *adj.* Empty; not occupied.–The lot next door is *vacant.* There is nothing built on it.

va•ca•tion (vay-KAY-shən) *n. vacations.* A period of time away from school, work, or one's usual occupation to do as one chooses, to have fun or to rest.–Our summer *vacation* lasts three months.

vac•ci•nate (VAK-sə-nayt) *v. vaccinates, vaccinated, vaccinating.* Inoculate a person with a vaccine to make him safe from smallpox or some other particular disease for a number of years.–Mary was *vaccinated* before she started going to school.

vac•cine (VAK-sin *or* vak-SEEN) *n. vaccines.* A specially-made fluid containing disease germs, usually dead ones. When *vaccine* is injected into a person, the body produces antibodies to fight the germs. These antibodies remain in the bloodstream for a certain amount of time and protect the person against the disease should he come in contact with it.

vac•u•um (VAK-yuh-əm) *n. vacuums.* A space that is completely empty, even of air, such as the space inside a radio tube.

va•grant (VAY-grənt) *n. vagrants.* A tramp; a penniless wanderer.–A *vagrant* knocked at our door and asked Mother for some food.
–*adj.; vagrantly, adv.* Having no set course or direction; moving about aimlessly; wandering. – The *vagrant* suggestions that Tim made showed that he did not have any well-thought-out plan for the picnic. He just had a few general ideas.

vague (VAYG) *adj.; vaguely, adv.* Not clear; indefinite; hazy.–The *vague* outline of a ship could be seen in the fog.–Father's vacation plans are still *vague.*

vain (VAYN) *adj.* 1. Proud.–The girl is *vain.* She thinks she is beautiful and likes to look at herself in the mirror.
2. Worthless; useless.–Jack made a *vain* attempt to catch the ball, but it was far over his head.
–*In vain* means without success.–Jack's efforts to catch the ball were *in vain.* He couldn't reach it.

vale (VAYL) *n. vales.* A valley; low land between hills or mountains.

val•en•tine (VAL-ən-tyn) *n. valentines.* A card or other token of love or friendship sent on St. Valentine's Day, February 14.

val•et (VAL-it *or* val-AY) *n. valets.* A man servant who takes care of his master's clothes, aids him in dressing, and so on.–The prince's *valet* helped him prepare for the ball.

val•iant (VAL-yənt) *adj.* Brave.–The *valiant* fireman went into the burning building to save the child.

val•id (VAL-id) *adj.; validity, n.* 1. Backed by facts, knowledge, authority.–Bill's opinion is not *valid.* He does not know the facts. He is only guessing.
2. Legal.–The contract was not *valid* until Father signed it.
3. Based on a good reason. – Bill told his teacher that he was absent from school because he had been sick. The teacher said that it was a *valid* excuse.

va•lise (və-LEESS) *n. valises.* A traveling bag; a suitcase.–Grandmother packed her *valise* to come to the city.

val•ley (VAL-ee) *n. valleys.* Low land between two hills or mountains. – We went down the hill into the *valley.*

val•or (VAL-er) *n.* Great courage.–The sailor received a medal for *valor* for saving his shipmates from drowning. – The fire chief said that Tom's *valor* in rescuing the baby deserved great praise.

val•u•a•ble (VAL-yə-bəl) *n. valuables.* Things of special worth.–The woman keeps her *valuables* locked in a safe.
–*adj.* 1. Worth much money.–A mink coat is *valuable.*
2. Of great worth or necessity.–These papers are *valuable* to the owner although they are worthless to the man who found them.

val•u•a•tion (val-yoo-AY-shən) *n. valuations.* The amount of money a thing is declared to be worth.–The farmer's *valuation* of his farm was eight thousand dollars.

val•ue (VAL-yoo) *n. values.* 1. Worth in money; price.–The *value* of the house is ten thousand dollars; but the owner must sell it quickly, so he will take eight thousand.
2. Worth.–Bob's friendship is of great *value* to Jack.
–*v. values, valued, valuing.* Appreciate; attach worth or value to.–Jack *values* Bob's friendship.

valve (VALV) *n. valves.* A device which controls the pressure or flow of air, gas, water, or other fluid. Some *valves* are operated by pressure within and some are operated by hand.–Water faucets are *valves.*

van (VAN) *n. vans.* 1. A covered truck usually used for carrying furniture.–It took a large *van* to move all the furniture the family had.

2. The leading group of an army or other body that is moving ahead.

van•dal (VAN-dl) *n. vandals.* A person who destroys or damages things of beauty or of value on purpose.–The *vandals* broke into the museum and ripped several paintings.

vane (VAYN) *n. vanes.* A device, often in the shape of an arrow, which shows the direction the wind is blowing.

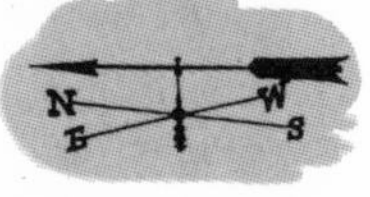

va•nil•la (və-NIL-ə) *n.* and *adj.* A flavoring extract made from the beans of the *vanilla* plant, which grows in warm places. – Mother flavored the candy with *vanilla.*

van•ish (VAN-ish) *v. vanishes, vanished, vanishing.* 1. Suddenly disappear.–The dog ran past us and *vanished* into the woods.
2. Disappear completely.–Mary learned to swim and her fear of the water *vanished.*

va•por (VAY-per) *n. vapors.* Moisture that can be seen.–Fog, mist, and steam are *vapors.*

var•ied (VAIR-eed) *adj.* Of different kinds.–Bob's collection of shells is *varied.* He has many kinds of shells.
–*v.* One form of the verb *vary.* – The sick child's condition hasn't *varied* during the night. His condition has not changed.

va•ri•e•ty (və-RY-ə-tee) *n. varieties.* 1. A wide selection of many different kinds.
2. A kind; a type.–The store has a new *variety* of cabbage for sale.

var•i•ous (VAIR-ee-əss) *adj.* 1. Several; different.–People from *various* countries took part in the program.
2. Varied; of different kinds. – There were *various* styles of dresses in the window.

var•si•ty (VAHR-sə-tee) *n. varsities.* An athletic team representing a university, college, school, etc., in any sport. The *varsity* is usually the first-string squad.

var•y (VAIR-ee) *v. varies, varied, varying.* 1. Change; make or become different.–The direction of the wind *varies* often.–The boy *varies* his handwriting so we won't know whose it is.
2. Be different. – The houses on this street *vary* in size, style, and color.

vase (VAYSS) *n. vases.* A vessel to put flowers in or to set on a table or mantel just for its beauty.

vast (VAST) *adj.; vastly, adv.; vastness, n.* Very large or great, especially covering much space.–A *vast* forest covers the mountains.

vat (VAT) *n. vats.* A tub, a barrel, or other large container for holding liquids.–The grocer keeps a *vat* of vinegar and a *vat* of pickles down in the cellar of his store.

Vat•i•can (VAT-ə-kən) *n.* 1. The palace of the Pope, head of the Roman Catholic Church. The *Vatican* includes a library, several museums, art galleries, and chapels, as well as St. Peter's Basilica and the living quarters of the Pope and his assistants. The *Vatican* is in Vatican City, a section of Rome. 2. The papal power; the authority of the Pope.–The *Vatican* has declared that all men should work toward peace and brotherhood.

vaude•ville (VOHD-vil *or* VAW-də-vil) *n.* A theatrical entertainment or variety show. *Vaudeville* usually features acts or performances that include comedy, songs, dances, and acrobatics.

vault (VAWLT) *n. vaults.* 1. A small room, usually of stone, for keeping the dead.
2. A strong room where things are safe and protected.

veal (VEEL) *n.* Calf meat.–*Veal* is often used for stew.

veg•e•ta•ble (VEJ-tə-bəl) *n. vegetables.* A plant that has parts which are used for food. –Spinach is a leafy *vegetable.* We eat the leaves.–Beans and peas are *vegetables.* We eat their pods or their seeds.–Carrots and beets are *vegetables.* We eat their roots.

veg•e•tar•i•an (vej-ə-TAIR-ee-ən) *n. vegetarians.* Someone who eats only vegetables or vegetable products; someone who does not eat meat. *Vegetarians* believe that human beings should not eat meat.

veg•e•ta•tion (vej-ə-TAY-shən) *n.* Plants, trees, and other growing things.–Where the soil is poor, there is little *vegetation.*

ve•hi•cle (VEE-ə-kəl) *n. vehicles.* A car, truck, bus, wagon, sleigh, or other means used for carrying persons and goods from place to place. *Vehicles* run on wheels or runners.

veil (VAYL) *n. veils.* A piece of very thin or fancy lacy material that you can see through. –Many hats have *veils* on them for trimming. –The bride's *veil* was very long and trailing. –*v. veils, veiled, veiling.* Cover or hide; put a veil over.–In some countries it is the custom for women to *veil* their faces in public.

vein (VAYN) *n. veins.* 1. One of the blood vessels in the body that carry the blood back to the heart.–Look at the under part of your wrist and you can see some of your *veins.*
2. Any line, crack, ridge, or long thin marking, as the *veins* in marble and in leaves, or a *vein* of mineral deposit in a rock.

ve•loc•i•ty (və-LAHSS-ə-tee) *n. velocities.* Speed, or how fast a thing travels.–The weather report says that the *velocity* of the wind today is twelve miles per hour.

vel•vet (VEL-vət) *n. velvets; velvety, adj.* A very soft cloth of silk, rayon, or cotton, with a thick, short nap.–*Velvet* dresses are beautiful.–Baby's skin is as soft as *velvet.*

ven•dor (VEN-der) *n. vendors.* A peddler; a man who sells things from a cart, wagon, or truck.–We bought a bag of peanuts from a peanut *vendor.*

ve•neer (və-NIR) *n. veneers.* 1. A thin layer of good wood laid over a cheaper wood.–This table has a walnut *veneer.*
2. Surface polish.–The boy had only a *veneer* of good manners. The boy behaved well at times, but if he forgot himself he was apt to be rude.

ven•er•ate (VEN-ə-rayt) *v. venerates, venerated, venerating.* Regard with reverence, admiration, or respect; hold in awe; worship.–The students *venerate* their old professor.–Many ancient peoples *venerated* idols.

venge•ance (VEN-jənss) *n.; vengeful, adj.* Punishment in return for injury; revenge. –The natives sought *vengeance* for the killing of their chief.
–*With a vengeance* means with unusual force, violence, or energy.–The hurricane winds were blowing *with a vengeance.*

ven•i•son (VEN-ə-zən) *n.* Deer meat. *Venison* tastes much like beefsteak, but it tastes stronger.–Robin Hood and his Merry Men ate *venison.*

ven•om (VEN-əm) *n.; venomous, adj.* 1. The poison of an animal such as a snake, scorpion, or spider.–Venomous animals inject their *venom* into their enemies by biting or stinging.
2. Spite; envy; general unfriendliness or ill will.–The jealous woman showed her *venom* by her cruel remarks.

vent (VENT) *n. vents.* An opening for letting something out.–Open the chimney *vent* or the room will fill up with smoke.
–*v. vents, vented, venting.* Give free expression to; discharge; let out.–The enraged man *vented* his anger by slamming the door.

ven•ti•late (VEN-tə-layt) *v. ventilates, ventilated, ventilating.* To change the air in an enclosed place by forcing the old, stale air out and letting fresh air in.–At home we *ventilate* the house by opening windows.–At school the rooms are *ventilated* by air pipes.

ven•tri•cle (VEN-trə-kəl) *n. ventricles.* Either of the two lower chambers of the heart. The right *ventricle* pumps used blood to the lungs to pick up a fresh supply of oxygen. The left *ventricle* pumps fresh blood to the arteries that supply the rest of the body.

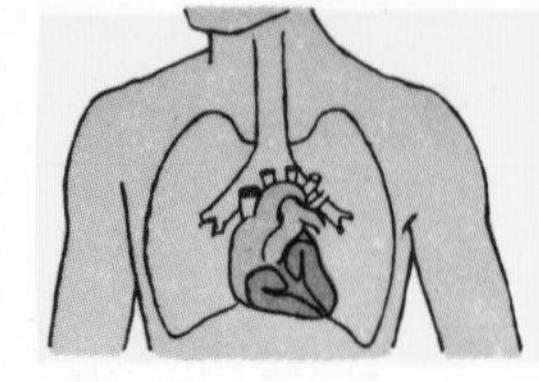

ven•tril•o•quist (ven-TRIL-ə-kwist) *n. ventriloquists.* A person who can speak so that his voice seems to be coming from some other person, animal, or thing.–The *ventriloquist* entertained the audience by carrying on a mock conversation with his wooden dummy.

ven•ture (VEN-cher) *n. ventures.* Something one sets out to do in which there is a danger of injury or loss.–Father's new business *venture* has been a success.
–*v. ventures, ventured, venturing.* 1. Dare; take a chance.–Jack *ventured* to say what he thought about the plan.–Mary did not *venture* a second request for spending money after Father said no.
2. Risk; put in danger.–The fireman *ventured* his life to save Joe from the burning house.

Ve•nus (VEE-nəss) *n.* 1. The ancient Roman goddess of spring, gardens, beauty, and love.
2. The second planet from the sun. *Venus* is the most brilliant of all the planets. At times it can be seen with the naked eye in the middle of the day.

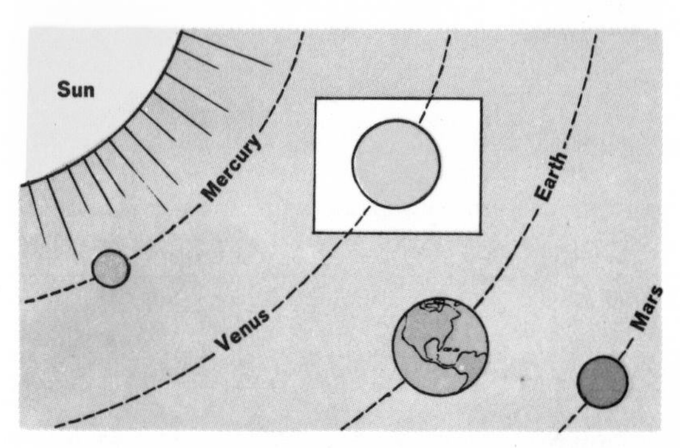

verb (VERB) *n. verbs.* A word that describes an action or a state of being.–The following words are *verbs:* sing, hear, do, ate, is, was.

ver•bal (VER-bəl) *adj.* 1. Dealing with words; in words.–The teacher asked for a *verbal* illustration. She did not want any pictures.
2. Expressed by word of mouth; spoken; oral.–He received *verbal* instructions. He was told what to do.

ver•dict (VER-dikt) *n. verdicts.* The decision of a jury after a trial in court.–The *verdict* of the jury in the murder case was "guilty." They decided that the man who was on trial was really the one who had done the killing.

verge (VERJ) *v. verges, verged, verging.* Have a tendency to; be on the border of.–The confusion was so great that the meeting *verged* on riot.

–*On the verge of* means on the edge of, or at the point after which something else will happen. – Mary was *on the verge of* tears after she found that her new dress was dirty.

ver•i•fy (VAIR-ə-fy) *v. verifies, verified, verifying.* Prove to be true; check the accuracy of.–Bill told his teacher that Tom had started the fight. Tom said Bill had started it. Tom's account was *verified* by two witnesses. Bill had lied.–Please *verify* the spelling of this word. Check to see whether it is spelled correctly.

ver•min (VER-mən) *n. sing.* and *pl.* Insect pests or other small animals that annoy, disgust, or bother people.–Flies, bugs, lice, mice, and rats are all *vermin.*

Ver•mont (ver-MAHNT) *n.* A dairying and vacation state in northeastern United States, particularly known for producing more maple sugar and maple syrup than any other state.

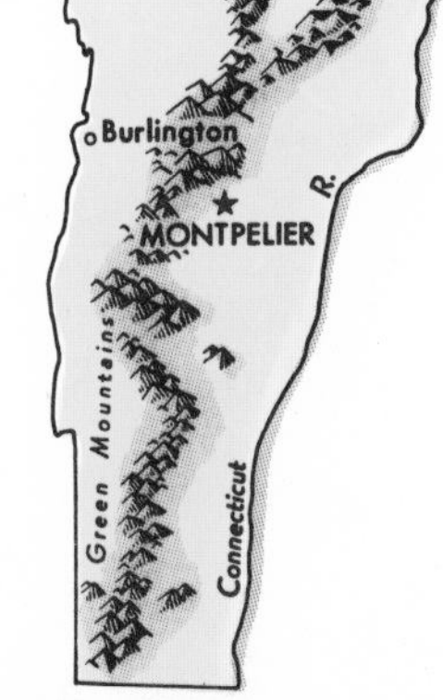

ver•sa•tile (VER-sə-tl) *adj.* Having many skills, abilities, or uses; capable of doing many things well. –Arthur is a *versatile* musician. He can play six different instruments well.–Father bought a *versatile* tool. It can be used as a hammer, screwdriver, file, and can opener.

verse (VERSS) *n. verses.* 1. A stanza; a group of lines that go together in a poem or song. –Do you know the second *verse* of "The Star-Spangled Banner"?

2. Poetry. – Robert Louis Stevenson wrote *verse* for children.

ver•sion (VER-zhən) *n. versions.* 1. A translation, especially of the Bible. – There are several *versions* of the Bible.

2. One side of a story, as related by two or more persons.–Tom's *version* of the argument is different from Bob's.

ver•sus (VER-səss) *prep.* Against (used especially in law and sports). – One of the world's great boxing matches was Joe Louis *versus* Max Schmeling.

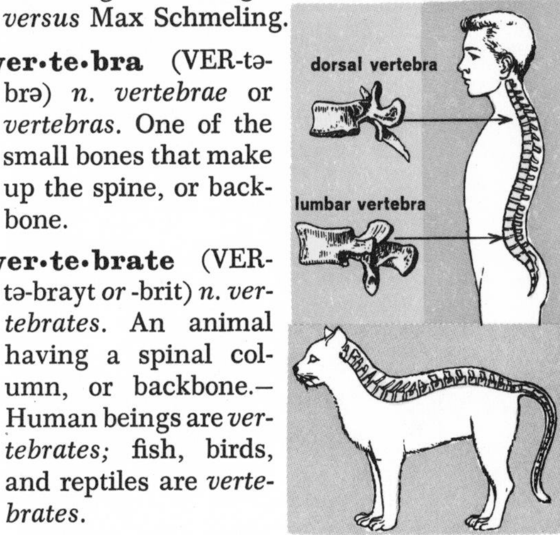

ver•te•bra (VER-tə-brə) *n. vertebrae* or *vertebras.* One of the small bones that make up the spine, or backbone.

ver•te•brate (VER-tə-brayt *or* -brit) *n. vertebrates.* An animal having a spinal column, or backbone.–Human beings are *vertebrates;* fish, birds, and reptiles are *vertebrates.*

ver•ti•cal (VER-tə-kəl) *adj.; vertically, adv.* Standing straight up and down; not leaning. –The flagpole stands in a *vertical* position.

ver•y (VAIR-ee) *adj.* and *adv.* 1. Extremely; exceedingly.–Mother is *very* kind to us.

2. Same. – The *very* day school started, I came down with the measles.

3. Mere.–The *very* idea of winter makes me shiver.

ves•pers (VESS-perz) *n. pl.* (Sometimes spelled with a capital "V.") Late afternoon or evening prayers; the religious service attending such prayers.–The church bell tolled for *Vespers.*

ves•sel (VESS-əl) *n. vessels.* 1. A pot, bowl, cup, dishpan, or anything that is hollow and will hold liquids or other substances.

2. A ship or boat; any craft that carries people on the water.

3. One of the tubes that carry the blood through one's body.

vest (VEST) *n. vests.* A short, sleeveless garment.–Men sometimes wear *vests* under their suit jackets.

ves•ti•bule (VESS-tə-byool) *n. vestibules.* A hall or passage between the outer door and the inside of a house, apartment, or building.–Mother left her umbrella in the *vestibule.*–There is a candy counter in the *vestibule* of the office building.

vest•ment (VEST-mənt) *n. vestments.* A robe or outer garment, especially one worn by a clergyman.–The bishop put on his *vestments* for the special service.

vet•er•an (VET-er-ən) *n. veterans.* 1. A person who has been in service in the army or the navy.

2. A person who has worked at the same kind of work for a long time.–The old actor is a *veteran* of the stage.

vet•er•i•nar•i•an (vet-rə-NAIR-ee-ən) *n. veterinarians; veterinary, adj.* A doctor who treats the diseases of dogs, cats, horses, cows, and other animals.–When Jack's dog was sick, Jack took him to a *veterinarian.*

ve•to (VEE-toh) *v. vetoes, vetoed, vetoing.* 1. When a President of the United States refuses to sign a congressional bill, he *vetoes* it. A bill which has been *vetoed* by the President can only become a law if two-thirds of the members of both Houses of Congress vote for it.

2. Refuse to approve; not give consent to. –When it started to rain, Mother *vetoed* our plans for a picnic.

3. Vote down.–Any of the five permanent member nations of the United Nations Security Council can *veto* a motion by voting against it. Any negative vote from one of these nations kills a motion.

vex (VEKS) *v. vexes, vexed, vexing.* Make angry; annoy.–The boys' jokes *vexed* their football coach.

vi•a (VY-ə) *prep.* By way of; by a route going through.–The letter was sent *via* air mail.–He went to Mexico *via* Texas. He passed through Texas in order to get to Mexico.

vi•a•duct (VY-ə-dukt) *n. viaducts.* A bridge over a road, a part of a city, a low place, etc. A *viaduct* is built to carry trains, trucks, or automobiles. *Viaducts* improve the safety and speed of transportation.

vi•al (VY-əl) *n. vials.* A small bottle or container, usually of glass. Medicines, chemicals, and perfumes are some of the things kept in *vials.*

vi•brate (VY-brayt) *v. vibrates, vibrated, vibrating.* Shake rapidly; swing or move quickly back and forth.–The strings of musical instruments *vibrate* and give off tones. –*vibration, n. vibrations.*

vice (VYSS) *n. vices.* An evil or bad habit.–Envy and pride are traditionally considered *vices.*

vice-pres•i•dent (vys-PREZ-ə-dənt) *n. vice-presidents.* The official whose rank is second to or just below that of the president.–The *vice-president* substitutes for the president when necessary, taking over his duties and responsibilities.

vi•ce ver•sa (VY-sə VER-sə). Just the reverse.–Jack likes to play tricks on Mary, and *vice versa.* Mary likes to tease Jack, too.

vi•cin•i•ty (vi-SIN-ə-tee) *n. vicinities.* A neighborhood; a section near or around a place.–Mr. Jones lives in the *vicinity* of the school. He lives near the school.

vi•cious (VISH-əss) *adj.; viciously, adv.; viciousness, n.* Savage; mean; spiteful. – The keeper fed the *vicious* tiger through the bars of his cage. The keeper wouldn't go into the cage for fear of being bitten.

vic•tim (VIK-tim) *n. victims.* A person or animal killed or harmed by a happening.–The *victims* of the hotel fire were removed to a hospital.–Jack the Ripper killed his *victims* with a knife.

vic•tor (VIK-ter) *n. victors.* A winner.–We were the *victors* in the football game.–The *victors* in war are the ones who conquer.

vic•to•ri•ous (vik-TOR-ee-əss) *adj.; victoriously, adv.* Winning; conquering.—Our side was *victorious*. We defeated the other team.

vic•to•ry (VIK-tə-ree) *n. victories*. A success. —Our *victory* in this game made us the champions of the league.

vid•e•o (VID-ee-oh) *adj.* Having to do with television, especially the receiving or sending of an image.—The actors are rehearsing for a *video* performance. They are going to do a television show.

view (VYOO) *n. views*. 1. A scene; that which is seen.—The *view* from the mountaintop was beautiful.
2. A thought; an idea; an opinion.—Father spoke his *views* on the election. — Father asked Mother for her *view* on the color he had chosen to paint the kitchen.
3. Sight.—The airplane soon came into *view*.
—*v. views, viewed, viewing*. 1. Think about; consider.—The doctor *viewed* Mary's illness with alarm. He was worried about it.
2. Look at.—We *viewed* the race from the bridge.

view•point (VYOO-point) *n. viewpoints*. 1. A spot from which a person views something. — He could see the entire valley from his *viewpoint* on top of the mountain.
2. A point of view or attitude; the way a person feels about something.—Your *viewpoint* on certain things may differ from mine, but that does not mean we can't be friends.

vig•il (VIJ-əl) *n. vigils*. 1. The act of staying awake, especially during the hours for sleep; a night watch; a watching at any special time. — The sentry kept a careful *vigil* all through the night.—The doctor's *vigil* was a difficult one. He had to stay awake and give careful attention to his patient all through the night.
2. (Usually plural) An evening church service, especially on the night before a religious festival.—Are you going to take part in the *vigils* on Christmas Eve?

vig•or (VIG-er) *n.* Strength and great energy. —After eating and resting, the man worked with more *vigor*.

vig•or•ous (VIG-er-əss) *adj.; vigorously, adv.* Strong and energetic. — Rest, exercise, and healthful food kept the players *vigorous*.

vi•king (VY-king) *n. vikings*. (Sometimes spelled with a capital "V.") One of the pirates, or sea robbers, who sailed the seas and raided the coasts of Europe during the eighth, ninth, and tenth centuries. The *vikings* came from Scandinavia.

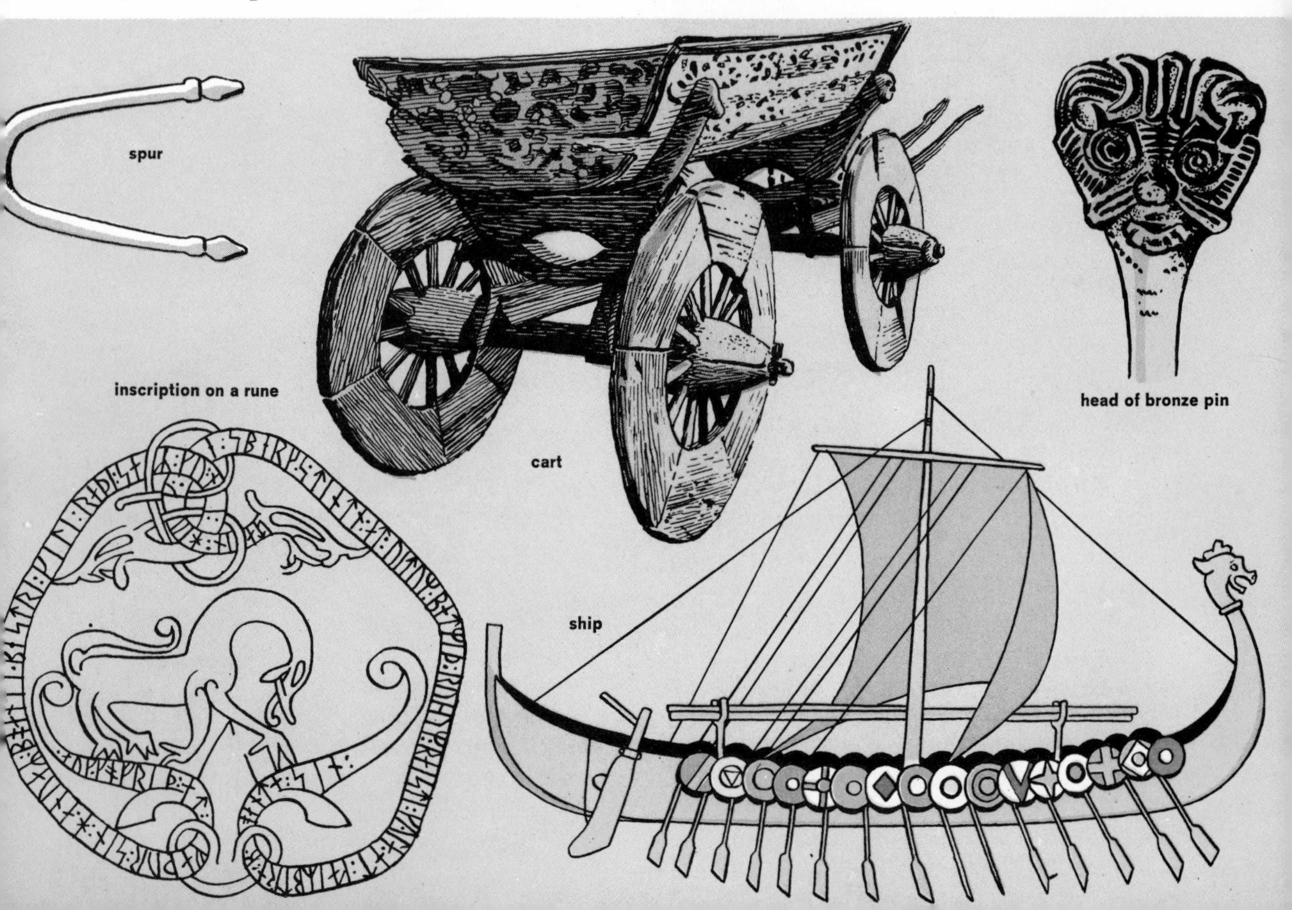

vile (VY-əl) *adj. viler, vilest.* Bad; very bad; wicked.–What a *vile* smell!–He was a *vile* man; nothing seemed to be too evil for him to do or say.

vil•lage (VIL-ij) *n. villages.* 1. A place smaller than a town, where a few people live in dwellings that are close together.
2. The people in a village.–The whole *village* came to put out the fire.

vil•lain (VIL-ən) *n. villains.* A wicked person.–Who took the part of the *villain* in the Western movie you saw?

vine (VYN) *n. vines.* A plant that climbs, or crawls on the ground.–Cucumber *vines* crawl. – Morning-glory *vines* climb.

vin•e•gar (VIN-ə-ger) *n.* A sour liquid used in salads, pickles, etc.–Cider that stands a long time turns into *vinegar.*

vine•yard (VIN-yerd) *n. vineyards.* A place where grapes are grown; a grape plantation. –France is famous all over the world for its fine *vineyards.*

vi•o•la (vee- *or* vy-OH-lə) *n. violas.* A musical instrument that looks like a violin, but is somewhat larger. The *viola* has a deeper, lower tone than the violin.

vi•o•late (VY-ə-layt) *v. violates, violated, violating.* Break (rules or laws).–Children who *violate* the rules of the school may be punished.–Citizens who *violate* the laws of the city may be put into jail.
–violation, n. violations.

vi•o•lence (VY-ə-lənss) *n.* Strength; force; roughness.–The storm struck with great *violence;* it hurt many people and did much damage.

vi•o•lent (VY-ə-lənt) *adj.; violently, adv.* Strong; intense; rough. – A *violent* storm lashed the shore and did much damage. – Jack has a *violent* temper.

vi•o•let (VY-ə-lit) *n. violets.* 1. A tiny purple, blue, white, or sometimes yellow flower which blooms in the spring.–We gathered *violets* near the brook.
2. Purplish-blue.

vi•o•lin (vy-ə-LIN) *n. violins.* A musical instrument with strings. The *violin* is played with a bow. It is the highest-pitched stringed instrument.

vi•o•lin•ist (vy-ə-LIN-ist) *n. violinists.* A person who plays the violin.

Vir•gin (VER-jin) *n.* Mary, the Mother of Jesus Christ.

vir•gin (VER-jin) *adj.* 1. Pure; spotless.–The hill was covered with *virgin* snow. There were no footprints or marks on it.
2. Not used, touched, or disturbed by man. –The hunter didn't hear or see any sign of another human being in the *virgin* forest.

Vir•gin•ia (ver-JIN-yə) *n.* A forest-covered, mountainous state on the east coast of the United States, important for its farm, dairy,

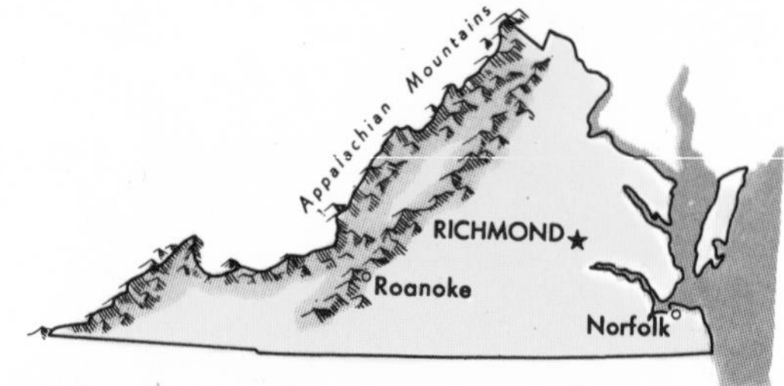

and lumber products, its minerals, and various kinds of building stone. Beautiful natural caverns are found in *Virginia.*

vir•tue (VER-choo) *n. virtues; virtuous, adj.* Goodness; a good quality.–Honesty is a *virtue.* It is a quality one must have to be good.

vi•rus (VY-rəss) *n. viruses.* One of the agents that cause various diseases such as measles, colds, and smallpox. *Viruses* are very tiny and can be seen only with special microscopes.

vise (VYSS) *n. vises.* A clamp used for holding a piece of material while one works on it. It can be opened and closed by means of a screw.–Bob put the wood in the *vise.*

vis•i•bil•i•ty (viz-ə-BIL-ə-tee) *n. visibilities.* 1. Range of vision.–There was so much fog that *visibility* was poor.
2. The clearness with which an object can be seen.–Because of the fog, ground *visibility* was poor. It was hard to see the ground.

vis•i•ble (VIZ-ə-bəl) *adj.* Able to be seen.–The airplane flew so high that it was not *visible* from the ground. It could not be seen from the ground.

vi•sion (VIZH-ən) *n. visions.* 1. The ability to see; eyesight.–The girl's *vision* is poor. She doesn't see well.
2. Anything that is seen in the imagination or in a dream.–The woman had a *vision* of her son, whom she had not seen for years.

vis•it (VIZ-it) *n. visits.* A call; a period of staying as a guest.–We made a short *visit* to our great-grandmother's house.
–*v. visits, visited, visiting.* Go or come to see; be a guest.–Grandma *visited* us. She came to see us and stayed with us awhile. She was our guest.

vis•i•tor (VIZ-it-er) *n. visitors.* A person who comes for a visit; a guest.–Grandmother was a *visitor* at our house.

vi•sor (VY-zer) *n. visors.* The part of a cap that sticks out in front. –The *visor* on the ball player's cap kept the sun out of his eyes.

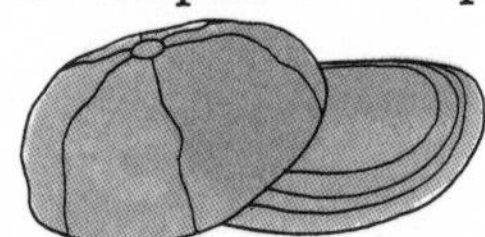

vis•u•al (VIZH-uh-əl) *adj.; visually, adv.* Having to do with seeing or sight.–We learn much through *visual* aids, through things that can be seen.

vis•u•al•ize (VIZH-uh-ə-lyz) *v. visualizes, visualized, visualizing.* Picture in one's mind. –It is hard to *visualize* something that one has never seen, no matter how well it has been described.

vi•tal (VY-tl) *adj.; vitally, adv.* 1. So important that life depends on it.–Food and rest are *vital* to life.
2. Of great importance.

vi•ta•min (VY-tə-min) *n. vitamins.* Any of certain substances found in foods that are needed to make us well and strong. Different kinds of foods contain different kinds of *vitamins. Vitamins* are named after the letters of the alphabet, as *vitamin* A, B, etc.

vi•va•cious (vy-VAY-shəss) *adj.; vivaciously, adv.* Lively; gay; lighthearted; spirited.–Alice is a *vivacious* girl. She is usually the life of the party.

viv•id (VIV-id) *adj.; vividly, adv.; vividness, n.* 1. Bright; clear.–Mary's dress is a *vivid* blue.
2. Clear; plain.–I have a *vivid* picture in my mind of the hat that I want to buy.

vo•cab•u•lar•y (voh-KAB-yə-lair-ee) *n. vocabularies.* 1. The words that a person knows and uses in writing and speaking.–Our teacher has a large *vocabulary.*–Using a dictionary will help you increase the number of words in your *vocabulary.*
2. A list of words and their meanings, arranged alphabetically, or according to the abc's.

vo•cal (VOH-kəl) *adj.; vocally, adv.* Having to do with the voice; expressed with the voice. –*Vocal* organs are the parts of the mouth and throat that we use in talking. The tongue, lips, and *vocal* cords are some of the *vocal* organs.

vo•ca•tion (voh-KAY-shən) *n. vocations.* Trade or work; the kind of work one does for a living.–A doctor's *vocation* is curing or healing sick people.–A mechanic's *vocation* is working with machines.–A teacher's *vocation* is teaching.

voice (VOISS) *n. voices.* The sound made by the speech organs (mouth, tongue, throat), as in speaking or singing.–The boy's *voice* was loud and clear. He spoke well.
–*v. voices, voiced, voicing.* Speak; express by saying aloud.–The man *voiced* the reasons he had for voting against the mayor.

void (VOID) *n. voids.* 1. Empty space. – John watched the rocket roar into the *void.* He watched it speed into empty space and disappear from view.
2. A feeling of emptiness due to a loss. – There was a *void* in Tim's life when his dog was lost.
–*v. voids, voided, voiding.* 1. Make something lose its effectiveness. – Our club members voted to *void* the old constitution and pass the new one.
2. Empty; get rid of.–To understand my new idea, you must *void* your mind of all prejudice.
–*adj.* 1. Lacking; empty; being without. – Jim's statement seems to be *void* of meaning. He doesn't seem to have said anything. –Bill's story was *void* of truth. It didn't have a word of truth in it.
2. Having no legal force. – The Supreme Court declared the law unconstitutional. They declared it *void.*

VOLCANO

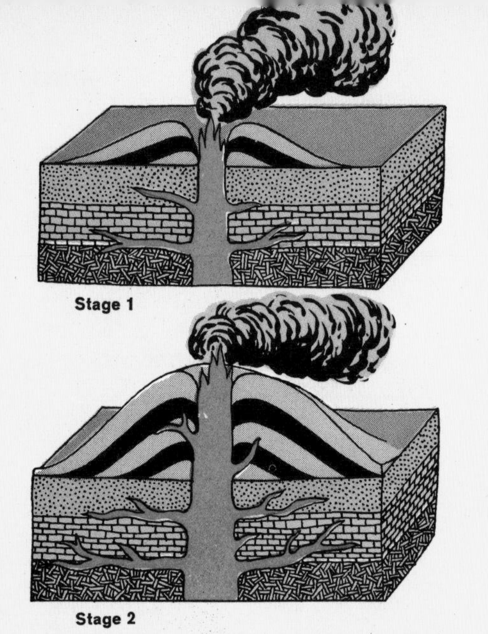

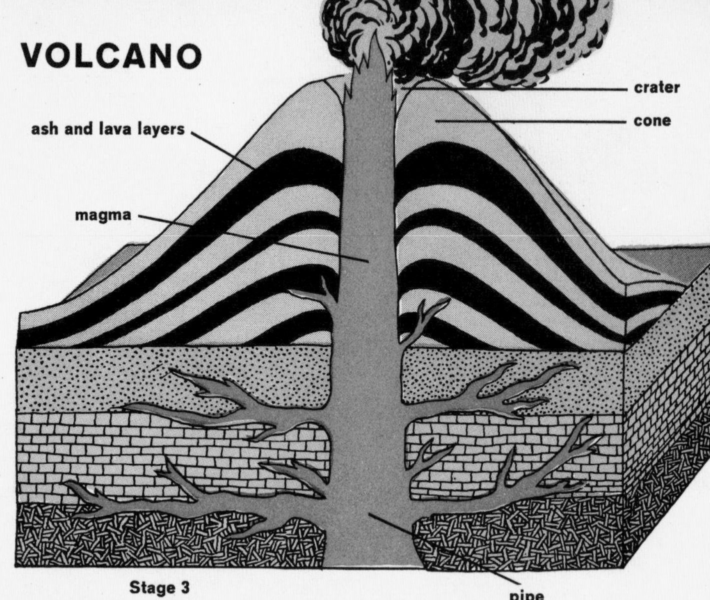

vol•ca•no (vahl-KAY-noh) *n. volcanoes.* A hole in the earth's crust through which lava and gases are thrown out in occasional eruptions. The material thrown out usually builds up into a large cone with a crater in the top.

volt (VOHLT) *n. volts.* A measuring unit that tells you how much force is being used to produce an electric current.

volt•age (VOHL-tij) *n.* Electric power or force, measured in volts.–The radio station has a transmitter of very high *voltage* for broadcasting signals over great distances.

vol•ume (VAHL-yəm) *n. volumes.* 1. A book. –This bookcase holds many *volumes.*
2. One book in a set of books.–Some books are so long that they are printed in several *volumes.*
3. Amount of space occupied; size in cubic inches, feet, etc.–What is the *volume* of this box? How much space does it take up?

vol•un•tar•y (VAHL-ən-tair-ee) *adj.; voluntarily, adv.* Done of one's own choice.–The work Mary did was *voluntary.* No one forced her or asked her to do it. She offered to do it.

vol•un•teer (vahl-ən-TIR) *n. volunteers.* A person who offers to do some task or service. –In small towns the fire department is made up of *volunteers.*
–*v. volunteers, volunteered, volunteering.* Offer to do something; offer one's services without being asked or told to do so.–The man *volunteered* to help put out the fire. – Men *volunteer* to serve as paratroopers.

vote (VOHT) *n. votes.* An expression of one's choice by a method decided on beforehand. Each hand raised or each piece of paper showing what or whom you choose is a *vote.*
–*v. votes, voted, voting.* Express one's choice by a method decided on beforehand, such as raising the hand or writing on a paper called a ballot what you want or whom you choose for an office.–The children who wanted Jack for their captain *voted* for him by raising their hands.

vot•er (VOH-ter) *n. voters.* A person who votes or has the right by law to vote.–Mother and Father are *voters;* their names are registered on a list of people who have the right to vote.

vow (VOW) *n. vows.* A promise.–Mary made a *vow* to study more.
–*v. vows, vowed, vowing.* Make a promise. – Mary *vowed* to Mother and Father that she would study more.

vow•el (VOW-əl) *n. vowels.* The letters a, e, i, o, u, and sometimes y are *vowels.*

voy•age (VOI-ij) *n. voyages.* A trip or journey by sea or over water.–The *voyage* took us across the Atlantic Ocean.
–*v. voyages, voyaged, voyaging.* Travel over water; make a voyage.–We *voyaged* across the Atlantic Ocean.

vul•gar (VUL-ger) *adj.; vulgarly, adv.* Coarse; not nice.–The boy's language is *vulgar.*–*Vulgar* language offends or hurts the feelings of people who have tact and good manners.

vul•ture (VUL-cher) *n. vultures.* A large bird that feeds on dead animals.

W w

W, w (DUB-əl-yoo *or* -yuh) *n. W's, w's.* The twenty-third letter of the alphabet.

wad (WAHD) *n. wads.* A small amount of any material squeezed together to make a lump or mass, as paper squeezed into a small ball, or paper *wad.*
–*v. wads, wadded, wadding.* Crumple or squeeze into a wad or lump.–The boy *wadded* his paper and put it into the wastebasket.

wad•dle (WAHD-l) *v. waddles, waddled, waddling.* Walk with short steps and swing from side to side.–Ducks *waddle.*

wade (WAYD) *v. wades, waded, wading.* 1. Walk along in water.–Children like to *wade* in the pond.
2. Struggle ahead.–We *waded* through the work in spite of many interruptions.
3. Cross; walk through (a body of water).–The horses *waded* the river.

waf•fle (WAHF-əl) *n. waffles* and *adj.* A cake cooked on a special iron (*waffle* iron) that marks it into small squares. *Waffles* are made of a batter containing eggs, flour, baking powder, and milk.

wag (WAG) *n. wags.* A swinging motion. – The dog answered Bob's question with a *wag* of his tail.
–*v. wags, wagged, wagging.* Move or swing from side to side.–The dog *wags* his tail to show that he is happy or friendly.

wage (WAYJ) *n. wages.* Pay; money given for work done, especially if reckoned by the hour.–The boy works for a *wage.* He works for fifty cents an hour.
–*v. wages, waged, waging.* Carry on (war).–The people *waged* war against the rats.

wa•ger (WAY-jer) *n. wagers.* A bet.–Many people make *wagers* on horse races. They bet money that a certain horse will win a race. If the horse they choose wins, they get back more money than they put up. If it does not win, they lose their money.
–*v. wagers, wagered, wagering.* Bet; make a wager.–In some states it is against the law to *wager* on horse races.

wag•on (WAG-ən) *n. wagons.* 1. A horse-drawn vehicle used to carry loads, such as an ice *wagon* or a vegetable *wagon.*

2. A toy vehicle drawn by hand or used for coasting.–Jimmy has a new red *wagon.*

waif (WAYF) *n. waifs.* 1. A lost, homeless person, especially a child.–The woman took the poor, hungry *waif* home and fed him.
2. A stray animal.–The shepherd found the lost sheep and brought the *waif* back.

wail (WAYL) *n. wails.* 1. A loud cry of pain or grief.–The dog gave out a *wail* when he was locked out of the house.
2. A mournful sound.–We heard the *wail* of the wind in the night.
–*v. wails, wailed, wailing.* 1. Cry loudly from pain or grief. – We could hear the woman *wailing* because her child was lost.
2. Make a sad sound.–The cold wind *wailed* in the night.

waist (WAYST) *n. waists.* 1. The middle part of the body, between the hips and the ribs.–A belt is worn around the *waist.*
2. The part of a garment that goes around the waist.–Mother took in the *waist* of her dress.
3. A woman's garment that covers the upper part of the body; a blouse.–A *waist* is worn with a suit or skirt. It covers the body from the hips or the *waist*line to the neck.

wait (WAYT) *n.* The act of staying until something happens; the time spent while being ready for something to happen. – The train was late, so we had a long *wait.*
–*v. waits, waited, waiting.* 1. Stay until some event happens.–You can see Mother if you *wait* for her. She is not here now.
2. Put off; delay.–I'm going to be late. Do not *wait* dinner for me. Do not put off serving dinner until the time that I arrive.
–*Wait on* means to serve.–A kind lady *waited on* us in the store. She sold us some candy.

wait•er (WAY-ter) *n. waiters.* A man who serves food at a table.–The *waiter* at the restaurant served William an extra dish of ice cream for dessert.

wait•ress (WAY-trəss) *n. waitresses.* A woman who serves food at a table.–The *waitress* at the hotel brought me a clean napkin.

waive (WAYV) *v. waives, waived, waiving.* Set aside for the time being; give up freely, as a right to something.–The lawyer *waived* his right to question the witness at that time. He decided to question him later.

wake (WAYK) *v. wakes, waked* or *woke, waking.* 1. Rouse or become roused from sleep; stop sleeping.–I *wake* when the alarm clock rings. The alarm *wakes* me.
2. Stir; begin activity. – The flowers and trees *wake* in early spring. They show signs of life and begin to grow.
3. Become alert; show interest.–The girls *woke* up when the comedy picture was shown.

wake•ful (WAYK-fuhl) *adj.* Sleepless. – Mother had a *wakeful* night. She could not sleep.

wak•en (WAYK-ən) *v. wakens, wakened, wakening.* 1. Wake; rouse out of sleep. – I *waken* when the alarm clock rings. The alarm clock *wakens* me.
2. Stir; begin activity.–The flowers *waken* in the spring.

walk (WAWK) *n. walks.* A trip on foot.–We went for a *walk* in the woods. We didn't ride; we went by foot.
–*v. walks, walked, walking.* 1. Go forward on foot, more slowly than in running.–Do not *walk* on the grass. Do not step on it.
2. Take for a walk.–Bob *walked* the dog around the block. He took him slowly around the block.

walk•ie-talk•ie (WAW-kee-TAW-kee) *n. walkie-talkies.* A radio set capable of sending and receiving messages, yet small enough to be carried about. *Walkie-talkies* were first used by soldiers in World War II.

wall (WAWL) *n. walls.* 1. One of the sides of a room or a building.–Pictures hang on the *walls* of the living room.–*Walls* separate the rooms in a house.
2. A fence built of solid material, such as stone or brick.–Many ancient cities had stone *walls* built around them.

wall•board (WAWL-bord) *n. wallboards.* An artificial board made of cane or wood fiber, or pressed wood shavings or sawdust. *Wallboard* comes in large sheets. It is used instead of wood, plaster, or other materials for such things as walls, closets, and panels.

wal•let (WAHL-ət) *n. wallets.* A leather case, which folds shut like a book, for carrying paper money and personal papers. – Father keeps a picture of his family in his *wallet.*

wal•lop (WAHL-əp) *v. wallops, walloped, walloping.* Hit hard; beat.–The little boy *walloped* the bully. He hit him very hard.

wal•low (WAHL-oh) *v. wallows, wallowed, wallowing.* Roll or wade in.–Pigs *wallow* in mud and water.

wal•nut (WAWL-nut) *n. walnuts* and *adj.* 1. A large nut, good to eat, with a very rough shell.–English *walnuts* are more easily cracked than black *walnuts.*
2. The tree on which walnuts grow.
3. The dark wood or lumber of the walnut tree.–Father's desk and chair are made of *walnut.*

wal•rus (WAWL- *or* WAHL-rəss) *n. walruses.* A large sea animal with tusks. The *walrus* is found in the cold North. Its skin is used for leather.

waltz (WAWLTSS) *n. waltzes.* 1. A kind of ballroom dance with a smooth, regular rhythm.–In the old-fashioned *waltzes,* the dancing couples whirled round and round very swiftly.
2. A piece of music written in three-quarter time, or having three beats to a measure.
–*v. waltzes, waltzed, waltzing.* Dance a waltz.
–Mother and Father like to *waltz.*

wam•pum (WAHM- *or* WAWM-pəm) *n.* Beads once used for money and ornament by the Indians of North America. *Wampum* was made of shells of dark purple or white. Dark beads were worth much more than white beads.

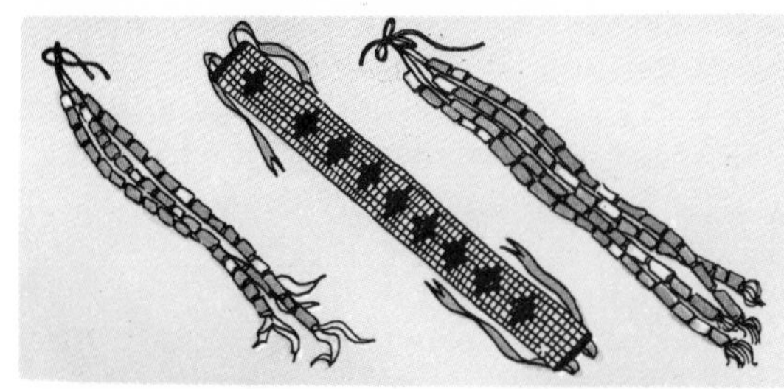

wand (WAHND) *n. wands.* A thin stick to hold in one's hand. – The fairy waved her magic *wand* and the six gray rats became six fine gray horses.

wan•der (WAHN-der) *v. wanders, wandered, wandering.* Roam; ramble; stray.–The children *wandered* through the woods. They went here and there for no special reason.

want (WAHNT) *n. wants.* A need; a thing one has to have.–The child's *wants* are few.
–*v. wants, wanted, wanting.* Desire or wish for.–Susan *wants* a doll with red hair.
–*In want* means to have a need for food, money, clothing, and other necessary things. –That family has always been *in want.* They have always been very poor.

war (WOR) *n. wars.* 1. Fighting over a period of time between two or more countries, or between parts of one country. *War* is carried on with guns, tanks, bomber planes, and other terrible weapons.
2. A planned fight.–Our teacher urged us all to join the *war* on heart disease by giving money.

war•ble (WOR-bəl) *n. warbles.* A trilling song.–We heard the *warble* of the canary.
–*v. warbles, warbled, warbling.* Sing a trilling song.–The birds *warbled* early each morning.

war•bler (WOR-bler) *n. warblers.* 1. A songbird.–Our canary is a *warbler.*
2. A singer.–Father calls Mary the *warbler* of the family, because she sings so much.

ward (WORD) *n. wards.* 1. A person left in the care of another person, or of a court.–The orphaned boy is the *ward* of his uncle; his uncle acts as his father.
2. A part of a hospital for certain kinds of patients. – People in a hospital who have catching diseases, such as measles, scarlet fever, or smallpox, are kept in a special *ward* by themselves.
3. A hospital room with beds for many patients.–When Father was in the hospital, he was in a *ward* until there was a private room for him.
4. One of several parts into which a city is divided.–People living in a certain *ward* vote in that *ward.*
–*v. wards, warded, warding.* Prevent; push (off).–He tried to *ward* off the blow with his arm, but he was too slow.–Grandmother is staying in the house today to *ward* off a cold.

ward•en (WOR-dn) *n. wardens.* A chief guard. – A prison *warden* is a person who guards or watches over a prison.–A fire *warden* is a person who sees that fire laws are obeyed.–A *warden* in a college takes care of rules about where the students live, what time they must come in at night, and the like.

ward•robe (WORD-rohb) *n. wardrobes.* 1. A piece of furniture with shelves and hooks for holding clothes.
2. All the clothes one has, or a whole outfit for a particular season or time.–Have you bought your winter *wardrobe* yet?–Mary's *wardrobe* is made up of dresses, sweaters, skirts, shoes, and other articles of clothing.

ware (WAIR) *n. wares.* 1. (In the plural) Goods; things for sale.–Simple Simon asked the Pieman if he might taste his *wares.*
2. Utensils, such as silver*ware,* kitchen*ware,* hard*ware,* copper*ware,* and tin*ware.*

ware•house (WAIR-howss) *n. warehouses.* A building or place for storing goods, machinery, and the like to be sold or used at some later date; a storehouse.–The firm's *warehouse* is located near the railroad yards.

war•fare (WOR-fair) *n.* War; conflict; fighting.–All nations must work together to end all *warfare.*

warm (WORM) *adj. warmer, warmest.* 1. Heated; somewhat hot; not cold.–Winter is cold. Spring is *warm.* Summer is *warmer.*
2. Able to keep or make somewhat hot.–We wear *warm* clothes in cold weather.
3. Hearty; cordial; glad.–Father received a *warm* welcome when he got home. We showed him that we were happy to see him.
4. Close; nearly right. – Tom hid the pen under the table. When Sue started to look under the chair for it, he said she was *warm.*
–*v. warms, warmed, warming.* Heat; make warm.–A fire *warms* a room by heating the air.–*Warm* your hands by holding them near the fire.

warm-blood•ed (WORM-BLUD-əd) *adj.* 1. Having warm blood, as mammals and birds. –Man, dogs, cats, pigeons, and many other animals are *warm-blooded.*
2. Warm in spirit or feeling.–The returning travelers are looking forward to a *warm-blooded* reception from their friends and relatives.

warmth (WORMTH) *n.* Moderate heat.–The *warmth* of the sun felt good on my face.

warn (WORN) *v. warns, warned, warning.* Tell ahead of time about some danger or unpleasant happening. – The boy *warned* the trainmen of a bridge that had been washed away.–Mother *warned* the children not to play with fire.–A dark cloud *warned* us of a storm.

warp (WORP) *n.* The lengthwise threads in cloth. The threads that go from side to side are called the woof.
–*v. warps, warped, warping.* Twist or curve out of shape. – The heat from the radiator *warped* the book that had been left on it.– We could not close the dresser drawer that had been *warped.*

war•rant (WOR- *or* WAHR-ənt) *n. warrants.* 1. A written order that gives one the right to do something.–The policeman had a *warrant* to arrest the man.
2. An excuse; a right; a fair cause.–You have no *warrant* to say such a thing.
–*v. warrants, warranted, warranting.* Justify. –Mary often gets more excited than the cause *warrants.* – The emergency *warranted* a change in the school rules.

war•ri•or (WOR- *or* WAHR-ee-er) *n. warriors.* A man who goes to war and fights.– Soldiers are *warriors.*

war•ship (WOR-ship) *n. warships.* A ship used for fighting in wartime.

was (WAHZ *or* wəz) *v.* One form of the verb *be. Was* is used with other words to help tell of something that has already happened.–I *was* sleepy last night, but I am wide awake today.–Jack *was* hungry before he ate; now he is not.–Rain *was* falling when I left for school, but it isn't now.

wash (WAHSH *or* WAWSH) *n.* A pile of things to be laundered.–Mother had a big *wash* today. There were many clothes to be cleaned.
–*v. washes, washed, washing.* 1. Clean by the use of water or some other fluid.–We *wash* our hands before we eat.–We *washed* our windows and floors today.
2. Carry; sweep. – The hard rain *washed* away the sand on the side of the hill.

wash•board (WAHSH- *or* WAWSH-bord) *n. washboards.* A piece of metal or glass, with ridges on it, in a frame. Clothes being washed are often rubbed on a *washboard* to loosen the dirt.

wash•er (WAHSH- *or* WAWSH-er) *n. washers.* 1. A washing machine.
2. A flat piece of metal, rubber, or other material with a hole in it used at the joints of pipes, hoses, etc., to make them tight and prevent leaking. *Washers* are also used to make nuts and bolts tight. – Father put a *washer* between the hose and the spray to keep the water from spurting out.

Wash•ing•ton (WAHSH- *or* WAWSH-ing-tən) *n.* 1. The first president of the United States, George *Washington.*
2. *Washington,* D. C.– The capital city of the United States, where the Federal Government is, and where the President lives.
3. A state on the west coast of the United States, the greatest lumbering and apple-growing state in the country. Grand Coulee Dam is in *Washington.*

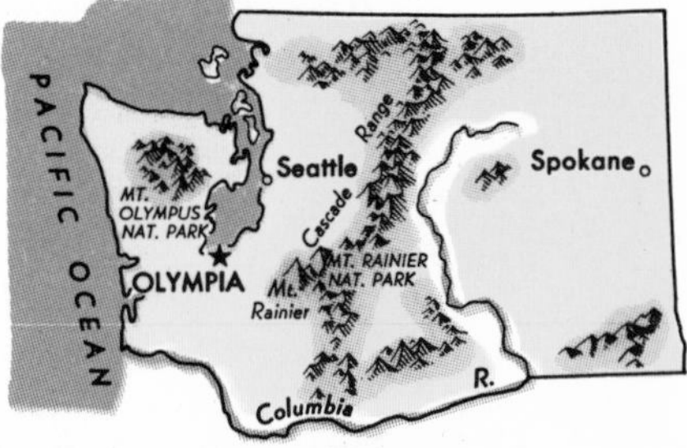

was•n't (WAHZ- *or* WUZ-ənt). Was not.– There *wasn't* an apple left after Jack and Bob found where they were.

wasp (WAHSP *or* WAWSP) *n. wasps.* A slim-bodied insect, something like a bee, that can sting sharply.

waste (WAYST) *n. wastes.* Any material that is left over and cannot be used.—Mother says there is a lot of *waste* on the roast; it has much fat and bone, which cannot be eaten.
—*v. wastes, wasted, wasting.* Not use, or use badly.—Do not *waste* your paper. Use up all of it, and do not take more than you need. Do not throw away anything that can be used again.
—*adj.* Useless; of no value; thrown away after being used.—We throw *waste*paper into the *waste*paper basket.

waste•ful (WAYST-fuhl) *adj.; wastefully, adv.* 1. Causing waste.—The old machines are *wasteful.* The new ones produce twice as much in the same time.
2. Extravagant; spending carelessly. – The rich young man is spoiled and *wasteful.*

watch (WAHCH) *n. watches.* 1. A small clock worn on a strap around the wrist, or in the pocket on a chain. We tell time by a *watch.*
2. A guard.—The Boy Scouts left a *watch* at the camp. He looked after the camp.
3. A turn to stand guard.—From eight o'clock until twelve was Bob's *watch.* He was supposed to stand guard at the camp during those hours.
—*v. watches, watched, watching.* 1. Look at.—We *watched* the circus parade going by.—Susan likes to *watch* Father shave.
2. Mind; care for.—Mary *watched* the baby all day.—Shepherds *watch* their sheep.
3. Look or wait for. – The cat *watched* the house all day for a chance to sneak in through the back door. – The baseball batter was *watching* for a slow pitch so that he could try to hit a home run.
—*Be on the watch for* means to look out for, or be on guard against.—The sailors on the Spanish Main were told to *be on the watch for* pirate ships.

watch•man (WAHCH-mən) *n. watchmen.* A man whose duty it is to watch or guard something.—A *watchman* at a railroad crossing watches for trains, and warns people when one is coming.

wa•ter (WAW-ter *or* WAHT-er) *n. waters.* The liquid that fills the oceans, seas, lakes, rivers, etc.—Rain is *water.*—We drink pure *water.*—We swim in *water.*—Tears are salty *water.*
—*v. waters, watered, watering.* Put water on. —Mary *watered* the flowers so that they would grow.

wa•ter col•or (WAW-ter *or* WAHT-er KUL-er) *water colors.* 1. Paint made for mixing with water.—We paint some pictures with oil paint, or paint mixed with oil, and some pictures with *water colors.*
2. A picture painted in water colors.—Bob likes to paint *water colors* of oldtime sailing ships at sea.

wa•ter•fall (WAW-ter-fawl *or* WAHT-er-fawl) *n. waterfalls.* A stream of water pouring from a high place. – We waded up the brook as far as we could go, and had our lunch by the *waterfall.*

wa•ter lil•y (WAW-ter *or* WAHT-er LIL-ee) *water lilies.* A plant that grows in water. It has white, yellow, or pink blossoms, and large, flat, green leaves that float on the water.

wa•ter•logged (WAW-ter-lawgd *or* WAHT-er-lawgd) *adj.* Containing so much water as to be hard to manage; over-soaked with water.—The canoe was *waterlogged.* The wood had soaked up so much water that it was unable to float.

wa•ter•mel•on (WAW-ter-mel-ən *or* WAHT-er-mel-ən) *n. watermelons.* A large melon with a green rind, and large, flat, black or white seeds. A *watermelon* is a deep pink or red color inside. The juice is sweet.

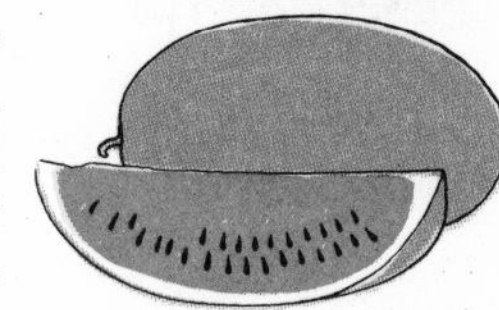

wa•ter•proof (WAW-ter-proof *or* WAHT-er-proof) *v. waterproofs, waterproofed, waterproofing.* Treat something so water will not go through it.—Grandfather put tar on the roof of his barn to *waterproof* it.
—*adj.* Not absorbing water; keeping water out. —Bob's raincoat is *waterproof.*—Galoshes are *waterproof,* too.

wa•ter•shed (WAW-ter-shed *or* WAHT-er-shed) *n. watersheds.* 1. An area from which water is drained, or shed, into lakes, rivers, reservoirs.
2. A chain of hills or mountains separating two or more of these water-shedding areas.

wa•ter va•por (WAW-ter *or* WAHT-er VAY-per). Water spread in the air as a gas; tiny drops of water. *Water vapor* is formed when water is heated to a point just below boiling. At the boiling point, water becomes steam.

wa•ter•way (WAW-ter-way *or* WAHT-er-way) *n. waterways.* A river, canal, lake, etc., on which boats travel.

wa•ter wheel (WAW-ter *or* WAHT-er hweel) *water wheels.* A wheel turned by flowing water to make power to run a machine. – The old mill was run by a *water wheel.*

watt (WAHT) *n. watts.* A unit for measuring electric power.–Light bulbs under sixty *watts* should not be used for reading. They don't transmit enough electrical power to give off sufficient light. They are not bright enough.

wat•tle (WAHT-l) *n. wattles.* 1. The red flesh on the underside of the necks of turkeys, chickens, and some other birds. 
2. An easily bent stick or twig. – William stuck some *wattles* together with clay and made a fine hut.

wave (WAYV) *n. waves.* 1. A moving ridge made by the rising and falling of water.–The cork bobbed up and down on the *waves.*

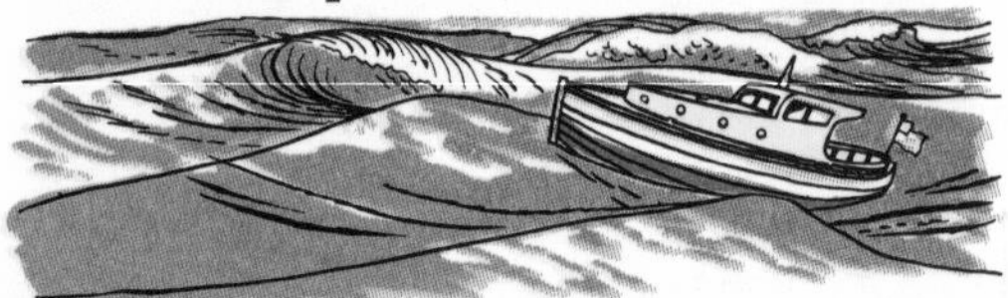

2. A ripple.–The hairdresser set Mother's hair in *waves.*
–*v. waves, waved, waving.* 1. Put waves in.–The hairdresser *waved* Mother's hair.
2. Move back and forth in the air.–The flag on the pole *waves* in the wind.–The children *waved* their hands to say good-by.

wa•ver (WAYV-er) *v. wavers, wavered, wavering.* 1. Sway; move from side to side or back and forth.–The sign hanging over the drug store *wavered* in the strong wind.
2. Shake; tremble; flicker.–When Sue asked Father not to scold her, her voice began to *waver.* Her voice began to tremble. – The flame *wavered.* It flickered.
3. Hesitate; be uncertain or undecided.–Tom *wavered* before making a decision. He wasn't too sure about what he should do.

wax (WAKS) *n.* 1. A yellowish-white substance that is secreted by bees and used in making honeycombs.–*Wax* can be molded when it is warm, and dries solid when it gets cold.–The material that some candles are made of is called *wax.*
2. A polish used on the surface of furniture, floors, automobiles, etc.
–*v. waxes, waxed, waxing.* Put wax on.–Father *waxes* the car to protect the finish.

way (WAY) *n. ways.* 1. A path; a direction.–The cows had trodden a *way* through the pasture.–A large man made his *way* through the crowd.–Show me the *way* to your house.
2. A distance.–It is a long *way* to school.
3. In a certain direction.–The girls went that *way.*
4. A plan; a method; a means.–Bob thought of a *way* to get the rabbit out of the trap.
5. A desire; what one wishes.–Mother didn't want us to go at first, but we got our own *way.* We went in the end.
6. A respect.–Bob's story was the best one in several *ways.* It was exciting, the people in it talked like real people, and it was clearly written.–In some *ways* Mary acts younger than Jack.
7. A manner.–Mother has a sweet *way* about her.–People from other lands have different *ways.*

we (WEE) *pron.* You and I; one or more others and myself.–*We* must hurry or *we* shall be late.–*We* all spelled all the words right in our class today.

weak (WEEK) *adj. weaker, weakest; weakly, adv.* 1. Not strong.–Baby was *weak* after her sickness.–The footbridge is too *weak* to hold many people.
2. Not easy to believe.–The boy's excuse was *weak.* It didn't sound true.
3. Not very good.–We have a *weak* ball team. –Jack is a little *weak* in history.
4. Containing very little of the important part.–*Weak* coffee has much water and little coffee in it.–Adding too much water to soup makes it *weak.*

weak•en (WEE-kən) *v. weakens, weakened, weakening.* Lose strength.–Sickness caused the old man to *weaken.*

weak•ness (WEEK-nəss) *n. weaknesses.* 1. A lack of energy or strength.–After his sickness, the man's *weakness* forced him to rest.
2. A defect.–There is a serious *weakness* in your argument.
3. Something one cannot resist.–Candy is Bob's *weakness;* he cannot help eating it.

wealth (WELTH) *n.* 1. Riches.–Ed is a man of great *wealth.* He has much money and property.
2. Much, or a large amount.–Mary has a *wealth* of dark brown hair.

wean (WEEN) *v. weans, weaned, weaning.* Get a child or young animal used to food other than its mother's milk.–The calves on Mr. Brown's farm have been *weaned.* They no longer drink their mothers' milk. They now eat grass, hay, and grain.

weap•on (WEP-ən) *n. weapons.* Anything used in fighting.–Guns, bows and arrows, swords, and clubs are *weapons.*

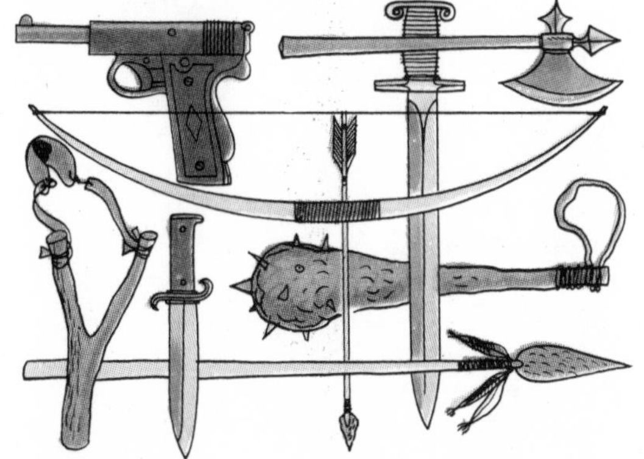

wear (WAIR) *n.* 1. Clothing.–Men's *wear* is sold in the men's department of the store.
2. Service; amount of time something can be used.–This suit will give you good *wear.* It will last a long time.–Father can get a little more *wear* out of his old shoes.
–v. wears, wore, wearing. 1. Carry or have on the body, as clothing or an ornament.–People *wear* clothes. They put them on to cover their bodies and to keep themselves warm.–Women *wear* earrings on their ears, rings on their fingers, and bracelets on their arms.
2. Rub or be rubbed away; make or become smaller, thinner, etc., through use. – The eraser on my pencil is *wearing* down. It will soon be all used up.–Mary's shoe *wore* a hole in her stocking.–Running water *wore* away the rocks in the river.

wea•ry (WIR-ee) *adj. wearier, weariest; wearily, adv.; weariness, n.* Tired; worn out. –Father is *weary* after his day's work.

wea•sel (WEE-zəl) *n. weasel* or *weasels.* A quick, small, slender animal that eats birds, mice, and other small animals.

weath•er (WETH-er) *n.* The heat, coldness, wetness, or other condition of the air.–In hot *weather* the air is hot or warm. In rainy *weather* the air is wet. In cold *weather* the air is cold.

weath•er•cock (WETH-er-kahk) *n. weathercocks.* A device, often cut or formed in the shape of a rooster, or a cock, that turns to show the direction in which the wind is blowing.

weave (WEEV) *n. weaves.* A kind or design of weaving. – Mother's skirt has a coarse *weave;* the material is rough.
–v. weaves, wove, weaving. Make (cloth or other fabric) by putting threads or strips under and over other threads or strips.–Children *weave* baskets of grass reeds.

weav•er (WEE-ver) *n. weavers.* A person who makes cloth, rugs, mats, etc., by weaving.

web (WEB) *n. webs.* 1. A network.–The picture shows a spider's *web.* Spiders spin *webs* to catch insects in.

2. The skin that joins the toes of certain swimming animals, such as ducks and beavers.

webbed (WEBD) *adj.* Having the toes joined by webs.–Ducks and geese have *webbed* feet. Their toes are joined by skin. *Webbed* feet help them swim.

wed (WED) *v. weds, wedded, wedding.* Marry; become man and wife.–"With this ring I thee *wed,*" said the bridegroom at the wedding.

we'd (WEED). 1. We had.–*We'd* better go now.
2. We would.–*We'd* be cold if we had no coats.

wed•ding (WED-ing) *n. weddings.* A service or ceremony at which a man and a woman are married.–Many *weddings* take place in church.

wedge (WEJ) *n. wedges.* A V-shaped piece of wood or metal used to split wood and to keep objects in position.–We put a *wedge* under the door to keep it open.
–v. wedges, wedged, wedging. Force; push; crowd in.–A stranger *wedged* his way through the crowd.

Wednes•day (WENZ-dee) *n. Wednesdays.* The day after Tuesday. *Wednesday* is the fourth day of the week.

weed (WEED) *n. weeds.* A plant that is useless or that grows where it is not wanted.—*Weeds* crowd out other plants in the garden.
—*v. weeds, weeded, weeding.* Clear of weeds.—Grandfather *weeds* the garden every week. He pulls up the weeds.

week (WEEK) *n. weeks.* 1. The seven days beginning with Sunday.
2. Seven days one right after the other.—Bob has been in the country for a *week.*
3. The five or six working days of the week.—A school *week* has five days in it.

week•day (WEEK-day) *n. weekdays.* Any day of the week but Sunday; or, sometimes, any day of the week but Saturday and Sunday.

week end or **week-end** (WEEK-end) *week ends* or *week-ends.* The holidays at the end of the week, usually Saturday and Sunday.—We go to school during the week and play during the *week end.*

week•ly (WEEK-lee) *n. weeklies.* A magazine or paper printed each week.—We take two *weeklies.*
—*adj.* Occurring every week.—Grandmother pays us a *weekly* visit. She comes to see us every week.
—*adv.* Once a week.—We pay for the newspaper *weekly.*

weep (WEEP) *v. weeps, wept, weeping.* Cry.—When Mary broke the dish, she started to *weep.*

wee•vil (WEE-vəl) *n. weevils.* A kind of small beetle with a hard-shelled back. *Weevils* eat grain, and often get into breakfast foods and flour.

weigh (WAY) *v. weighs, weighed, weighing.* 1. Find out how heavy something is.—Bob *weighed* himself on the scale.—The grocer *weighs* the sugar to be sure that he gives you the right amount.
2. Be of a certain weight or heaviness.—The baby *weighed* six pounds when she was born.
3. Bend or press (down).—The trees were *weighed* down with snow. The heavy snow made them bend over.
—*Weigh one's words* means to carefully consider what one is about to say or write; to carefully choose the words one is going to use in speaking or writing.—*Weigh your words* before you speak. Make sure that you say just what you want to say.

weight (WAYT) *n. weights.* 1. How heavy a thing is; how much a thing weighs on the scales.—Bob weighs eighty pounds. His *weight* is eighty pounds.
2. A piece of heavy material used to hold something down.—Father has a lead paper-*weight* on his desk. He puts it on his papers so that wind will not scatter them.

weird (WIRD) *adj. weirder, weirdest; weirdly, adv.; weirdness, n.* Strange; ghostlike; mysterious.—The wind made *weird* sounds as it whistled through the trees.

wel•come (WEL-kəm) *n. welcomes.* A greeting (usually kind or warm).—We gave Father a warm *welcome* when he came home from his long business trip.
—*v. welcomes, welcomed, welcoming.* 1. Greet or receive gladly.—The people of the city *welcomed* the soldiers on their return home.
2. Allow; permit.—I *welcome* you to borrow any one of my books.
—*adj.* 1. Gladly received.—We always feel *welcome* at Grandmother's home.
2. Permitted.—You are *welcome* to stay at my house for the week end.
—People often say, "You are *welcome*" when they have been thanked for something.—When John thanked Mary for her gift, she said, "You are *welcome.*"

weld (WELD) *v. welds, welded, welding.* Join pieces of metal by heating them and pressing them together.—Father will *weld* the ends of the wires together. He will join them by heating them till the metal is soft, and then pressing them together.

well (WEL) *n. wells.* 1. A hole dug or drilled in the ground to reach gas, oil, or water.
2. Anything like a well.—An ink*well* holds ink.
—*adj.* 1. In good health.—Grandfather is *well.* He isn't sick.
2. Right.—It is *well* that you study your spelling words.
—*adv. better, best.* 1. Nicely; in the right or desired way.—Everything went *well* until we came to the obstacle on the road.—Mary sings *well.*
2. Thoroughly. — Chew your food *well* before you swallow it.

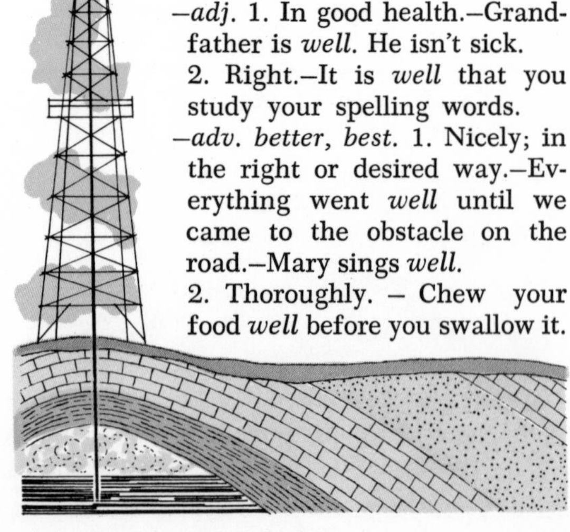

we'll (WEEL). 1. We will.–*We'll* make it to the top.
2. We shall.–*We'll* be late if you don't hurry.

well-known (WEL-NOHN) *adj.* Known by many people.–President Franklin D. Roosevelt was *well-known.* He was known by people everywhere.

welt (WELT) *n. welts.* A long swollen place on the skin caused by a blow.–The cruel man beat the horse until its back was covered with *welts.*

went (WENT) *v.* One form of the verb *go.*–Bob came to school at noon and *went* home at three o'clock.

wept (WEPT) *v.* One form of the verb *weep.* –The children *wept* when their dog was lost.

were (WER) *v.* One form of the verb *be.*–We *were* sorry you didn't come.–You are late today and you *were* late yesterday.–If I *were* hungry, I would eat some food; but I am not hungry, so I shall not.

we're (WIR). We are.–*We're* ready for school now.

weren't (WERNT). Were not.–We *weren't* ready for school when Father left the house.

west (WEST) *n., adj.,* and *adv.*
1. The direction in which the sun sets.–If you stand with your face to the north, *west* is on your left.

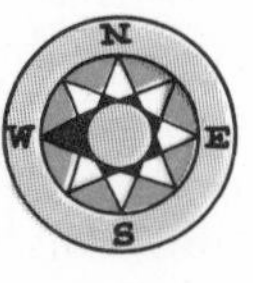

2. (Spelled with a capital "W.") The section of the United States lying west of the Mississippi River.–Johnny said that if he could have his wish he would live in the *West* and be a cowboy.
3. (Spelled with a capital "W.") Europe and the Americas are sometimes referred to as the *West.*

west•ern (WESS-tern) *adj.* 1. From, in, of, or to the west.–Bob lives in the *western* part of town.
2. (Spelled with a capital "W.") Having to do with the West.

West Vir•gin•ia (WEST ver-JIN-yə) *n.* A state of forest-covered mountains and rich plateaus in eastern United States, noted for hardwood and tobacco products and the production of soft coal.

west•ward (WEST-werd) *adj.* and *adv.* Toward the west.–The boy turned the corner and went *westward.* He went in a *westward* direction.

wet (WET) *v. wets, wetted, wetting.* Soak, or put a liquid on.–Bob *wets* his hair with water before he combs it.
–*adj. wetter, wettest.* 1. Covered or soaked with water or other liquid.–The grass is *wet* with rain.–The towel is *wet.*
2. Rainy.–We had *wet* weather during our vacation.
3. In liquid form; not hardened; not dry.–The paint is still *wet.*

we've (WEEV). We have.–*We've* six minutes to wait.

whale (HWAYL) *n. whales.* A big sea mammal that looks like a fish. The *whale* is the biggest animal in the world.

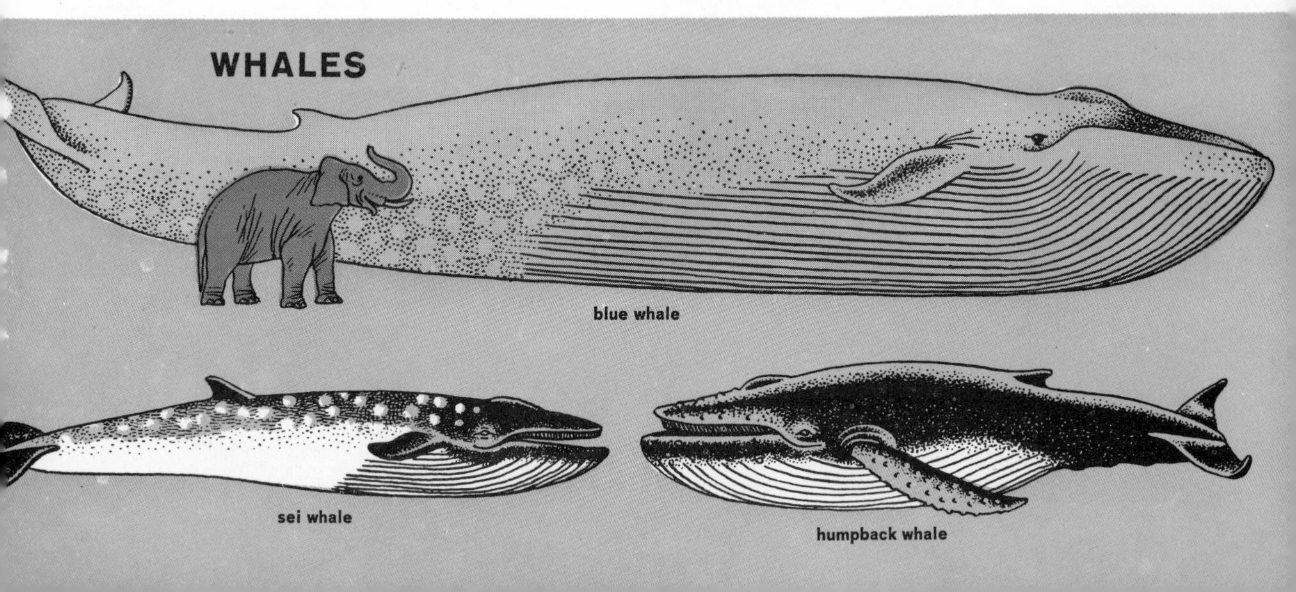

wharf (HWORF) *n. wharves.* A large dock at which boats can load or unload.

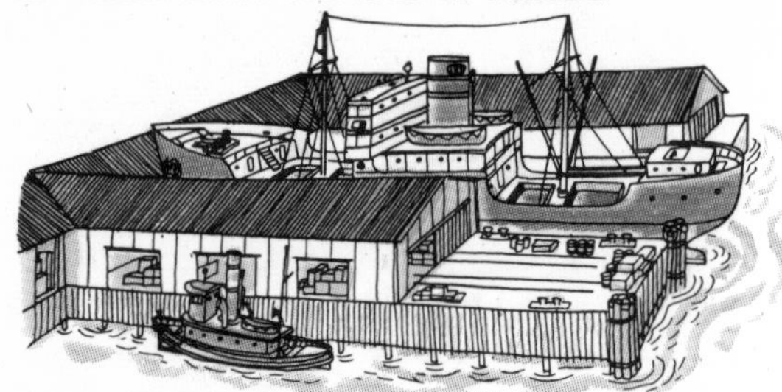

what (HWAHT *or* hwut) *adj., adv.,* and *pron.* 1. A word used to ask questions.–*What* is that noise?–*What* is the name of your teacher?–*What* book do you want?–*What* does he mean?
2. Anything that; something that.–Say *what* you want.–The hungry child ate *what* was left over.

what•ev•er (hwaht-EV-er) *adj.* Of any kind. –He may have *whatever* book he wishes.
–*pron.* 1. Anything that.–Eat *whatever* you want to eat.
2. No matter what.–Come tomorrow, *whatever* happens.

what's (HWAHTSS *or* hwutss). What is.–*What's* in the basket?

wheat (HWEET) *n.* An important grain, from which flour, bread, cereals, and other foods are made.–Farmers grow *wheat.*

wheel (HWEEL) *n. wheels.* A round object that turns about its center.–*Wheels* make machines go.–Cars, wagons, and trains run on *wheels.*

wheel•bar•row (HWEEL-bar-oh) *n. wheelbarrows.* A little vehicle with two legs and one wheel, and pushed by two handles. A *wheelbarrow* is used for carrying small loads.–A man can push a *wheelbarrow* filled with sand, stones, or dirt.

wheeze (HWEEZ) *v. wheezes, wheezed, wheezing.* Breathe heavily with a whistling sound.–When Father has a cold, he *wheezes* and sneezes.

when (HWEN) *adv.* At what time.–*When* do you get up?
–*conj.* 1. At the time that.–We eat *when* we are hungry.
2. After the time that.–Do you want me to throw the ball to you *when* I catch it?
3. Although.–Bob bought two pencils *when* he needed only one.

when•ev•er (hwen-EV-er) *adv.* and *conj.* When; any time that.–Some children eat *whenever* they are hungry.–You may go home *whenever* your work is done.

where (HWAIR) *adv.* 1. In what place.–*Where* did you put your book?
2. At what place.–*Where* did you stop?
3. To what place.–*Where* was the letter sent?
4. From what place.–*Where* did you get that hat?
–*conj.* In or at the place in which.–John is going to sit *where* I usually sit. He is going to sit in my chair.

wher•ev•er (hwair-EV-er) *adv.* Any place that.–*Wherever* you go, I shall go.

whet (HWET) *v. whets, whetted, whetting.* 1. Sharpen by grinding or rubbing, as the edge of a blade or tool.–The hunter was *whetting* his knife with a stone.
2. Stimulate; make keen or eager.–The delicious smell of Mother's cooking always *whets* my appetite. It makes me feel hungrier than I was before I smelled it.

wheth•er (HWETH-er) *conj.* 1. No matter if. –*Whether* it rains or snows, we shall go to the party.–*Whether* you like it or not, I shall do it.
2. If.–Mary didn't know *whether* Bob was home or not.
3. I did not know *whether* to go.

which (HWICH) *adj.* and *pron.* 1. What one. –*Which* girl sits here?–*Which* is the path we should take?
2. That.–We play games *which* we like.

while (HWYL) *n.* A time.–Father will be home in a little *while.*
–*v. whiles, whiled, whiling.* Spend or pass (time).–Bob *whiles* away his time loafing.
–*conj.* 1. During the time that.–*While* we were eating, the doorbell rang.–Tom didn't want to wash the dishes *while* his sister went to the movies.
2. Although.–*While* Mother spoke loudly, I didn't hear her. I was making too much noise.
–*Worth one's while* means that a certain thing that one does is worth doing, that it is worth the time and effort used to do it.–Since Bill was poor in geography, the teacher gave him some extra books to read. She felt that reading them would be *worth his while.*

whim•per (HWIM-per) *n. whimpers.* A sobbing little cry.—We didn't hear a *whimper* from Baby when she fell down.
v. whimpers, whimpered, whimpering. Whine or cry in low, broken sounds.—The dog *whimpers* when he is cold.

whin•ny (HWIN-ee) *n. whinnies.* The cry of a horse.—The pony gave a *whinny* when he saw the apple.
—v. whinnies, whinnied, whinnying. Neigh, or give a whinny. – Roosters crow. Dogs bark. Horses *whinny.*

whip (HWIP) *n. whips.* A lash, usually with a handle or grip.—The horseman carries a *whip.*
—v. whips, whipped, whipping.
1. Beat; strike.—The cruel man *whipped* the dog for running away.
2. Beat with a beater.—Mary *whipped* the cream to make it thick and fluffy.

whip•poor•will (HWIP-er-wil *or* hwip-er-WIL) *n. whippoorwills.* A bird that flies by night. The *whippoorwill* lives on insects. It seems to say its own name when it calls.

whir or **whirr** (HWER) *n. whirs* or *whirrs.* A buzzing sound.—We heard the *whir* of the engines as we passed the factory.
—v. whirs, whirred, whirring. Spin or move fast and make a buzzing sound.—The wheels of Grandmother's sewing machine *whir.*—Sally's top *whirs* when she spins it.

whirl (HWERL) *n. whirls.* A spinning circle. —My head seems to be in a *whirl,* I am so excited.
—v. whirls, whirled, whirling. Turn round and round; spin.—A top *whirls.*—The children *whirled* about the room.—The boy *whirled* the rope about his head.

whirl•pool (HWERL-pool) *n. whirlpools.* Water that whirls round and round in a swift circle.—*Whirlpools* often upset boats.

whirl•wind (HWERL-wind) *n. whirlwinds.* Air or wind blowing round and round, fast and fiercely. A *whirlwind* is a violent windstorm.

whisk (HWISK) *n. whisks.* A sweep or brush. —One *whisk* of the hand and Mary's desk was cleaned.
—v. whisks, whisked, whisking. 1. Sweep or brush away with a light, easy motion.—Mary *whisked* the scraps of paper from her desk.
2. Dash; dart; quickly move.—When the dog chased the cat, she *whisked* up a tree.

whisk•er (HWISS-ker) *n. whiskers.* 1. A long, stiff hair that sticks out from the sides of the mouth.—Our white kitten has long black *whiskers.*
2. The beard; stiff hair growing on the cheeks, upper lip, and chin of a man.—Father shaves off his *whiskers* in the morning.

whis•key or **whis•ky** (HWISS-kee) *n. whiskies.* A liquor made from wheat or other grains.

whis•per (HWISS-per) *n. whispers.* A soft, hissing sound, under the breath.—Mother has a cold and can speak only in a *whisper.*
—v. whispers, whispered, whispering. 1. Speak under the breath with a soft, hissing sound.—When Father is asleep, we *whisper.*
2. Make a low rustling sound.—The wind *whispered* through the leaves on the trees.
3. Tell secretly from one to another.—It was *whispered* about that the teacher wore a wig.

whis•tle (HWISS-əl) *n. whistles.* 1. A little hollow instrument that makes a shrill note when you put it to your lips and blow through it; any device, big or little, for making such a sound. – The policeman blew a *whistle* to tell the children when to cross the street.—The engineer blows the train *whistle.*

2. A whistlelike sound.—We heard the *whistle* of the whippoorwill.
—v. whistles, whistled, whistling. 1. Pucker up the lips and blow through them to make the sound of a whistle.—Jack *whistles* for his dog.
2. Make a sound like a whistle.—The wind *whistles* through the trees.

white (HWYT) *n. whites.* The color of snow. —Mother picked *white* for the color of the house paint.
—adj. Of the color white.—Mother's hair is coal-black; Grandmother's hair is *white.*—Wild daisies usually have *white* petals.

whit•en (HWYT-n) *v. whitens, whitened, whitening.* Make white; bleach. – Mother hangs the clothes in the sun to *whiten* them.

white•wash (HWYT-wahsh *or* -wawsh) *v. whitewashes, whitewashed, whitewashing.* Whiten with a liquid substance, usually made of water and lime. – Tom and his friends are *whitewashing* the fence.

whit•tle (HWIT-l) *v. whittles, whittled, whittling.* 1. Cut off chips or pieces of wood with a knife.
2. Carve or cut out in a shape.–Bob *whittled* a doll for Sally.

whiz or **whizz** (HWIZ) *n. whizzes.* A humming sound.–The batter heard the *whiz* of the ball.
–*v. whizzes, whizzed, whizzing.* Fly with a buzzing or humming sound.–Bob threw the ball so hard that it *whizzed* by the boy who was batting.

who (HOO) *pron.* 1. What person; which people. – *Who* would like to go with me? Would you, Mary?–*Who* opened the window?
2. That.–The boy *who* is singing this song is my brother.

whoa (HWOH) *interj.* Stop.–The farmer says *"Whoa!"* to his horses when he wants them to stand still.

who•ev•er (hoo-EV-er) *pron.* Anyone who; any person that.–*Whoever* guesses what I have in my hand may have it.

whole (HOHL) *adj.; wholly, adv.* 1. Complete; entire.–We couldn't play checkers because we did not have a *whole* set of checkers. Some pieces were missing.–The fat man ate a *whole* pie. He ate all of it.–The *whole* family came. Everybody in the family came, from Grandfather to the baby.
2. All in one piece.–Do you want to eat the apple *whole,* or would you like it cut up?

whole•sale (HOHL-sayl) *adj.* Having to do with buying or selling in large quantities.–Mr. Jones is in the *wholesale* drug business. He buys drugs in large quantities from the manufacturers and then sells them to retail druggists.

whole•some (HOHL-səm) *adj.; wholesomely, adv.; wholesomeness, n.* Healthful; good for one's health.–Fruits and vegetables are *wholesome* foods.

whom (HOOM) *pron.* What person; which people.–To *whom* shall I give the book?–*Whom* do you like better, Bob or Jack?

whoop•ing cough (HOO-ping *or* HUHP-ing kawf). A disease, usually of children. *Whooping cough* makes a person cough and whoop. Children catch it by getting near others who are sick with it.

whose (HOOZ) *pron.* 1. Which person's.–*Whose* book is this? To whom does it belong? Is it yours, Mary's, or Jack's?
2. The man *whose* hat blew off is Father.–Mary, *whose* cold was worse, did not go out today.

why (HWY) *adv.* For what reason.–*Why* were you late?–I don't see *why* you don't come with us.

wick (WIK) *n. wicks.* The soft cord in a candle or the loosely woven tape in an oil lamp that draws up the wax or oil to be burned for light.

wick•ed (WIK-id) *adj.; wickedly, adv.; wickedness, n.* Bad or sinful.–The *wicked* king was sorry for his bad deeds when he saw how unhappy he had made the people.

wide (WYD) *adj. wider, widest* and *adv.* 1. Broad.–One path was so narrow that only one person could walk in it. The other was *wide* enough for two people to walk side by side.
2. As far as it will open.–We open the windows *wide* when we go to bed.

wid•en (WYD-n) *v. widens, widened, widening.* Make or become wide.–The workmen will *widen* the narrow street so that more cars can use it.

wide•spread (WYD-SPRED) *adj.* 1. Spread out.–The boy is standing with his feet *widespread.* His feet are far apart.
2. Spread over or covering a wide area; widely extended.–The storm is *widespread.* –The young singer is enjoying *widespread* popularity.

wid•ow (WID-oh) *n. widows.* A woman whose husband is dead, and who has not married again.

wid•ow•er (WID-oh-er) *n. widowers.* A man whose wife is dead, and who has not married again.

width (WIDTH) *n. widths.* Distance across or from side to side; how wide a thing is.–The *width* of my desk is two feet.–The *width* of the river is fifty feet.

wield (WEELD) *v. wields, wielded, wielding.* Hold in the hand and use.–Jack is never happier than when he is *wielding* a paintbrush.

wife (WYF) *n. wives.* A married woman.–Mother is Father's *wife.*

wig (WIG) *n. wigs.* A covering of false hair worn on the head. Some bald-headed people wear *wigs.*–Actors often wear *wigs* to make them look like someone else.

wig•gle (WIG-əl) *v. wiggles, wiggled, wiggling.* Move uneasily back and forth.–Children sometimes *wiggle* in their seats.

wig•wam (WIG-wahm *or* -wawm) *n. wigwams.* A hut made of poles covered with strips of bark. Some Indians of America lived in *wigwams.*

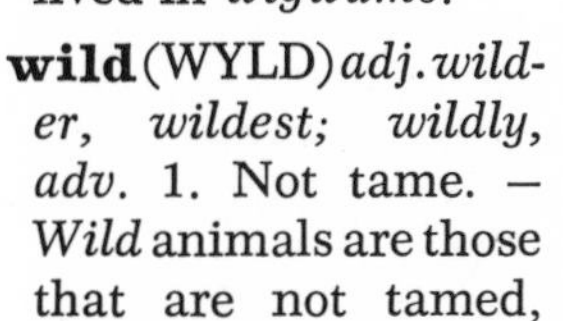

wild (WYLD) *adj. wilder, wildest; wildly, adv.* 1. Not tame. – *Wild* animals are those that are not tamed, those which man cannot control.–Lions and tigers are *wild* animals.

2. Not cultivated; not taken care of by people.–*Wild* flowers are flowers that grow by themselves in the fields and woods, and by the roads.

–*adv.* Without cultivation; without control.–Daisies and violets grow *wild.*–The children ran *wild.*

wild•cat (WYLD-kat) *n. wildcat* or *wildcats.* A fierce wild animal that looks like a large cat. *Wildcats* eat the flesh of other animals.

wil•der•ness (WIL-der-nəss) *n.* A land where no people live.–While riding through the West, Bob and Mary passed through miles of *wilderness.* There was no sign of any people, and the only growing things grew wild.

will (WIL) *n. wills.* 1. Wish or desire; determination.–Tom is intelligent, but he is also lazy. He has no *will* to succeed.

2. A paper written according to law which tells what shall be done with a person's belongings after he is dead.–Grandfather has made a *will* leaving all his possessions to Grandmother.

–*v.* 1. One form of the verb *be.*–Father *will* be home early.–You *will* hear the bells at six o'clock if you listen.–It *will* be getting dark earlier now that winter is coming.

2. Be willing to.–Mary *will* sing if she is asked.

will•ing (WIL-ing) *adj.* Ready; pleased.–Bob is *willing* to do the work.

will•ing•ly (WIL-ing-lee) *adv.; willingness, n.* Gladly.–Mary did the work *willingly.* She didn't mind doing it at all.

wil•low (WIL-oh) *n. willows.* A kind of tree or bush. – Some *willows* are called weeping *willows.* Their branches bow down as if they were sad.

wilt (WILT) *v. wilts, wilted, wilting.* Wither; droop down; lose strength.–Flowers that are picked and left out of water soon *wilt.*

win (WIN) *v. wins, won, winning.* Succeed; gain a victory; reach a goal.–We *win* ball games by playing better than the other team. –We *win* a spelling contest by spelling better than the other team. – Our team *won* the victory.–Mary *won* the bet from Bob. She was right.

wince (WINSS) *v. winces, winced, wincing.* Shrink or draw back quickly. – The horse *winced* when the driver hit him with the whip.

wind (WIND) *n. winds; windy, adj. windier, windiest.* 1. Air that is moving.–The *wind* blew the apples off the tree.

2. Breath.–The runner was tired and out of *wind* after the race.

–*v. winds, winded, winding.* Make short of breath.–Climbing the stairs *winded* Father.

wind (WYND) *v. winds, wound, winding.* 1. Wrap or twine around; roll up. – The flag *winds* around the flagpole.–Bob *winds* his kite string into a ball.–Mother *winds* thread on the spool.

2. Turn a part of a machine to tighten a spring, so that the machine will go on working by itself.–Grandfather *winds* his watch every night. He turns the stem around and around so that the watch will go on ticking. –The children's phonograph has to be *wound* by hand.

3. Twist; go this way and that way.–A path *winds* through the woods.

wind•break (WIND-brayk) *n. windbreaks.* A shelter or protection from the wind. – A wall, a fence, a tree, a rock, or any other shelter may serve as a *windbreak.*

wind in•stru•ment (WIND IN-strə-mənt) *wind instruments.* A musical instrument that is played by blowing air through it.–Trumpets, horns, flutes, and fifes are *wind instruments.*

wind•mill (WIND-mil) *n. windmills.* A machine run by wind for pumping water.–The farmer has a *windmill* to pump water into his kitchen.–There are many *windmills* in Holland.

win•dow (WIN-doh) *n. windows.* An opening in a wall to let in air, light, and sunshine. – We open our *windows* at night for fresh air.

win•dow•pane (WIN-doh-payn) *n. windowpanes.* A piece of glass set in a window to keep out the weather.–The boy tossed a ball through the *windowpane* and broke it.

wind•pipe (WIND-pyp) *n. windpipes.* A tube that carries air from the throat to the lungs.

wind•shield (WIND- *or* WIN-sheeld) *n. windshields.* A heavy, and usually shatter-proof, piece of glass in the front of the body of an automobile to keep out rain, snow, dust, and wind.

wine (WYN) *n. wines.* A drink made from the fermented juices of fruits or other plants. *Wine* has some alcohol in it.

wing (WING) *n. wings.* 1. The part of a flying insect, bird, or bat that keeps it up in the air when flying.
2. Something like a wing in appearance or function, as the *wing* of an airplane.
3. Anything that sticks out from the side of a body or a main part of a thing.–Mother wants to have another *wing* built onto the house because we need more room.
4. A space off the stage at the right or left.–The actors stood in the *wings* until it was time for them to go on stage.
–*v. wings, winged, winging.* Fly. – The bird *winged* its way south.

wing•spread (WING-spred) *n. wingspreads.* The distance between the ends or tips of the wings of a bird, insect, or airplane. *Wingspread* is measured when the wings are stretched out as far as possible.

wink (WINGK) *n. winks.* 1. A quick opening and closing of the eyes; a blink.
2. (In the plural) A brief period of sleep.–Mother was so tired she said she was going to snatch a few *winks* before serving dinner.
–*v. winks, winked, winking.* 1. Open and shut the eyes quickly.–The fly buzzing near the baby's eyes made her *wink.*
2. Open one eye and close it as a signal to someone.–Can you *wink?*
3. Flicker; twinkle.–When Bob opened the door, the candles *winked.*

win•ner (WIN-er) *n. winners.* One that wins or has won.–Our team was the *winner.* It won the game.–Mary's story was the *winner.* It won the prize.

win•ter (WIN-ter) *n. winters.* The cold season of the year.–Spring, summer, autumn, and *winter* are the four seasons.
–*v. winters, wintered, wintering.* Spend the winter.–Our friends *wintered* in the South. They lived there all winter.

win•ter•green (WIN-ter-green) *n. wintergreens.* 1. A small plant with shiny leaves and red berries.
2. A flavoring for candy, ice cream, and cakes made from the oil of the leaves of the plant.

win•try (WIN-tree) *adj.* Having a resemblance to winter; like winter; cold or stormy. –Although the days are warm, the nights are *wintry.*

wipe (WYP) *v. wipes, wiped, wiping.* 1. Make a thing dry or clean by rubbing.–Mary *wiped* the dishes for Mother. – Mother *wiped* the floor with a mop.
2. Rub away. – *Wipe* the jelly from your mouth.

wire (WYR) *n. wires.* 1. A strand or thread of metal.–*Wire* carries electricity for telephones, electric lights, and other things.

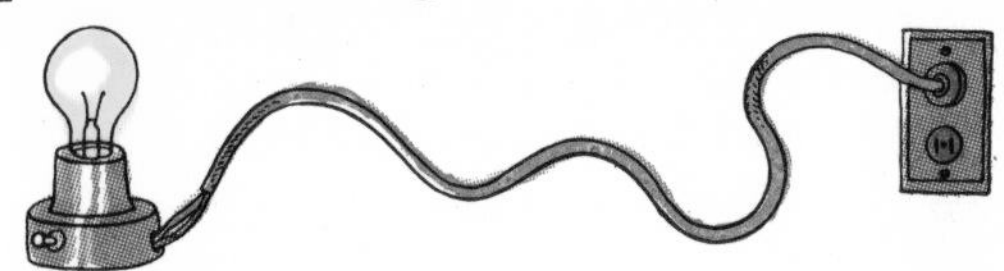

2. A telegraph message; a telegram.–When Father was away, he sent us a *wire* telling us he would be home on Sunday.
–*v. wires, wired, wiring.* 1. Put a wire around. –Father *wired* the box that he sent to Grandmother.
2. Put electric wires in.–We shall *wire* the garage so that we can have a light in it at night.
3. Send a message by telegraph. – Father *wired* us that he would be home on Sunday.

wire•less (WYR-ləss) *n. wirelesses.* A message sent by radio, or without the use of wires.–The ship received a *wireless* from the shore.

Wis•con•sin (wiss-KAHN-sən) *n.* A beautiful, largely agricultural state in north central United States. Dairy farming and general farming, vegetable canning, manufacturing machinery, leather, paper, and furniture are its chief industries.

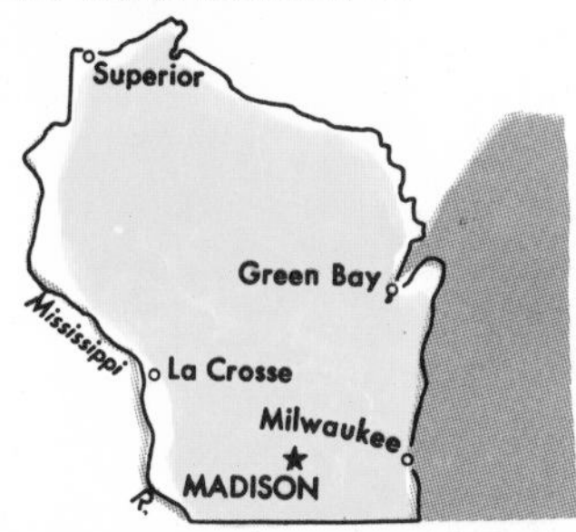

wis•dom (WIZ-dəm) *n.* Good judgment; ability to use one's knowledge to help oneself and others.

wise (WYZ) *adj. wiser, wisest; wisely, adv.* Having wisdom.–Father is *wiser* than Jack because he has lived so much longer. He knows more.

wish (WISH) *n. wishes.* 1. A desire.–John's *wish* is to have a pony of his own.
2. An expressed desire. – Bob made a *wish* when he blew out the candles of his birthday cake. He said he wanted a bicycle.
–*v. wishes, wished, wishing.* 1. Want; desire. –I *wish* I had a dog.–King Midas *wished* that everything he touched would turn to gold.
2. Express hope to (a person) for (something pleasant).–I *wish* you a happy birthday.

wisp (WISP) *n. wisps.* A small strand or bunch of strands.–The bird carried a *wisp* of grass to its nest and wove it in to line the nest.–Bob dropped a *wisp* of hay when he fed the calf.

wit (WIT) *n. wits.* 1. The ability to understand quickly and to express one's thoughts cleverly.
2. (In the plural) Mind; senses.–The Halloween ghost frightened us out of our *wits.*

witch (WICH) *n. witches.* An ugly old woman believed to have magic power.–In fairy tales *witches* ride on brooms.

with (WITH or WITH) *prep.* Accompanying; going together. – Mary said to her friend, "Please come *with* me. Let us go together."– We eat butter *with* bread.–Here comes Bob *with* his dog.

with•draw (with- *or* with-DRAW) *v. withdraws, withdrew, withdrawing.* 1. Draw or pull back.–When the cat scratched Mary's foot, Mary *withdrew.*
2. Leave; go away. – The firemen had to *withdraw* from the burning building or be injured.

with•er (WITH-er) *v. withers, withered, withering.* Dry up; become lifeless; fade. – Flowers *wither* unless they have water.

with•hold (with- *or* with-HOHLD) *v. withholds, withheld, withholding.* Hold or keep back; check.–The company *withholds* part of Father's wages each week for taxes.–The police *withheld* the angry mob.

with•in (with- *or* with-IN) *adv.* and *prep.* 1. Inside; inside of.–The boy is hiding *within* the house.
2. Not beyond. – Is the shelf *within* your reach?

with•out (with- *or* with-OWT) *adv.* and *prep.* 1. Not having; not with. -- We went *without* lunch. – We can do *without* many things. We can get along even if we do not have many things.
2. On the outside; outside of.–Those within the house called to those *without.*

wit•ness (WIT-nəss) *n. witnesses.* A person who knows and can give proof that something happened.
–*v. witnesses, witnessed, witnessing.* 1. See.– We *witnessed* the fight.
2. Testify to having seen; act as witness.– Father *witnessed* Mr. Jones's signing of the paper. Father wrote his name on the paper to show that he saw Mr. Jones sign the paper.

wit•ty (WIT-ee) *adj. wittier, wittiest.* Having or showing wit; quick, clever, and amusing.—Edward is quite *witty.* He says things that are clever and funny.

wives (WYVZ) *n. pl.* More than one *wife.*—King Solomon had many *wives.* He married many times.

wiz•ard (WIZ-erd) *n. wizards.* A person who is thought to have magic power, or power to do what seems impossible.

wob•ble (WAHB-əl) *v. wobbles, wobbled, wobbling.* Move shakily; tremble.—The sick boy's legs *wobbled* when he walked.

woe (WOH) *n. woes.* Trouble; sorrow.—The knight's heart was heavy with many *woes.*

woke (WOHK) *v.* One form of the verb *wake.* —Baby went to sleep but soon *woke.*

wolf (WUHLF) *n. wolves.* A wild animal that looks something like a police dog.—*Wolves* eat other animals.

wolf•hound (WUHLF-hownd) *n. wolfhounds.* A kind of large dog once used in hunting wolves.

wolves (WUHLVZ) *n. pl.* More than one *wolf.*

wom•an (WUHM-ən) *n. women.* A grown female person.—A girl grows to be a *woman.*—Mother is a *woman.*

wom•en (WIM-ən) *n. pl.* More than one *woman.*—Mother belongs to a club for *women.*

won (WUN) *v.* One form of the verb *win.*—We *won* the ball game. The other team lost.

won•der (WUN-der) *n. wonders.* 1. Surprise. —Bob's eyes opened with *wonder* when he saw his new pony.
2. Awe.—We watched the sunset in *wonder.*
3. Strange, wonderful thing.—Niagara Falls is one of the *wonders* of the world.
—*v. wonders, wondered, wondering.* 1. Want to know.—I *wonder* what my present will be.
2. Be surprised.—I shouldn't *wonder* if it is a new coat.

won•der•ful (WUN-der-fuhl) *adj.; wonderfully, adv.* 1. Full of surprising or delightful things.—Our trip was *wonderful.* It was full of fun and surprises.
2. Causing one to feel wonder. – Niagara Falls is a *wonderful* sight. It is amazing.

won't (WOHNT). Will not.—I *won't* do it.

woo (WOO) *v. woos, wooed, wooing.* Make love to; court.—In the fairy tale the prince *wooed* the beautiful maiden. He made love to her and asked her to marry him.

wood (WUHD) *n. woods.* 1. The part of a tree under the bark; the inside part of a tree.—We burn *wood* to cook with and to keep us warm.—*Wood* is cut into boards and used to build houses, furniture, boxes, and many other things.
2. (Usually in the plural) A place where many trees grow.—The children like to play in the *woods.*

wood•chuck (WUHD-chuk) *n. woodchucks.* An animal of the same family as rabbits and rats. *Woodchucks* sleep all winter in tunnels which they dig in the ground. They come out for food in the spring. *Woodchucks* are also called ground hogs.

wood•cut•ter (WUHD-kut-er) *n. woodcutters.* A man who cuts down trees and chops up wood.

wood•ed (WUHD-əd) *adj.* Covered with many trees.—The hills are *wooded.*

wood•en (WUHD-n) *adj.* Made of wood.—Some houses are *wooden;* some are made of bricks.—The children marched like *wooden* soldiers.

wood•land (WUHD-lənd) *n. woodlands.* Land covered with many trees.—There is a small stretch of *woodland* near our house.

wood•peck•er (WUHD-pek-er) *n. woodpeckers.* A bird that pecks holes in the bark of trees to catch insects that live under the bark. The feathers in a *woodpecker's* tail are stiff to help him in climbing up tree trunks.

woods (WUHDZ) *n. sing.* and *pl.* A forest; a place where many trees grow close together. —The children went to the *woods* to play.

wood wind (WUHD wind) *wood winds.* A wind instrument such as the oboe, clarinet, flute, bassoon, piccolo, and English horn.

woof (WOOF) *n.* The threads that go from side to side across a piece of cloth. The lengthwise threads are called the warp.

wool (WUHL) *n. wools.* The soft, curly hair of sheep.–A sheep's body is covered with *wool.* –*Wool* is made into yarn, cloth, and clothes.

wool•en or **wool•len** (WUHL-ən) *n. woolens* or *woollens.* Clothing made of wool.–The store had a sale of *woolens.*
–*adj.* Made of wool.–*Woolen* clothes are very warm.–*Woolen* blankets keep us warm at night.

wool•ly (WUHL-ee) *adj. woollier, woolliest.* Like the wool on a sheep's back.–Mother has a *woolly* blanket.

word (WERD) *n. words.* 1. A group of letters that stands for one idea. Several *words* that express one thought make a sentence.–The first *word* that Baby spoke was "Mamma."
2. Promise.–I give you my *word* that I will not tell our secret.
3. A message; news.–Father is on a trip, and we have had no *word* from him yet.
4. A short conversation.–Mother had a *word* with Mary's teacher about Mary's work.

wore (WOR) *v.* One form of the verb *wear.*– I wear a clean dress every day. Yesterday I *wore* my best dress.

work (WERK) *n. works.* 1. Anything we do in an effort to make or get something we want.–Bob did some *work* on his model boat.
2. Task.–Father said he had some *work* for Tim. He asked Tim to mow the lawn and to rake the leaves.
3. A trade; a vocation; the thing one does to make a living.–Being a doctor, a mechanic, a clerk, or a teacher is *work.*–Mother's *work* is in the home. She washes, cleans the house, cooks, sews, and takes care of the baby.
–*v. works, worked, working.* Run; operate. – Our car will not *work.* It needs repairs.

work•er (WERK-er) *n. workers.* 1. A person who works.–Bob is a hard *worker* when he is doing something that interests him.
2. A person who works for wages. – The *workers* in the factory asked for higher wages.

work•man (WERK-mən) *n. workmen.* A man who works, especially one who works with his hands.–A gang of *workmen* unloaded the truck.

work•shop (WERK-shahp) *n. workshops.* A shop or room in which work is done.–Santa Claus has many elves in his toy *workshop.*

world (WERLD) *n. worlds.* 1. The earth. – The *world* is round. – Ships sail round the *world.*

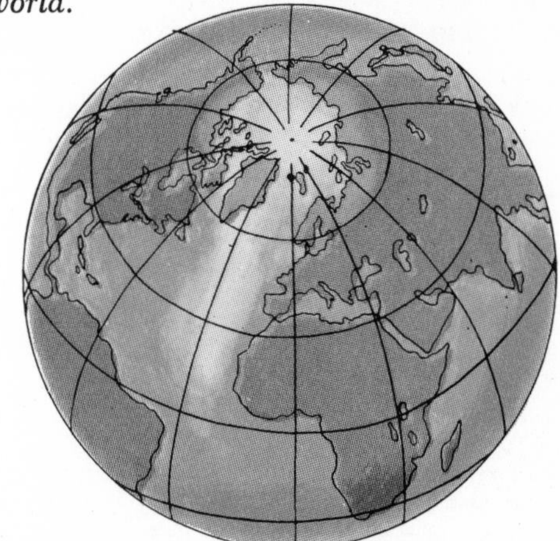

2. All the people living on earth.–The *world* will soon hear the good news.

worm (WERM) *n. worms.* A small, slender animal that wriggles along or through the ground.–Robins eat *worms* that live in the ground and are called earth*worms.*
–*v. worms, wormed, worming.* Wriggle.–The boy *wormed* his way through the crowd so that he could see the parade.

worn (WORN) *v.* One form of the verb *wear.* –I wear this hat every day. I have *worn* it for a year.

worn-out (WORN-OWT) *adj.* Made worthless by wear or use. – Mother threw away Mary's *worn-out* shoes. They had been used until they could be worn no longer.

wor•ry (WER-ee) *n. worries.* An anxious or troubled feeling.–*Worry* over the baby's sickness is very tiring to Mother.
–*v. worries, worried, worrying.* 1. Trouble; bother.–Do not *worry* Baby by teasing her.
2. Feel troubled and anxious.–Mother *worries* when we are late from school.

worse (WERSS) *adj. worst. Worse* means the opposite of better.–Bad, *worse,* worst are the opposites of good, better, best.–Father was sick this morning, and tonight he is *worse.*

wor•ship (WER-ship) *v. worships, worshiped, worshiping.* 1. Show deep or loyal respect for.–We go to church to *worship* God. We pay respect to God.
2. Hold dear.–The man *worships* his little daughter.

worst (WERST) *adj. Worst* means the opposite of best.–Bad, worse, *worst* are the opposites of good, better, best.–Bob is the best boy in school; Bill is the *worst.*–The fire was the *worst* that we had ever seen.

worth (WERTH) *n.* The amount (a sum of money) will buy.–Give me a dime's *worth* of candy.
–*adj.* 1. Equal to in value.–What is your ball *worth*? How much money would it take to buy it?
2. Have a fortune of.–The king is *worth* millions of dollars.
3. Good enough for.–Mary's story is *worth* reading. It is good enough to read out loud.

worth•less (WERTH-ləss) *adj.* Having no value or worth; not usable.–These worn-out clothes are *worthless.*

worth•while (WERTH-HWYL) *adj.* Worth or worthy of time, trouble, interest, or effort. –Reading good books is a *worthwhile* form of relaxation.

wor•thy (WER-thee) *adj. worthier, worthiest.* 1. Deserving.–The soldier's bravery is *worthy* of praise.–The Red Cross is *worthy* of our help.
2. Having worth; admirable.–Abraham Lincoln was a *worthy* gentleman. He was an excellent man whom many people admired.

would (WUHD) *v.* 1. Wished to; wanted to; was willing to.–Bob said that he *would* play ball with our team.
2. *Would* is used to express a condition.–I *would* tell you if I knew. The only reason I don't tell you is that I do not know.
3. Is willing to.–Bob *would* play ball every day if he had time.
4. *Would* is used to show that something went on regularly for some time.–In summer the children *would* go for long walks in the country.
5. *Would* is used to make a request more polite.–*Would* you close the door for me?
6. Wish.–I *would* that I lived in the country.

would•n't (WUHD-nt). Would not. – I *wouldn't* go if I were you.

wound (WOOND) *n. wounds.* An injury, especially from being shot, cut, bruised, or burned.
–*v. wounds, wounded, wounding.* Hurt; injure.–A bullet *wounded* the man in the leg.

wound (WOWND) *v.* One form of the verb *wind.*–Father *wound* the clock last night.

wove (WOHV) *v.* One form of the verb *weave.* –Grandmother *wove* a rug out of strips of colored rags.

wo•ven (WOH-vən) *v.* One form of the verb *weave.*–Cloth is *woven* from threads.

wran•gle (RANG-gəl) *n. wrangles.* A dispute; a quarrel.–The boys got into a *wrangle* over who was to bat first.
–*v. wrangles, wrangled, wrangling.* Quarrel; argue angrily.–Mother told the children not to *wrangle* over their toys.

wrap (RAP) *n. wraps.* An outer garment worn for warmth.–The children took off their wet *wraps* in the hall.
–*v. wraps, wrapped, wrapping.* Cover closely with paper or other material; fasten up.–We *wrap* our presents on Christmas Eve.

wreath (REETH) *n. wreaths.* A ring of leaves or flowers. – Mother hung Christmas *wreaths* in the windows.

wreathe (REETH) *v. wreathes, wreathed, wreathing.* Encircle; put a ring around.–They *wreathed* their heads with dandelions.

wreck (REK) *n. wrecks.* What is left of anything after it has been damaged badly by a fire, a storm, or some other accident.
–*v. wrecks, wrecked, wrecking.* Destroy or damage badly.–The driver *wrecked* his automobile by running it into a delivery truck.

wreck•age (REK-ij) *n.* What is left after something has been wrecked or badly damaged by fire, storm, or other accident.–We saw the *wreckage* of a boat damaged by a storm.

wreck•er (REK-er) *n. wreckers.* 1. A man who tears down old or damaged houses, machinery, cars, etc. He saves the materials and parts that can be sold and used again.
2. The machine or car a wrecker uses to haul away wreckage.

wren (REN) *n. wrens.* A small songbird. *Wrens* often build nests in birdhouses made for them.

wrench (RENCH) *n. wrenches.* A tool for holding and turning nuts or bolts.–Father tightened the nut on the wheel with a *wrench.*
–*v. wrenches, wrenched, wrenching.* Twist or sprain. – You may *wrench* your back if you carry too heavy a load.

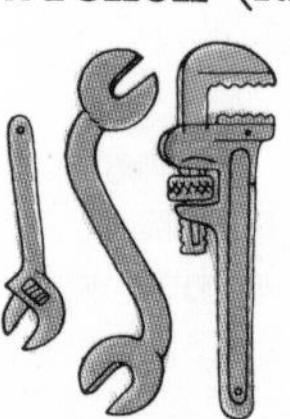

wres•tle (RESS-əl) *v. wrestles, wrestled, wrestling.* Take part in a sport in which each athlete tries to throw the other to the ground. – These boys are *wrestling.*

wres•tler (RESS-ler) *n. wrestlers.* A person who wrestles.

wretch•ed (RECH-id) *adj.; wretchedly, adv.; wretchedness, n.* 1. Very unhappy.–The lonely old man was *wretched* over the loss of his dog.
2. Poor; miserable; uncomfortable. – The poor family was living in a *wretched* house at the edge of town.

wring (RING) *v. wrings, wrung, wringing.* Twist and squeeze. – Mary *wrings* out the dishcloth. She twists and squeezes it between her hands to get the water out.

wring•er (RING-er) *n. wringers.* A machine with rollers that turn in opposite directions, for squeezing the water out of clothes that have been washed.–The *wringer* broke the buttons on Father's shirt.

wrin•kle (RING-kəl) *n. wrinkles.* A little ridge, fold, or line.–The old woman has many *wrinkles* in her face.–Clothes that have not been ironed have *wrinkles* in them.
–*v. wrinkles, wrinkled, wrinkling.* Make folds or ridges in.–Do not *wrinkle* your fresh dress before the party.–Mary *wrinkles* her forehead when she does arithmetic.

wrist (RIST) *n. wrists.* The joint between the hand and the arm.–You wear a watch or a bracelet on your *wrist.*

write (RYT) *v. writes, wrote, writing.* 1. Form letters and words.–Mary likes to *write* on the blackboard with chalk.–*Write* your name at the top of the paper.
2. Think up and set down in words.–Jack *wrote* a story called "The Robber's Revenge."
3. Write a letter.–Father *writes* to Mother every day when he is away.

writ•er (RY-ter) *n. writers.* 1. A person who can write or form letters and words.–Tom is not a good *writer.* He cannot spell very well.
2. An author; a person who makes up stories, poems, or articles, and has them published.–Who is your favorite *writer?*

writ•ing (RY-ting) *n. writings.* Something written.–My favorite author's *writings* fill twenty books.
–*v.* One form of the verb *write.*–Mary is *writing* her name on the blackboard.

writ•ten (RIT-n) *v.* One form of the verb *write.*–My letter to Grandmother is all *written* now. I have finished it.

wrong (RAWNG) *v. wrongs, wronged, wronging.* Do something to someone that is not just.–Sally accused Bob of not returning the book he had borrowed from her. Bob said Sally had *wronged* him; he said he had put the book on her desk that morning.
–*adj.; wrong* and *wrongly, adv.* 1. Not right or good.–It is *wrong* to lie or to steal.
2. Not true or correct. – This answer is *wrong.* It is not the right answer to the question.–That is the *wrong* way to play the game. You are not following the rules.
3. Mistaken; not proper.–It is *wrong* not to thank someone for a present.
4. Not meant to be turned upward or seen.–This wallpaper has a right side and a *wrong* side.–Mary put her sock on *wrong* side out.
5. Not as it should be; out of order.–Something is *wrong* with this watch. It won't work. – Is anything *wrong* with you this morning? Don't you feel well?
6. Not the one wanted or meant. – You brought me the *wrong* book. I wanted a different one.

wrote (ROHT) *v.* One form of the verb *write.* –I write stories in school. Yesterday I *wrote* one about my first piano lesson.

wrought i•ron (rawt Y-ern). A form of iron that can easily be forged, bent, shaped, or welded. *Wrought iron* is used for such things as fences, furniture, and ornaments.

wrung (RUNG) *v.* One form of the verb *wring.* – When I had *wrung* the water out of the washcloth, I hung it up.

Wy•o•ming (wy-OH-ming) *n.* A state that lies within the widest part of the Rocky

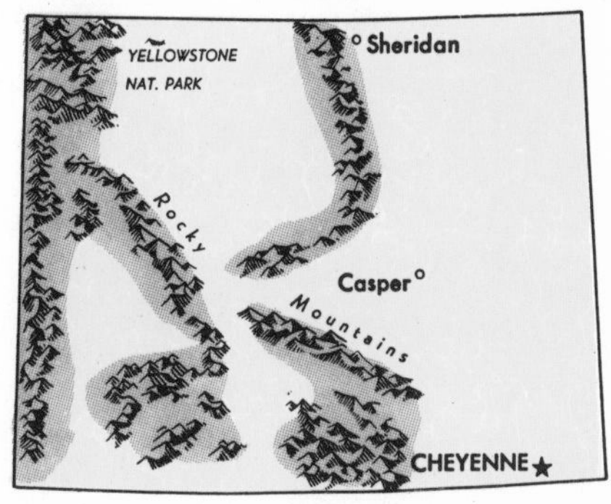

Mountains, in western United States. *Wyoming* is noted for the famous Yellowstone National Park, the oldest national park in the United States.

X x

X, x (EKS) *n. X's, x's.* The twenty-fourth letter of the alphabet.

Xmas (EKS-məss) *n. Xmases.* A short way of writing the word Christmas.–The seal on the package said, "Do not open until *Xmas.*"

X ray (EKS RAY) *X rays; X-ray, adj.* 1. A strong ray, something like light, that can go through certain substances, and even through a person's body. *X rays* are used to see whether bones are broken, or whether the lungs or the roots of teeth are diseased.

2. A picture taken with the help of an X ray. –I saw the *X ray* of Jack's broken arm.
–*v. X-rays, X-rayed, X-raying.* Take an X-ray picture of.–The dentist *X-rayed* Bob's teeth. He examined them by the use of X rays.

xy•lo•phone (ZY-lə-fohn *or* ZIL-ə-fohn) *n xylophones.* A musical instrument which consists of a series of bars of wood or metal. A *xylophone* is played by striking the bars with wooden hammers.

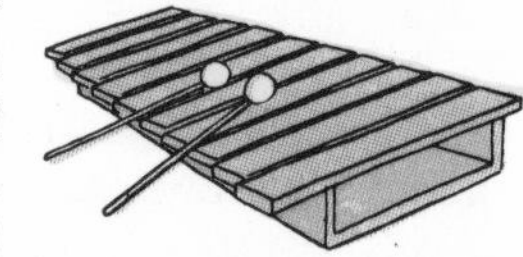

Y y

Y, y (WY) *n. Y's, y's.* The twenty-fifth letter of the alphabet.

yacht (YAHT) *n. yachts.* A boat used for pleasure or for racing.–There was a strong wind blowing the day that we went for a sail on Ed's *yacht.*
–*v. yachts, yachted, yachting.* Sail in a yacht. –Ed and I like to *yacht.*

yak (YAK) *n. yaks.* A very large wild ox found in Tibet and other parts of Asia. Some *yaks* have been tamed and are used for domestic purposes.

yam (YAM) *n. yams.* The root of a certain food plant. A *yam* is a kind of sweet potato, deep orange in color. – Mother makes candied *yams* by cooking them in brown sugar and butter.

yank (YANGK) *v. yanks, yanked, yanking.* Pull suddenly and sharply; jerk.–The rude boy *yanked* the ball away from his friend and threw it over the fence.

Yan•kee (YANG-kee) *n. Yankees.* 1. A nickname given to people in the northern part of the United States, particularly in the Northeast.
2. A nickname given to the people in the United States by people of foreign countries.

yard (YAHRD) *n. yards.* 1. The space, lawn, or ground around a house.–The children play in the *yard.*
2. An area shut in by a fence or a wall, and used for a special purpose.–The boys built a snow fort in the school*yard.*–We go by the church*yard* on our way home from school.–The cows stood in the barn*yard.*–Trains go to railroad *yards* for repairs.
3. A unit of measure equal to 3 feet or 36 inches. A *yard* is about as long as the distance from a grown person's nose to his fingertips when his arm is held out straight from the shoulder.–Mother bought a piece of ribbon one *yard* long.

yard•stick (YAHRD-stik) *n. yardsticks.* A measuring stick 36 inches long.

yarn (YAHRN) *n. yarns.* 1. A thread made by drawing out and twisting wool, flax, cotton, or other fiber.–Stockings, sweaters, and caps are often made of *yarn.*
2. A story.–Grandfather tells us long *yarns* about the experiences he had as a boy.

yawn (YAWN) *n. yawns.* Opening the mouth and taking a long breath.–Mary was so tired that she could do nothing to hide her *yawn.*
–*v. yawns, yawned, yawning.* Open the mouth and take a long breath.–When Baby is sleepy, she usually *yawns* and shows her two new teeth.

yea (YAY) *n. yeas* and *adv.* 1. Yes.–When it was time to vote, John voted *yea.* He voted in favor of the resolution. Bill voted against the resolution. He voted nay.
2. Truly; indeed.–*Yea,* that's the way life is.

year (YIR) *n. years.* The time it takes the earth to go around the sun. A *year* has 365 days, 52 weeks, or 12 months in it. Leap *year,* which comes every four *years,* has 366 days in it.

year•ling (YIR-ling) *n. yearlings.* An animal one year old or in its second year of life.–Of all the horses in the stable, the trainer likes the *yearling* most. He likes the one-year-old colt best of all.

year•ly (YIR-lee) *adj.* and *adv.* 1. Once a year.–The Junior Prom is a *yearly* event at our school.
2. Each year.–Bob gets fifty dollars *yearly* for spending money.

yearn (YERN) *v. yearns, yearned, yearning.* Long (for); want very much. – The lonely child *yearns* for letters or post cards from his friends.

yeast (YEEST) *n.* A substance used in making bread. – *Yeast* causes bubbles, which makes bread light. It makes the bread dough rise.

yell (YEL) *n. yells.* A scream; an outcry.–We heard the boy's *yell* from the second-story window of the old house.
-*v. yells, yelled, yelling.* Scream; cry out loudly.–The boys *yelled* when the bear got loose.

yel•low (YEL-oh) *n. yellows.* The color of butter. – Billy thinks we should paint the dining room *yellow.*
–*v. yellows, yellowed, yellowing.* Turn yellow. –The old newspaper had *yellowed* with age. It had turned yellow.
–*adj. yellower, yellowest.* Of the color yellow. –The living room is the only *yellow* room in the house.
–*Yellowish* means somewhat yellow.

yel•low fe•ver (YEL-oh FEE-ver). A dangerous infectious disease occurring in warm or tropical climates. *Yellow fever* is carried by a certain type of mosquito and transmitted by its bite.

yel•low jack•et (YEL-oh jak-it) *yellow jackets.* A wasp that has bright yellow stripes on its back. A *yellow jacket's* sting hurts.

yelp (YELP) *n. yelps.* A sharp cry or bark.– The *yelp* of his dog brought Jack running to see what was wrong.
–*v. yelps, yelped, yelping.* Bark sharply.–The dog *yelps* when he is hurt.

yen (YEN) *n. sing.* and *pl.* 1. The unit of money in Japan. One hundred *yen* is about twenty-seven cents in United States money.
2. Desire or longing.–Tom has a *yen* to go to the movies. He has a keen desire to see a motion picture.

yeo•man (YOH-mən) *n. yeomen.* 1. In England, a farmer who owns only a small farm. –The old *yeoman* worked hard, plowing his small field and tending his few crops.
2. An attendant, servant, or guard in the service of a king or a noble. – There are one hundred *yeomen* in the royal army. There are one hundred guards in the royal army.
3. A petty officer in the United States Navy. A *yeoman's* rank is equivalent to that of a sergeant in the United States Army.

yes (YESS) *n. yeses* and *adv.* The opposite of no.–We say *yes* when we agree or are willing.–Will you go with me? *Yes,* I would like to go with you.

yes•ter•day (YESS-ter-dee *or* -day) *n. yesterdays, adj.,* and *adv.* The day right before today; the day just past.–Today is Monday; *yesterday* was Sunday.

yet (YET) *adv.* and *conj.* 1. Up to now; before this time.–The train has not come *yet.* We are waiting for it.
2. Still; even now. – The bells are ringing *yet.* You can still hear them.
3. At some time to come.–I will learn to play the piano *yet.*
4. Still; even.–The wind blew harder *yet* when we turned the corner.
–*As yet* means up to the present time, up till now.–Bill hasn't done it *as yet,* but he will when he gets a chance.

yew (YOO) *n. yews.* 1. An evergreen tree or shrub having fine-grained wood and dark green foliage. *Yews* grow in Europe, Asia, and parts of Africa and North America.

2. The wood of such a tree. – Bows for shooting arrows were generally made of *yew* because the wood is so tough and elastic.

yield (YEELD) *n. yields.* An amount produced.–Four bushels is a large *yield* for a small tree.
–*v. yields, yielded, yielding.* 1. Produce; give forth.–The peach tree *yielded* four baskets of fruit.
2. Give in.–Father *yielded* to Mary's coaxing and let her go to the show.
3. Give up ground; surrender.–The soldiers would not *yield* to the enemy.

yo•ga (YOH-gə) *n.* In the Hindu religion, a union of the human mind with the mind of God. To attain *yoga* a man must control his body and mind to such a degree that he can overcome consciousness of the world around him and release his mind to God.

yoke (YOHK) *n. yokes.* 1. The top part of a dress that is cut separately from the dress. –Sally's yellow dress has a white *yoke* with a bright red ruffle around it.

2. A wooden framework placed over the necks of two animals so that they will work together. – The man fixed the animals' *yoke*.
–*v. yokes, yoked, yoking.* Harness; put a yoke on.–The two oxen were *yoked* together.

yolk (YOHK *or* YOHLK) *n. yolks.* The yellow part of an egg.–Mary likes the *yolk* of the egg best.

yon•der (YAHN-der) *adj.* and *adv.* Over there; at that place. – Look at the sunset *yonder*.

yore (YOR) *adj.* and *adv.* An ancient word meaning olden times, or long ago. The word is used today only in the phrase *"of yore."*– The book contains a dozen tales *of yore*.

you (YOO) *pron. sing.* and *pl.* The person or persons to whom one is speaking or writing. –*You* may go home now.–*You* are bigger than I am.–All of *you* come with me.

you'd (YOOD). A short way of writing you had or you would.–*You'd* see better if you sat nearer to the window.–Before *you'd* walked with us a mile, *you'd* be tired.

you'll (YOOL). You will.–If you do not hurry, *you'll* be late.

young (YUNG) *n.* Babies.–A cat carries her *young* by the backs of their necks.–A dog's *young* are her puppies.
–*adj. younger, youngest.* Not old; not many years old.–Babies are very *young* children.– Boys and girls are *young*.–The peach tree is *young*. It was planted not very long ago.

young•ster (YUNG-ster) *n. youngsters.* A child; a young person.–The *youngsters* at the party played games.

your (YUHR) *adj.* and *pron.* Belonging to the person or persons to whom one is speaking or writing.–*Your* nose, *your* toes, *your* hands are all parts of you. *Your* dress belongs to you.

you're (YUHR). You are.–*You're* taller than I am.–*You're* going to be late.

yours (YUHRZ) *pron.* Something that belongs to the person to whom one is speaking or writing.–This hat is *yours;* that one is mine.–My eyes are blue; *yours* are brown.

your•self (yuhr-SELF) *pron. yourselves.* 1. You alone.–If you want your work done well, do it *yourself*. Don't expect somebody else to do it.
2. Your own self. – Dress *yourself* quickly, for breakfast is ready.

your•selves (yuhr-SELVZ) *pron. pl.* Mother said to us, "You must play by *yourselves* today, for your friends are away."

youth (YOOTH) *n. youth* or *youths.* 1. Older boys and girls.–The high school was built for the *youth* of our town.
2. A young man.–The letter was sent by a *youth* in search of a job.

youth•ful (YOOTH-fuhl) *adj.; youthfully, adv.; youthfulness, n.* Young. – Mother's green dress makes her look *youthful*.–Grandmother is *youthful* in her ideas. She thinks like a young person.

you've (YOOV). You have.–*You've* written to Grandmother, haven't you?

yule (YOOL) *n. yules.* An old-fashioned word for Christmas.

Z z

Z, z (ZEE) *n. Z's, z's.* The twenty-sixth and last letter of the alphabet.

zeal (ZEEL) *n.; zealous, adj.; zealously, adv.* Enthusiasm; warm and active interest; eager desire.–The children worked with great *zeal* to put on the annual school show.

ze•bra (ZEE-brə) *n. zebras.* An animal that looks something like a horse, but has black and white stripes going around its body.

ze•nith (ZEE-nith) *n. zeniths.* 1. That point in the sky directly above any observer or place on earth.
2. The highest point; the peak; the summit. –The actor is at the *zenith* of his career. He is at the top. He has never before been so popular, or earned so much money, or acted so well.

zeph•yr (ZEF-er) *n. zephyrs.* A soft, gentle wind that comes from the west; any gentle wind.

zep•pe•lin (ZEP-ə-lin) *n. zeppelins.* A kind of balloon that can be steered; a dirigible.–People can ride in a *zeppelin.*

ze•ro (ZIR-oh *or* ZEE-roh) *n. zeros* or *zeroes.*
1. The figure [0] which comes before 1. –When the temperature is *zero* [0°], it is very cold.
2. Nothing; none.–Jack has slept all morning. The amount of work he has done amounts to *zero.*
3. A grade meaning that no answer has been correct.–Mary had every answer wrong in the arithmetic test, so her mark was *zero* for that day.

zest (ZEST) *n.; zestful, adj.* Hearty flavor; sharp interest; keen enjoyment.–The hungry boys ate their food with *zest.*

zig•zag (ZIG-zag) *n. zigzags, adj.,* and *adv.* A figure that has short, sharp turns.
–*v. zigzags, zigzagged, zigzagging.* Move back and forth making sharp turns.–The airplane *zigzagged* in the sky.

zinc (ZINGK) *n.* A soft, bluish-white metal.

zin•ni•a (ZIN-ee-ə) *n. zinnias.* A bright-colored late summer flower.–*Zinnias* last for a long time.

zip (ZIP) *v. zips, zipped, zipping.* Fasten with a zipper.–Tom is *zipping* the bag. He is fastening it.

zip•per (ZIP-er) *n. zippers.* A slide fastener. *Zippers* are often used instead of buttons or laces on trousers, skirts, dresses, jackets, etc.

zith•er (ZITH-er) *n. zithers.* A musical instrument having up to forty-five strings stretched over a flat sounding box. – The *zither* is played with the fingers and a small piece of ivory, metal, or other material.

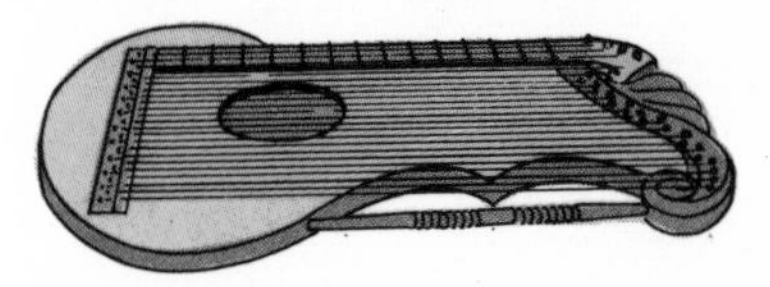

zo•di•ac (ZOH-dee-ak) *n.* In going around the sun, the earth always moves in a certain path. Out in the heavens there is a belt of stars that circles this path. That belt of stars is the *zodiac.* It can be divided into twelve constellations, or picture-groups of stars. Among them are "Taurus, the Bull," "Cancer, the Crab," and "Leo, the Lion."

zone (ZOHN) *n. zones.* 1. An area or place set aside for a special purpose. – The children waited in the safety *zone* for the bus.
2. One of the great divisions of the earth.–It is very hot in the Torrid *Zone.*–We live in the North Temperate *Zone.*–The Frigid *Zones* are very cold.

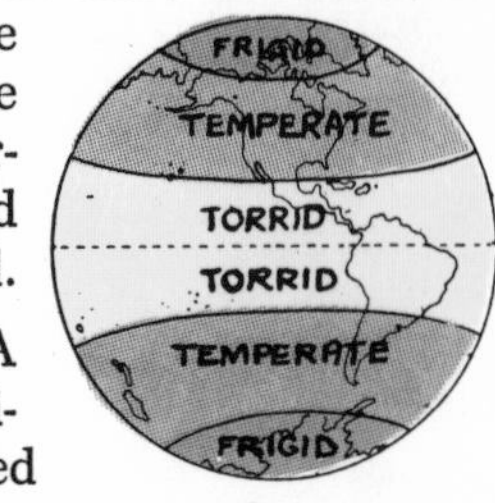

zoo (ZOO) *n. zoos.* A park where wild animals are kept in fenced yards or in cages, so that people can come and look at them. Most large cities have *zoos.* –Father took the children to the *zoo* to see the baby elephant.

zo•ol•o•gy (zoh-AHL-ə-jee) *n. zoologies; zoological, adj.* The science or study of animals and animal life.–Carrie and Hannah are going to college to study *zoology.* They will study everything from one-celled animals to human bodies.

Things You Will Want to Know

DAYS OF THE WEEK

Sunday	(Sun.)
Monday	(Mon.)
Tuesday	(Tues.)
Wednesday	(Wed.)
Thursday	(Thurs.)
Friday	(Fri.)
Saturday	(Sat.)

SEASONS OF THE YEAR

Winter – December 22 to March 20
Spring – March 21 to June 21
Summer – June 22 to September 20
Autumn – September 21 to December 21

MONTHS OF THE YEAR

January	(Jan.)
February	(Feb.)
March	(Mar.)
April	(Apr.)
May	
June	(Jun.)
July	(Jul.)
August	(Aug.)
September	(Sept.)
October	(Oct.)
November	(Nov.)
December	(Dec.)

SPECIAL DAYS

New Year's Day	January 1
Lincoln's Birthday	February 12
Valentine's Day	February 14
Washington's Birthday	February 22
St. Patrick's Day	March 17
Easter Sunday	March or April
Mother's Day	Second Sunday in May
Memorial Day	May 30
Flag Day	June 14
Father's Day	Third Sunday in June
Independence Day	July 4
Labor Day	First Monday in September
Columbus Day	October 12
Halloween	October 31
Election Day	First Tuesday after first Monday in November
Veterans Day (formerly Armistice Day)	November 11
Thanksgiving	Fourth Thursday in November
Christmas	December 25